D0214487

DATE			

CONTOURS
OF THE
FANTASTIC

**Contributions to the Study of
Science Fiction and Fantasy**

Great Themes of Science Fiction: A Study in Imagination and Evolution
John J. Pierce

Phoenix from the Ashes: The Literature of the Remade World
Carl B. Yoke, editor

"A Better Country": The Worlds of Religious Fantasy and Science Fiction
Martha C. Sammons

Spectrum of the Fantastic: Selected Essays from the Sixth International Conference
on the Fantastic in the Arts
Donald Palumbo, editor

The Way to Ground Zero: The Atomic Bomb in American Science Fiction
Martha A. Bartter

The Legacy of Olaf Stapledon: Critical Essays and an Unpublished Manuscript
Patrick A. McCarthy, Charles Elkins, and Martin Harry Greenberg, editors

Strange Shadows: The Uncollected Fiction and Essays of Clark Ashton Smith
Steve Behrends, editor, with Donald Sidney-Fryer and Rah Hoffman

Welsh Celtic Myth in Modern Fantasy
C. W. Sullivan III

When World Views Collide: A Study in Imagination and Evolution
John J. Pierce

From Satire to Subversion: The Fantasies of James Branch Cabell
James Riemer

The Shape of the Fantastic: Selected Essays from the Seventh International
Conference on the Fantastic in the Arts
Olena H. Saciuk, editor

The Poetic Fantastic: Studies in an Evolving Genre
Patrick D. Murphy and Vernon Hyles, editors

In the Image of God: Theme, Characterization, and Landscape in the Fiction of
Orson Scott Card
Michael R. Collings

CONTOURS
OF THE
FANTASTIC

Selected Essays from the
Eighth International Conference on
the Fantastic in the Arts

Edited by MICHELE K. LANGFORD

Contributions to the Study of Science Fiction and Fantasy, Number 41
Marshall B. Tymn, Series Editor

GREENWOOD PRESS
New York • Westport, Connecticut • London

Library of Congress Cataloging-in-Publication Data

International Conference on the Fantastic in the Arts (8th : 1987 : Houston, Tex.)
   Contours of the fantastic : selected essays from the Eighth International Conference on the Fantastic in the Arts / edited by Michele K. Langford.
      p.   cm.—(Contributions to the study of science fiction and fantasy, ISSN 0193–6875 ; no. 41)
   Includes bibliographical references.
   ISBN 0–313–26647–6 (lib. bdg. : alk. paper)
   1. Fantastic literature—History and criticism—Congresses.
2. Science fiction—History and criticism—Congresses.
I. Langford, Michele.   II. Title.   III. Series.
PN56.F34I58   1990
809'.915—dc20   89–23308

British Library Cataloguing in Publication Data is available.

Library of Congress Catalog Card Number: 89–23308
ISBN: 0–313–26647–6
ISSN: 0193–6875

First published in 1990

Greenwood Press, 88 Post Road West, Westport, CT   06881
An imprint of Greenwood Publishing Group, Inc.

Printed in the United States of America

The paper used in this book complies with the Permanent Paper Standard issued by the National Information Standards Organization (Z39.48–1984).

10 9 8 7 6 5 4 3 2 1

Contents

VII. The Fantastic World—Space and Time

Michele K. Langford

Introduction

The attention given to the fantastic has increased steadily in the last ten years, and the Eighth International Conference on the Fantastic in the Arts, held in Houston, Texas, in March 1987, reflects this interest. The conference guests attracted avid listeners from literature and the arts: Stephen Donaldson, guest of honor, author of the two *Thomas Covenant* trilogies that have made him one of the best known fantasy writers; Brian Stableford, guest scholar, who has published extensively on the history of science fiction and is himself a prolific science fiction novelist; Brian Aldiss, novelist, poet, and critic, author of more than two dozen books, many of which are considered science fiction classics; Vivian Sobchack who, along with her work on science fiction films, has written on semiotics, phenomenology, and documentaries; Michael Whelan, creator of more than 250 book cover paintings as well as other art; and Nancy Willard, author of prize-winning novels, collected stories, poetry, and numerous children's books.

But the fascination exerted by the fantastic is not limited to the growing numbers of literary and art critics. The conference included participants from the social and natural sciences, engineering and aeronautics, the military, and many representations from other fields who showed their enthusiasm for the world of the imaginary, the dream, the uncanny, the paranormal, and all forms of speculative fiction.

Many factors explain the current interest in the fantastic. As science has progressed through the twentieth century, we have become increasingly aware that a solved mystery often reveals a deeper one; hence, the necessity in medicine, physics, space exploration, and other scientific endeavors, to "dream" possible solutions, to extrapolate from known facts, and to speculate on the future.

On the sociopsychological level, perhaps the most significant factor in Western culture is a prevailing climate of *fin de siecle*, to which is added a *fin de millennium* syndrome. The nostalgia produced by the end of an era and the anxiety brought forth by the beginning of a new one are magnified by the myths surrounding the events to befall humankind after the year 2000. Recent science fiction films that bridge the future, the present, and the past are successful, in part, because they answer the needs and aspirations of our epoch.

The notion of separation in terms of centuries and millennia is, of course, an arbitrary one, and it is agreed that almost nothing ever begins or ends at the precise date of the turn of the century. Yet the approach of a new century creates a sense of rupture and feelings of uneasiness and anxiety. Other events can certainly cause unrest in society and provoke a general feeling of anxiety. The atomic explosion in 1945 is often pinpointed as an event that conditioned the demeanor of a whole period following it. But these fears were precise and could be eased by taking precautions that now seem puerile, such as enduring classroom drills and building bomb shelters. Nothing can prepare us for the uncertainties of the future. What would a third world war be like? Can we deal with the new and baffling diseases and increased pollution, terrorism, and urban violence likely to befall us?

If we agree with Roger Caillois that the fantastic signifies anxiety and rupture, we see what an important role it plays in reflecting the contemporary social consciousness. It does not constitute merely an escape from reality, as is often stated; instead, it allows us to visualize what the future may bring and thus to focus our fears. But, most of all, the fantastic provides a coherence of its own in our overinformed, disinformed, confused postmodern world, relieving our sense of disarray in our never-ending quest to understand our destiny.

On the personal level, the fantastic world has never ceased to exert its enchantment for those who, from childhood, have retained the sense of wonder, the need to understand mystery, and the desire to decode the undeciphered. But the limits between reality and fantasy—the inner and outer worlds—are more and more unclear, and it has become increasingly difficult for scientists to separate them.

Psychological experiments have shown that what people see when they look at an object depends on who they are and on their interests at the moment. A pilot sees a bird and thinks of flight; a hunter sees in the bird a target and food. For some of us, the fantastic owes its attraction precisely to its ability to defy limits and to escape conclusive definitions. There are as many forms of the fantastic as there are ways to visualize the outer world—a world that we see not with the eyes, but with the soul.

For the critic involved in the fantastic, the problem of perceived reality becomes crucial. A critic's approach to the fantastic in literature and art includes an implied notion of what, for him or her, constitutes reality—a perception that is inseparable from the mind of the reader/observer. Ideally, the critic's methodology would reflect an awareness of his own *parti pris* and sense of reality.

As for the creator of fantasy, he answers a primordial need of human beings. For Walter Scott, the belief in wonder has its origin in the human condition.

The world created by the fantasticor becomes visible, and therefore accessible, to the nostalgic curiosity of the reader. Considering this idea further, we see that this given visualization is, in a sense, the opposite of poetry, because to be effective, the poet's art must never be apparent in what he or she makes visible: hence the problems posed by sincerity in the art that tormented many major poets. In opposition, for the inventor of fantasy, everything resides in the artifice created. If sometimes the fantasist works like a magician, showing what does not exist, redefining and transforming reality, he or she also works like a puppeteer who deliberately shows the strings that hold together the creation, but for whom the challenge resides in making the public forget about them or, more precisely, accept them as the conditions of a genre. The artifice is thus incorporated in the visualization for the creation of the imagery. The fantastic, as a mode of expression, is therefore an artistic affirmation, a *prise de position* on the part of the author who is situated "just this side" of reality the better to highlight the confines of each domain.

It is not surprising, however, that many poets create fantasy and that many authors of fantasy or science fiction, such as Nancy Willard, Brian Aldiss, Thomas Disch, Ursula K. LeGuin, Joe Haldeman, and Orson Scott Card, are also poets. These two forms of expression complement each other. Problems posed by sincerity and expression of self are temporarily suspended for the writer of fantasy, only to impose themselves later more vividly. Inversely, for the poet, the writing of fantasy allows a temporary escape from the same problems. Nevertheless, whatever an author writes or an artist creates, the work remains unmistakably his or her own, and what Cocteau calls the "signature" is always included in the creation.

In the present volume, the ninth in a series of collected essays from the International Conference on the Fantastic in the Arts, we seek to outline the contours of the fantastic, not with a heavy and continuous line, but as an artist sketches a portrait, leaving empty spaces and using a line that in turns thickens and becomes elusive. Our intent is to give a perspective of the territory covered by the fantastic, showing the diversity in the field and the matching variety of approaches in the attempt to comprehend it. Each essay brings its own method of investigation—phenomenological, theoretical, historical, sociological, psychological, textual—in an effort to situate the border between reality and fantasy and the passage from one to the other.

The twenty-two papers in *Contours of the Fantastic* begin with a section on fantasy and discontinuity. In his essay, Aldiss shows that many major authors, including Balzac, Dickens, Poe, Aldous Huxley, C. S. Lewis, and Tolkien, have at some point suffered a discontinuity in their private life (in a sense, this "fatal break" constitutes their signature). The writing of fiction, and particularly fantasy, becomes a consolation for maternal deprivation either from death or lack of motherly love. The next two papers concern individual works. William Lomax underlines the importance of *The Last Man* in the work of Mary Shelley as well as its place in the broader context of science fiction. He demonstrates how the novel is based on a reversal of linear time that makes it an epic of human history in reverse. Through a similarly close investigation, Leonard Heldreth situates *The Zoo Story* in relationship to Albee's work and other stories of the time. He shows how the characters in the play manipulate reality, transforming it into compensatory and often destructive fantasy that, in turn, affects reality. In his theoretical essay "The Self, the Referent, and the Real in Science Fiction and the Fantastic," Peter Malekin chooses four authors, Len, Pynchon, Kubin, and Delany, to analyze language and the relationship between mind, language, and object.

The second section pertains to national fantasy. It begins with Brian Stableford's paper on "The British and American Traditions of Speculative Fiction," in which he compares and contrasts the development of the genre in these two countries that share a common language. Joseph Andriano and Bud Foote each turns his attention to one text in particular. Using a post-Jungian perspective, Andriano analyzes love and death in Le Fanu's *Carmilla*, a masterpiece of nineteenth-century British horror fantasy often compared to Coleridge's *Christabel*. Foote, in *"The Panchronicon: A New Hampshire Yankee in Queen Elizabeth's Court,"* situates this novel by Harold Steele MacKaye within time travel fiction, assessing the new ideas that appear in it and the extent to which it is indebted to other works, in particular Twain's *Yankee*. Next, Joyce Watford elects two novels, *The Palm Wine Drinkard* by Amos Tutuola and *Things Fall Apart* by Chinua Achebe, to illustrate the specificity of the West African fantastic novel.

The third section shifts to children's literature. More than literature intended exclusively for children, it is a childlike perception of the fantastic that provides the inspiration for the texts discussed in this section. The first paper, by Nancy Willard, "Making the Dreamed Earth," gives an account of the way in which the fantastic erupted in her life. She discusses the events that contributed to a fantastic vision of the world and the people who gave birth to the characters in her books. In the following essay, Jules Zanger analyzes two of the most familiar characters for young Americans, Dorothy and Tarzan, working toward a theory of national fantasy. Next, Michael Clifton investigates Baum's creative vision and the author's ambivalence toward his own creation.

The fourth section relates to science fiction and fantasy films, beginning with Vivian Sobchack's essay "Terminal Culture: Science Fiction Cinema in the Age of the Microchip." There she discusses the sharp break that occurred in science fiction films in the last decade and examines the sociocultural and political context surrounding it. The following two papers center on specific issues in films: Lisa Heilbronn traces the rejection of science that accompanies the search for knowledge in Science Fiction films, and Sharon Russell poses the problems of novelization in *Dead and Buried* and *Nomads* by Chelsea Quinn Yarbro.

The following section—fusion, transfusion, and transgression in the fantastic—approaches specific forms of fantasy. First, Joe Sanders investigates Christian horror in fiction, assessing the aesthetic and religious ideas expressed. Second, Cynthia Walker, in a close reading of *The Second Chronicles of Thomas*

Covenant, defines the concept of fusion actualized in vampirism and symbolized by the alloy contained in the white gold ring, and its opposite, transfusion. Then, Mickey Pearlman considers most of Muriel Spark's seventeen novels, following the author's evolution and working to isolate the fantastic element in the artist figure.

The last two sections trace more decisively the borders between fantasy and reality. In the section on the fantastic and science, Joe Feimer delineates each domain. His essay on Bram Stoker's *Dracula* demonstrates how Cartesian reason and a scientific approach to the study of the soul are challenged by the occult and the demonic preternatural. Greg Zentz, in his essay "Physics, Metaphysics, and Science Fiction: Shifting Paradigms for Science Fiction," points to the conceptual and verbal problems posed by the new physics and the attempts made by science fiction to deal with them.

The final section concerns space and time in the fantastic. Ingeborg Kohn's paper shows how America became part of the imagery of French thinking and discusses the role played by America's geography in the work of Hervé Guibert and Monique Wittig. Jack Voller's essay offers a link between one of the aspects of Todorov's theory of the fantastic, the moment of hesitation, and the concept of the sublime, which was first elaborated upon in the eighteenth century. Finally, David Miller investigates the interactions between fantasy and the fantastic in "Mommy Fortuna's Ontological Plenum: The Fantasy of Plenitude."

The prospect of giving frontiers to the fantastic, even frontiers conceived as sketchy contours, is of course paradoxical in terms, not unlike the quest to "reach the unreachable star." Each essay, in some sense, points to the fact that the cycle of the fantastic is, in turn, opaque, transparent, translucent, porous, transitory—forever changing. Yet the scrutinization of the confines of reality and fantasy imposes itself. As Descartes contended, our always-contested sense of reality can only be obtained by the comprehension of its opposite, phantasm. But perhaps more importantly, the fantastic represents one of the few true challenges of the mind, a challenge that is described in the last essay of this volume as follows: "Every morning somebody shows up with a dragon to be killed or a harp to be played, and I don't know how to do either." But as Brian Aldiss points out, the critic who chooses to investigate the fantasy of another being must "tread softly," for it often expresses the most profound of human experiences.

I would like to thank all those who participated in the conference and, in particular, the guest speakers who allowed me to include their papers in this volume. I am also very grateful for the help I received from my colleagues and from Sandi Ford and her staff at Pepperdine University.

I

Fantasy and Discontinuity

Brian W. Aldiss*

Fatal Breaks

The kinds of fiction in which we are most interested exhibit marked breaks between reality and the surreality represented in the story. H. G. Wells's *The War of the Worlds* begins in quite a humdrum way, with truthful portraits of the country around London. Then comes the surreal event, the alien invasion, and the break with the ordinary novel and reported reality has been made.

A casual glance at the biographies of the makers and shakers in the related fields of science fiction and fantasy indicates a grave discontinuity in many of their lives. I suspect that they wrote as they wrote because they found a way of exercising that discontinuity, with its attendant sorrow, in their fictions; we may regard them as true writers, who wrote for rewards other than financial ones.

In fiction, this break falls between the world as is and the world that was, or will be, or might be. In horror fantasy, for instance, we experience a break between the normal world and a world where a form of chaos prevails: today normal; tomorrow (or yesterday) chaos. Utopias stand at the opposite extreme. They tell us, "Today all is chaos. Tomorrow will be better, orderly, just." From Bacon and More to Wells and LeGuin, we see this kind of break. It ascends from chaos to order, from a world where nothing can be taken for granted to one where everything can.

Nonutopian science fiction—and most of it is dystopian—descends, like horror, from a more or less conventional world to an unconventional one. The break, the fatal break, lies in the present.

Why do writers choose this particular writing gambit, often sticking to it all their working lives, instead of choosing, say, the more usual gambit of writing about aspects of the world they already know?

*This essay was presented by Brian W. Aldiss, guest speaker, as a featured luncheon address.

I believe that the fatal break is the sign of a writer who has suffered a severe discontinuity in his or her private life, and generally early on, in the formative years. The discontinuity in life is echoed in fiction. In all genuine art, there is an element of compulsion: to write books continuously over a lifetime is not something that is "natural," that can be conceived as having been achieved naturally.

The only important things any novel can concern itself with are life, love, and death. Often one has to face death to live the life of an artist. Here are a few examples that come to mind easily—that is, authors who preferred to write what may be called fantasy or science fiction.

C. S. Lewis was not yet ten when his mother died. The shock resounded throughout his life, as if he had been branded with a special brand. He summarized the fatal break in these words: "It was sea and islands now. The great continent had sunk like Atlantis."

Lewis also suffered another discontinuity, not a private one, but a general discontinuity that affected the whole world. He saw action in World War I and was wounded. His sometimes close friend, J. R. R. Tolkien, was also involved in that war, and survived the Battle of the Somme. Tolkien could admit to several discontinuities. At the age of three he left South Africa, and at the age of twelve his mother died, leaving him and his sister orphaned. They then moved from the country to Edgbaston, in Birmingham. From the windows of the house where he went to live, the countryside could be seen only distantly, over the rooftops and chimneys.

In both Lewis and Tolkien, one witnesses a response to the desolation that opened to them. Tolkien wrote diaries only when he was miserable, and both he and Lewis turned to the writing of fiction as consolation—fantasy fiction.

Someone has defined fantasy worlds as places to which no hypothetical vehicles can transport us, as against science fiction worlds, to which possible future spaceships or time machines may take us. Certainly no vehicle can take us to Middle Earth; it lies firmly within the fantasy orbit, beyond reach of ion jet or matter-transmitter. In Lewis's trilogy, he begins with a rocket ship, but in the second volume, interestingly enough, he retreats further from realism and reverts to celestial means of transport. In his Narnia books, one need only walk through a wardrobe to reach the magic world. But—first find your wardrobe.

Aldous Huxley's mother died suddenly of cancer when he was fourteen. His sister Margaret wrote of that final break, "I lost my mother, my home, my school, living in the country and my governess, all at one blow." Writing of someone else in similar circumstances to himself, Huxley once put his own situation in a nutshell: "There remained with him, latent at ordinary times but always ready to come to the surface, a haunting sense of the vanity, the transience, the hopeless precariousness of all merely human happiness."

Another blow was to befall Aldous at the age of 20, when his elder brother, Trevenen, "the hub of the family wheel," as Margaret, Aldous's sister, called him, committed suicide. Huxley's best-known science fiction novel began well into the future, very unexpectedly for those days, in the Year of Our Lord 632, as if to signify a deep rift between the past and what is to come. *Ape and Essence* displays at least as dramatic a break.

Later in life, Huxley went to visit H. G. Wells in the south of France—in some trepidation, for Wells saw *Brave New World* as defeatist. Wells also suffered breaks, though less disastrous ones than Huxley's. But for a sensitive boy, it was enough that his mother, Sarah, suddenly left her husband and young Wells and went off to be housekeeper in a big house. It was a desertion that took him a long while to come to terms with.

Perhaps it needs little to persuade a sensitive young person to turn to fantasy or science fiction nowadays, when those modes are so popular. When the modes scarcely existed, the break must necessarily have been greater. Certainly one could scarcely think of a series of misfortunes graver than those that afflicted Mary Shelley, commencing with the death of her mother, Mary Wollstonecraft, in childbirth. I have dealt with her life in *Trillion Year Spree*, so I will say no more here. Much of her injured, orphaned, and chilled sensibilities went into the making of her forlorn monster.

So one might go on with this catalog of early maternal deaths among fantasists. The mother of the originator of the Gothic, Horace Walpole, died when he was twenty. George MacDonald, he of the North Wind much loved by C. S. Lewis, lost his mother at the age of eight. Rudyard Kipling, Saki, and P. G. Wodehouse were all brought up by aunts, and aunts play villainous roles in the fantasies of the first two at least, while Wodehouse's aunts are a world unto themselves.

That monster of letters Balzac cried, "I have had no mother," according to his biographer, Stefan Zweig, so abysmally did his mother treat him. But let us not allow ourselves to be led into the miseries of the continent of Europe.

I will not labor the list longer. Not all those who lose their mothers or fathers in childhood become writers, never mind writers of fantasy; nor is the loss of a parent sufficient to qualify one as a fantasy writer. Nevertheless, that sense of the fragility of all merely human happiness, as Huxley put it, haunts, I believe, a good proportion of the most valued fantasy. One cannot be too exact about so imprecise a thing as deprivation, but let's say that the mind has a less fixed abode when natural maternal love is missing. It shows a tendency to wander, and sometimes to wander creatively. The term fantasy has many meanings; in one sense, fantasy denotes a sickness of mental health, something to be poured out in the privacy of a psychiatrist's session. Maternal deprivation is often seen to contribute to extravagant states of mind. One of the great authorities on child care and mental health, Dr. John Bowlby, states the position simply: "This complex, rich, and rewarding relationship with the mother in early years, varied in countless ways by relations with the father and with the brothers and sisters . . . child psychiatrists and many others now believe to underlie the development of character and of mental health."

Even when these agonies are overgrown by later and more urgent experience, the wounds still show through as an underlying pattern. Those savage faces that press upon us in the world of Charles Dickens, each often seeming scarcely to acknowledge other living beings, can be traced to the young Dickens's spell of six months—no more—in the blacking factory. He could not bring himself to talk of that painful episode until late in life. He was wounded by his father's indifference and, as Edmund Wilson puts it in his telling essay "Dickens: The two Scrooges," "Charles never forgave his mother for having wanted to keep him working in the warehouse even after his father decided to take him out. 'I never afterwards forgot,' he wrote of her attitude at this time. 'I never shall forget. I never can forget.' "

With those awful words ringing in our ears, the most unforgiving in our language, we return to the fantasists pure and simple, or not so simple. I have, with the exception of a mention of Balzac, confined my comments to British writers; but what of that man—that American with an English mother—who was Edgar Allan Poe? There, in some ways, is the perfect fantasist: fragmentary, tantalizing, a dealer in codes and riddles. His mother, you recall, was deserted by her husband. She was the leading actress of a small company of players. She died when her son was only two years old. This fatal break in Poe's life was indeed fatal. One can feel how he barely survived, by exercising his creative faculties, by pouring out his ravaged thoughts.

Shylock asked on behalf of the Jews, "If they prick us, do we not bleed?" The fantasy writers have often been pricked. They bleed, and that lifeblood is our profit.

I have spoken only of writers who are dead, but no doubt the same observation might be made of the living. Things do not change in that respect. If you looked behind the texts of such novels as *The Drowned World* and *Hothouse,* you might expect to come upon similar discontinuities.

The late Andrei Tarkovsky, master of the cinema, saw films as a way of fixing time or of transposing reality. Fantasy is often a way of turning the clock back to a time when happiness was unquestioned. Perhaps the irrational side of our natures recognizes this and gives its grudging thanks to the writers. But I would say this to critics, "Tread softly, for you tread on our screams."

William Lomax

Epic Reversal in Mary Shelley's *The Last Man*: Romantic Irony and the Roots of Science Fiction

Mary Shelley's third novel, *The Last Man* (1826), languished for a century and a half in deep literary obscurity. It brought its author a modicum of success,[1] but the book virtually disappeared during the nineteenth century; Victorian optimism evidently found little inspiration in this most pessimistic of Romantic novels. Recently, however, the book has once again begun to attract critical attention, in part because the first new edition in 132 years appeared in 1965, in part perhaps because the pendulum of pessimism has swung back with the modern uneasiness over nuclear technology. Whatever the reason, the critical canon is growing, and *The Last Man* is being recognized as a significant work, both for Shelley scholarship and for an understanding of Romantic philosophy.[2]

The purpose of this study is to examine one aspect of the novel's structure that places *The Last Man* squarely in the developing tradition of Romantic irony and suggests that the novel is also a major text for our understanding of the origins of science fiction.

The story begins in 1818 with a visit to the Cave of the Cumaean Sybil in Naples, where the narrator discovers the scattered pages of an ancient manuscript. She organizes them—and they tell the story of Verney, the last man on Earth. In 2073, England has become a republic, and a group of characters (loosely based on the members of the Shelley-Byron circle) become involved in the social and political processes of the time. A war in Greece looses a deadly plague that slowly depopulates the entire world. The English survivors head for Greece, but all eventually die, leaving Verney as the Last Man. He records the history of man's destruction, then leaves his manuscript in the Sibylline Cave.

It is a simple story line, padded to fill out the three-volume format of the day, and is thus often dismissed as rambling and diffuse. The whole, however, is controlled by an underlying blueprint that is tight and logically consistent. Mary's intention in that blueprint is, I believe, to *reverse* the Christian narrative of creation by "decreating" the human race. By metaphorically reversing the flow of time, she destroys generic expectations conditioned by conventional biblical narrative, and produces, literally, a new genre (see Spark 157) which inverts Christian teleology and transforms narrative structures based on that teleology. By placing Verney's completed manuscript in the "timeless" Sibylline Cave (Sterrenburg 342), making it possible for a story written in the year 2100 to be found in the year 1818, Mary shatters the deterministic flow of linear time, which *must* have a stop in Christian teleology, and replaces it with a spiralling, indeterminate sequence that turns back upon itself and never ends—for if it did, why would Verney, the Last Man, bother to write a book? One of the more satisfying ironies in the book is that the "author" of the introduction tells us that the chaotic order of the story is explained by the disorder of the "leaves" in the Cave (Sterrenburg 343)—yet the story is, in fact, linear, rigorously ordered, complete, and logical—but *in reverse*. The introduction, then, is a carefully prepared clue to Mary's intention, which is to use traditional narrative form to destroy traditional narrative form, thereby subverting the Christian *telos* and philosophical world system.

It is a technique used frequently by Byron, who framed his pessimism about the Christian world view in the very narrative forms that had traditionally symbolized that world view. Thus he called *Cain* and *Heaven and Earth* "Mysteries," and the words "Vision" and "Phrophecy" appear in titles of major works. The introduction to *Cain* suggests Byron's familiarity with biblical forms and his desire to emulate them.[3] This technique adds ironic pungency to his poem "Darkness" (a possible influence on *The Last Man*), which uses the ancient dream-allegory format as a "scrim" through which we view what is by far Byron's most pessimistic and despairing vision of mankind and its future. By juxtaposing the pessimism of thought with the optimism of form, Byron establishes an authorial perspective that allows him to present a vivid sociocultural critique while avoiding both total despair and rigid didacticism. It is the strategy of the quintessential Romantic ironist, and it is the strategy used by Mary Shelley in *The Last Man*. In a sense, we may call the product of this generic reversal an "antistructure." That is, by using the "Mystery" form for *Cain*, Byron has produced an "anti-Mystery," or a work which calls into question the world-system and philosophy represented by the traditional Christian "Mystery." Similarly, "Darkness" we may call (albeit rather awkwardly) an "anti-dream-allegory." Following this pattern, *The Last Man* becomes "anti-epic"—the reverse of the Miltonic epic that so strongly influenced Mary.

It is in the reversal of linear time that we most dramatically see the anti-epic impulse that controls the structure of *The Last Man*. Simply stated, *The Last Man* is an epic novel that tells the story of human history in reverse. From the opening page, it is as if the clock of human experience had begun to run backward, and the characters, although they live on the surface according to the normal forward linearity of time, actually rehearse, in a matter of a quarter century of "real" time, the complete history of human life on Earth from the nineteenth century backward to the creation of Adam.[4]

This reversed historical sequence is most clearly presented in the evolution of the career of the narrator, Verney, who, of the major characters, undergoes the most radical changes. Those changes seem to be of two types—those of his inner life and those of his outer life—and they proceed in opposite directions.

Verney first appears to us as a wild savage—"My life," he writes, "was like that of an animal, and my mind was in danger of degenerating into that which informs brute nature" (12).[5] He wanders through "civilized England as uncouth a savage as the wolf-bred founder of old Rome" (9). He is physically imposing; mentally primitive. His sole motivation is revenge against all superior civilized beings, those who persecute and imprison him simply for exercising his desire for freedom. But then, having been caught repeatedly for poaching on lands belonging to the Earl of Windsor, he meets Adrian for the first time. At the moment Adrian confronts him, Verney's "savage revengeful heart, felt the influence of sweet benignity sink upon it" (17) and he "began to be human" (20). He becomes self-aware, his mind is opened to human sympathy, and he becomes sensitive to art. Above all, he becomes a social being and dedicates himself to human benevolence (25). Intellectually, he devotes himself to the world of books and lives in the imagination (55). Morally, he finds himself totally reformed, an image of virtue such that even the angelic Idris becomes interested in him (56). Socially and politically, he becomes a sensitive, benevolent aristocrat, beloved by the little people, a leader of men, a powerful ally of England's rulers. Under the immediate and powerful influence of Adrian, Verney is converted, almost overnight, into the epitome of a civilized being. Later, he becomes a visionary and develops, ultimately, into a god, for at the end he is the sole remaining civilized being in the universe, one who longs, godlike, for companionship, and one who creates, godlike, a new world in his ordering of the chaos of experience in a fictional narrative. He becomes a myth, a legend to those unknown souls who may, somehow, read the Sibylline leaves of his "scripture."

The cosmic irony of this is that the peak of his spiritual development coincides with the disappearance of his constituency. As his inner life flourishes, his outer life degenerates. This reversal is most obvious in the depopulation of the Earth, but Mary Shelley is not satisfied with the obvious and so plants a carefully structured sequence of symbols and images to show that we are indeed traveling backward from modern times to Genesis.

The first volume of the novel is the most contemporary of the three. Despite the date, Republican England is, politically and socially, England of the Regency. The book is, for a volume and a half, nothing more than a traditional novel of manners. But with the deadly rise of the plague, contemporary manners and civilized living gradually retrogress. Ordered society collapses, and social entropy increases. Soon biblical allusions begin to appear in reverse historical order. Like an Old Testament prophet, Verney begins to have visions of plague and death (146, 174). Then, as the remnant of survivors leaves England to seek a better place, Adrian becomes a Moses leading an exodus across the channel to a Promised Land. The vast abandoned resources of civilization, like manna from heaven, provide the wanderers with food and necessities. In France, Adrian has to deal with a false prophet who lures his followers into idolatry, but Adrian destroys him and leads his flock onward. Later, after wandering through the wilderness of France, Adrian finally mounts the pass through the Jura, and, to Verney, who alludes to Hebrew poetry, Adrian "seemed to behold something unexpected and wonderful; for, pausing, his head stretched out, his arms for a moment extended, he seemed to give an All Hail! to some new vision" (305). Adrian does make it through the mountains, but his death by drowning in the Adriatic prevents him from reaching the Grecian "Promised Land" that they all had envisioned. Then, as the survivors dwindle, flood imagery increases. In desolated England, Windsor had seemed an Ark, a "haven and retreat for the wrecked bark of human society" (189). Verney later compares the destruction of man by plague to the Flood (295), and eventually the "perennial flood" of ocean (320) takes his last companions from him. As the four remaining survivors reach Milan, Verney writes that "we made laws for ourselves, dividing our day" (313) as Adam, in Eden, had ordered his world by fiat. Earlier in the novel, Verney had referred to himself as the "father of all mankind" (113) and, as the Last Man, he ultimately tries to return the cosmos to chaos so he can recreate it in narrative:

> It is all over now—a step or two over those new made graves, and the wearisome way is done. Can I accomplish my task? Can I streak my paper with words capacious of the grand conclusion? Arise, black Melancholy! quit thy Cimmerian solitude! Bring with thee murky fogs from hell, which may drink up the day; bring blight and pestiferous exhalations, which, entering the hollow caverns and breathing places of earth, may fill her stony veins with corruption, so that not only herbage may no longer flourish, the trees may rot, and the rivers run with gall—but the everlasting mountains be decomposed, and the mighty deep putrify, and the genial atmosphere which clips the globe, lose all powers of generation and sustenance. Do this, sad visaged power, while I write, while eyes read these pages (318).

In an ironic echo of the Genesis story of creation, the plague takes seven years to destroy man and then rests (310).

The final ironic opposition occurs in the fact that, while the human race rapidly moves along a reversed linear time line toward annihilation, Verney, once he reaches the godlike peak of his evolution, discovers he has merely come in a circle and has returned to that state where he began: a wild savage and a pariah from society. After the shipwreck, he compares himself to Robinson Crusoe—"My hair was matted and wild. . . . The wild and cruel Caribbee, the merciless Cannibal . . . would have been to me a beloved companion . . . [for] his nature would be kin to mine" (326–27). He is startled when he accidentally sees himself in a mirror—"What wild-looking, unkempt, half-naked savage was that before me?" (331). He again refers to himself, as he had in the first chapter of his story, as akin to the "wolf-bred founder of old Rome" (338). He is again a nomad—now literally in the Rome to which he had only alluded at the beginning. In writing a narrative of his cyclic journey, he rehearses the entire epic quest, and he is firmly caught in endless repetitiveness for, as the Last Man, he is also automatically the First Man, as alone as Adam and no more hopeful than Adam.

Verney's inverted epic journey is, however, only the central strand which, like a backbone, supports the body of the novel's structure. Numerous subthemes, like ribs, branch from this central trunk. One is the quest for the Edenic Paradise that appears, both literally and metaphorically, throughout the novel. Considering the ultimate devastation of the plague, it would seem to be a futile quest. But for Mary Shelley, it is futile only as long as men insist on searching for Paradise in the traditional ways. The reversed time sequence of *The Last Man* represents such a search—and the result is indeed futility.

Simultaneously, however, Mary suggests that, while dreams of the Paradise of Christian myth are vain, a Paradise *is* available in human society and human love. From the beginning, Verney yearns for the solace of human society; even as a savage, warring against civilization, he paradoxically wishes to belong to it (12). His interior development through the novel is a progression toward an ever more intense desire to serve his fellow human beings (107, 126). The Paradise of human society reaches its zenith in love of family and of friends and the love of man and wife. Numerous instances of such love are scattered through the novel, too many to cite, but it is important to note that such individual love is inevitably as physical as it is spiritual. Perdita, for example, is obsessed with the idea of living next to her husband's tomb (150–52). Merrival, the astronomer, who has apparently lived his life in a haze of speculative ether, actually loses his mind when his family dies, and he, too, like Heathcliff, insists on being near their dead bodies (220–21). The most intense spiritual and moral strengths, the greatest happiness, emerge from close family and personal relationships in the novel, and the greatest despair grows out of the loss of such relationships. It is in the continuing physical proximity of sympathetic, loving human beings that Mary's characters find Paradise, as temporary as it may be. This Paradise, too, is lost at the end of the novel, but the crucial difference is that the Paradise of human society *did exist* when humanity populated the Earth, whereas the inverted quest for a Christian Paradise, one free of death (321), is futile because it has never existed for man since the original expulsion from Eden. The first is only metaphorically lost in narrative and can be regained in narrative—and implicitly regained, therefore, in the "narrative" of human life— whereas the latter has never been regained and never will be, given the nature of the human fall.

Mary sets up, in Raymond, a vivid and kinetic symbol of the gradual loss of this human Paradise. The Byronic Raymond oscillates between the poles of love and heroism—and to Mary Shelley, these are direct oppositions. Raymond is continually torn between passion for love and passion for greatness. He tastes the former in his life with Perdita, but when Evadne reenters his life and he experiences the conflicts of dual passions, he turns violently against the "necessities" of the heart (47). He denounces passion (though he, ironically, is the most passionate of men), for it is a continual source of disorder (107) and a power over which he has no control (109). Raymond is a man who needs action (85), who thrives on power and acclaim, and the heart is a stumbling block for such a man (45). He revels in war (116), and he grows morose and gloomy without the pull and the satisfaction of glory (135, 141). Raymond is Mary's vision of the true *epic* hero—and he is inadequate in every way. It is significant that Raymond, the heroic leader, is the one who defies the commonsense caution of his soldiers and enters Constantinople to loose the plague onto the world (127). He puts heroism above love, and loses his life—the life which is the only source of Paradise for fallen man. It is a poignant but sincere irony that, when the survivors emigrate from England, Verney says that they leave the "land of heroism" (275).

Mary's true hero appears not in the foolhardy Raymond, but in her commemorative homage to her beloved Shelley, the Christlike Adrian, who cares for humanity, not for glory (185, 277). At his first meeting with the godlike Adrian, the savage Verney is almost immediately converted and "born anew" (19):

> He came up the while; and his appearance blew aside, with gentle western breath, my cloudy wrath: a tall, slim, fair boy, with a physiognomy expressive of the excess of sensibility and refinement stood before me; the morning sunbeams tinged with gold his silken hair, and spread light and glory over his beaming countenance. . . .
>
> As he spoke, his earnest eyes, fixed on me, seemed to read my very soul: my heart, my savage revengeful heart, felt the influence of sweet benignity sink upon it; while his thrilling voice, like sweetest melody, awoke a mute echo within me, stirring to its depths the life-blood in my frame. I desired to reply, to acknowledge his goodness, accept his proffered friendship; but words, fitting words, were not afforded to the rough mountaineer; I would have held out my hand, but its guilty stain restrained me. Adrian took pity on my faltering mien: "Come with me," he said. (17)

As the novel progresses, we soon perceive that, just as Verney's career follows Old Testament history in reverse, so Adrian's career follows the life of Christ forward. Early in the story, Adrian goes "insane" and wanders in the wilderness (49). Unlike Raymond, he is a peacemaker (116), and on two occasions, once in England and once in France, he rides boldly between opposing armies and, with words alone, forces men to lay down their arms and embrace each other (216–18, 276). He feeds the needy (171) and responds to the needs of humanity, gaining strength as the adversity of others increases (178). As the Protector of England after Ryland's humiliating abdication, Adrian is a true philosopher-king, constantly restoring order and performing miracles, leading like a "magician" (182). He tells Ryland that, if indeed "all the world has the plague," then "to avoid it, we must quit the world" (175). He is worshipped—"women kissed his hands, and the edges of his garments; nay, his horse received tribute of their embraces; some wept their welcome; he appeared an angel of peace descended among them" (276–77)—and he remains faithful to the "force of love" to the very end (311).

His power to "save" recurs often. An abandoned girl in the ruins of London pleads with Adrian: "save me" (242). Another girl, watching over her blind father in a Swiss church, cries to Adrian: "O save my father!" (307). In France, Adrian "saves" his followers while the false Prophet does not scruple to kill his to maintain power (278). He even intervenes to save the life of the man who attempts to assassinate him (295). Other characters frequently engage in "saving" acts, but with starkly contrasting results. Verney tries to save Perdita by drugging her and carrying her off; as a result, she drowns herself (154–55). He tries to save Adrian from the massive responsibilities of the Protectorship, but fails (183–84); both Perdita and Adrian chastise him as "unkind." Verney resolves to "save" his family (180), but more than once he abandons them to follow Adrian (185, 293).

The intentional irony of all this is that, for all of Adrian-Shelley-Christ's heroics, he ultimately fails as a Christ while succeeding as a human being. He essentially accomplishes all that Christ accomplished *on Earth*, but as a savior of his race, he is impotent even to save himself. There will be no resurrection from his watery grave. Mary Shelley is here presenting, I think, a Byronic view of Christ, one that sees the great act of sacrifice on the cross as an ultimately useless one.[6] "Adrian" is Mary Shelley's true sacrificial hero, and he lives the dedicated, consecrated life that she sees as the only true moral life. But "Christ" fails to remove the universal plague from man's nature, fails to save either the lives of individuals or the life of the race. The nature and destiny of man is out of his hands and in the control of a Necessity—a "natural" plague (140)—which is omnipotent. Before the inexorable force of that Necessity, *nothing* human is effective, for it is the "nature" of man. Burkean politics fail (165); military might collapses into chaos (217); rank and privilege dissolve into a universal democracy of misery (212); speculative science, out of touch with practical realities, goes mad in a disordered world (209, 220–21); above all, the promises of religion—the old, traditional sanctuary of a disintegrating world—prove to be empty and useless in combating the plague that has arisen from the city of Constantinople, the home of the very Church itself. There is no sanctuary in Westminster Abbey, for Verney sees a chorister die at the very moment that prayers for salvation rise up to heaven (205). The churches fall silent and die as Verney and Adrian prepare to leave London (241).

Now is the future state for Mary Shelley; they are one and the same. Present and future revolve around each other in a timeless, cyclic dialectic that totally shatters the Christian teleology rooted in linear time, beginning in Genesis and ending in Apocalypse. Mary does not want an *end* to anything except pain; she has suffered through the premature deaths of her entire circle of companions, and she finds eternal life in an endless spiral of love and sociability that even the death of the race cannot halt. As Verney approaches the Eternal City of Rome, he looks neither to the future nor the past, but only to the present (303, 310, 325). He no longer has prophetic visions. He throws away the stick on which he had been marking days, for he realizes he no longer needs it (333). He hears only "the voice of dead time" (336).

In these complex juxtapositions and reversals—Christ and Adrian, Raymond and Adrian, Adrian and the Prophet, love and heroism, time and eternity, Eden and the Paradises of this world, inner and outer life, and many others— Mary Shelley has woven a complex texture of irony designed to shatter the assumptions and traditions of an outmoded worldview—outmoded because it failed to justify or soothe the inexpressibly deep pain of personal experience. *The Last Man* is an epic story that inverts and ironizes *Paradise Lost*, the last great epic produced by that worldview. It is anti-epic because, although its "outer form" is that of prose epic, its "inner form"[7] substitutes for Miltonic justification a vision of despair and annihilation. Neither Adam nor Christ can fulfill the epic role for Mary, and without the Christian epic hero, the only remaining figure of power is Satan—the plague of man's nature.

The Byronic juxtaposition of an outer form of Christian epic with an inner form of annihilation sets up a dialectic of narratives that allows Mary the flexibility to escape the trap of total despair. Thus, there is a *type* of epic hero in *The Last Man*, and there is a *type* of victory. Raymond, the classic epic hero, may fail, but Adrian, the apostle of love, does not. Adrian the Christ figure may fail, but Adrian the humanitarian does not. The Paradise of Genesis may be unattainable, but the Paradise of human companionship is not. The novel is pessimistic to the extent that the plague of man's "nature" inevitably over-powers man's hopes and aspirations but, just as the repetitive spiral of time in which Verney finds himself at the end implies a hope for a repetition of the human cycle, so the offer of alternatives implies the possibility of a different sort of salvation even as the old sort collapses.

It is this, I would argue, that is the crucial characteristic of *The Last Man* that connects it with modern science fiction. The central concern of science fiction is the creation not of alternate worlds or alternate futures, but of alternate myths. Alternate worlds and futures are only the metaphors that express the underlying myths of a culture's fundamental worldview. "A given culture," writes Hayden White, "is only as strong as its power to convince its least dedicated member that its fictions are truths" (1972). This is what we can no longer do for ourselves, for our "sustaining cultural myths . . . have one by one passed into the category of the fictitious" (6). With the collapse of the great mythic system of Christianity, new metaphors and new myths had to be found. They are necessarily located in other worlds and future times, for those are the only places new myths can settle; the dead past is the home of the old myth. Thus, out of Romantic pessimism and its artistic demolition of the past, science fiction arose. It is the dramatization of the search for new myths that characterizes science fiction. *The Last Man* has had little direct influence on subsequent literature, but it was an early efflorescence in English literature of a cultural consciousness that later crystallized in modern science fiction.

The term *anti-epic* means, then, not the destruction of epic, but the transformation of epic. Within the vastness of the sublime destruction of mankind there does exist a small seed of hope, a vision of a different kind of Paradise than that held out by Christian epic, and in her complex, subtlely integrated narrative, Mary Shelley reaches out, however feebly, to touch it. This is the most that can be expected of the Byronic Romantic who, looking unwillingly to the future, sees only Darkness. The Darkness, the plague, is not in the future, but in man's nature, and it is the plague that prevents man from ever attaining the Promised Land, the Paradise Garden, Eden—all of the mesmerizing mythical visions held out by the Christian world-system. *The Last Man* implies that as long as man continues to pursue such unattainable dreams, annihilation will continue to be the only result of the pursuit.

Like most major Romantics, Mary Shelley in *The Last Man* turns inward to find alternatives and thereby achieves a kind of solace through the domination of outer reality by inner, imaginative reality. And that, I believe, is the tap root of science fiction.

Notes

1. Contemporary reviews were generally favorable, and Mary received around £1,000 during the time it was in print. See Bigland 223, Gerson 234, Grylls 190.

2. The critical canon is yet small and therefore still manageable, but certain approaches or "schools" of thought have crystallized. One is that of the "Last Man" theme, the roots of which lay in the late eighteenth-century fascination with ruins and the decline of civilizations. With the anonymous English translation in 1806 of Grainville's *Le dernier homme*, it grew into a brief, minor fad that inspired works by Byron, Shelley, Beddoes, Campbell, Hood, and others (Palacio, Sambrook), and provided Mary with a convenient current subject for her novel, just as the Asian cholera working its way slowly toward England in the 1820s probably gave her the plague theme (Sambrook 31).

> The autobiographical approach has proven to be the most popular: Ultimately we must return to the fact that it is from her own experience of solitude, from the personal landscape of devastation she felt around her, that her wonderful story draws life. (Spark 165)

The obvious biographical correspondences of Adrian-Shelley, Raymond-Byron, and Verney-Mary make the novel an interesting roman à clef, but Mary herself remains the center of this approach. For Mary, says Hartley Spatt, the only real existence was that which was reenacted in the mind; the inner life is the only ordered, rational reality, for outer "reality" is chaos and death (532). This is why Verney must write his story even though no one remains to read it. He can convince himself of the reality of his experiences only by reenacting them in his mind and ordering them in a narrative, producing what John Clubbe, referring to Byron's poetry, has called an "objective correlative for a spiritual state" (27).

A third school, which we may call the sociopolitical approach, attempts to relate the novel to contemporary events. Lee Sterrenburg, for example, argues that Mary "translated her personal suffering into an ambitious, historically significant anatomy of the revolutionary age" (347). Others have seen in the novel a representation of her father's ideas (e.g., Spark 154–56), while yet others see it as a refutation of Godwinianism (e.g., El-Shater 94–105).

3. Byron wrote, rather sardonically, to Thomas Moore, on September 19, 1821, that he had titled *Cain* "A Mystery" "according to the former Christian custom, and in honour of what it probably will remain to the reader" (Byron 7: 216).

4. Even though the story takes place in the twenty-first century, the intent of the novel is clearly not prophecy or speculation. The only obvious scientific extrapolation is commercial balloon travel, and it has little to do with the story. The oft-mentioned prediction of the ascendance of the House of Windsor is, of course, simply a lucky hit. Most other aspects of the story are persistently Georgian in character. The only reason for placing the story in the future—the primary reason why all fantasy fiction is placed "other-where"—is to allow the imaginative flexibility of action necessary for such a prodigiously extravagant myth.

5. All page references to the novel, hereafter placed in the body of the text, are from Professor Luke's 1965 edition, published by the University of Nebraska Press. A reprint of this edition has recently been issued in England by Brian Aldiss (London: Hogarth, 1985).

6. To Francis Hodgson, on September 13, 1811, Byron wrote:

> The basis of your religion is *injustice*; the *Son of God*, the *pure*, the *immaculate*, the *innocent*, is sacrificed for the *guilty*. This proves *His* heroism; but no more does away with *man's* guilt than a schoolboy's volunteering to be flogged for another would exculpate the dunce from negligence, or preserve him from the rod. You degrade the Creator, in the first place, by making Him a begetter of children; and in the next you convert Him into a tyrant over an immaculate and injured Being, who is sent into existence to suffer death for the benefit of some millions of scoundrels, who, after all, seem as likely to be damned as ever. (Byron 2: 97)

7. These terms are used in Wellek and Warren 221.

Works Cited

Bigland, Eileen. *Mary Shelley*. London: Cassell, 1959.

Byron, Lord George Gordon. *Byron's Letters and Journals*. Ed. Leslie A. Marchand. Vol. 2. Cambridge: Harvard University Press, 1973.

————. *Byron's Letters and Journals*. Ed. Leslie A. Marchand. Vol. 7. Cambridge: Harvard University Press, 1978.

Clubbe, John. " 'The New Prometheus of New Men': Byron's 1816 Poems and *Manfred*." *Nineteenth-Century Literary Perspectives*. Ed. Clyde de L. Ryals. Durham, N.C.: Duke University Press, 1974.

El-Shater, Safaa. *The Novels of Mary Shelley*. Salzburg: Institut für Englische Sprache und Literatur, 1977.

Gerson, Noel B. *Daughter of Earth and Water*. New York: Morrow, 1973.

Grylls, R. Glynn. *Mary Shelley*. London: Oxford University Press, 1938.

Palacio, Jean de. "Mary Shelley and the 'Last Man'—A Minor Romantic Theme." *Revue de Litterature Comparee* 42 (January–March 1968): 37–49.

Sambrook, A. J. "A Romantic Theme: The Last Man." *Forum for Modern Language Studies* 2 (January 1966): 25–33.

Shelley, Mary. *The Last Man*. Ed. Hugh J. Luke, Jr. Lincoln: University of Nebraska Press, 1965.

Spark, Muriel. *Child of Light*. Hadleigh: Tower Bridge, 1951.

Spatt, Hartley S. "Mary Shelley's Last Men: The Truth of Dreams." *Studies in the Novel* 7 (Winter 1975): 526–37.

Sterrenburg, Lee. "The Last Man: Anatomy of Failed Revolutions." *Nineteenth-Century Fiction* 33 (December 1978): 324–47.

Wellek, Rene, and Austin Warren. *Theory of Literature*. New York: Harcourt Brace, 1949.

White, Hayden. "The Forms of Wildness: Archaeology of an Idea." *The Wild Man Within*. Ed. Edward Dudley and Maximillian E. Novak. Pittsburgh: University of Pittsburgh Press, 1972. 3–38.

Leonard G. Heldreth

From Reality to Fantasy: Displacement and Death in Albee's *Zoo Story*

Both those who regard *The Zoo Story* as one of Albee's "more realistic" plays (Woods 224) and those who see it as "part fantasy and part truncated realism" (Dubler 253) tend to focus on the connections with Ibsen and Strindberg.[1] An alternate approach is to see the play as a precursor of the fuller fantasies embodied in *The American Dream* and *Who's Afraid of Virginia Woolf*? Dubler asserts, "The common denominator of all incidents alluded to and situations enacted in *The American Dream* is that they involve private fantasies" (247), and the same evaluation holds true of *The Zoo Story*. Because Jerry's fantasies have an air of realism about them—Peter says Jerry described people "vividly"—and because Peter's fantasies are standard ones of the middle class, their illusory quality is less obvious than the fantasies in several of Albee's other plays.[2] Yet Peter's fantasy insulates him from the reality of people such as Jerry, and Jerry's fantasy leads him to death.

This theme of fantasy appears in two short stories that appeared before *The Zoo Story* and may have influenced Albee in writing the play. In 1953, Jean Stafford's "In the Zoo" was published in *The New Yorker*, and in 1955, Carson McCullers published "A Tree, a Rock, a Cloud"; *The Zoo Story* was produced in Germany in 1958. These stories have striking parallels with many of the elements and some of the ideas of Albee's one-act play. He was probably familiar with McCullers's work, since he later adapted *The Ballad of the Sad Cafe* to the stage; he may also have known Stafford's story, since "In the Zoo" received the O. Henry Award, First Prize, in 1955.[3] Noting the similarities between these stories and *The Zoo Story* may shed some light on the later work.

The initial scene of "In the Zoo" is virtually identical to the set of the play. In Stafford's story, two middle-aged women, Daisy and her unnamed sister, the narrator, are sitting on a park bench in the Denver Zoo, passing the time until the sister's train arrives. As Jerry throughout the play compares people to animals—the zoo animals, Peter's cats and parakeets, the landlady's dog—so the two women note the similarity between the animals they are watching and people they have known as children, and immediately both are plunged into a reverie on their past. Later in the story, they compare Mr. Murphy's pets to people, and the people in Mrs. Placer's boarding house to animals.

As Jerry tells Peter of his childhood and past experiences, so the narrator of "In the Zoo" relates the story of her childhood and youth. Jerry's mother died when he was between eleven and twelve, and about three weeks later his father was killed by a bus; the parents of the girls died "within a month of each other," when Daisy was ten and the narrator was eight. Jerry moved in with his aunt, who neither drank nor sinned (24), while the girls moved into a boarding house run by Mrs. Placer, who was equally dour and had "old cardboard boxes filled with such things as W.C.T.U. tracts and anti-cigarette literature and newspaper clippings relating to sexual sin in the Christianized islands of the Pacific" (114). Jerry, at the time of the play, lives in a boarding house whose landlady possesses traits of both Mrs. Placer, the girls' guardian, and Mr. Murphy, the drunk Irishman who gives them a dog. Jerry's landlady spies on him (28), while Mrs. Placer has spies all over town and ridicules the girls until "Daisy and I lived in a mesh of lies and evasions, baffled and mean, like rats in a maze" (111). Each afternoon Jerry's landlady drinks a pint of lemon-flavored gin, and Mr. Murphy, the girls' friend, stays drunk most of the time, gradually becoming "enfeebled with gin" (111).

The strongest parallel, however, between the two landladies is their use of fantasy. Jerry's landlady, in her drunken stupor, remembers, with a little urging from him, an affair with Jerry that never took place. Mrs. Placer, ridiculing everything from the girls' boyfriends to their achievements, constantly reshapes the facts brought to her by the girls until they suit her view of the world. The best example of her manipulation of reality is her reaction when Mr. Murphy offers the girls a puppy, a reaction that is first negative as she considers "this murderous, odiferous, drunk, Roman Catholic dog," and then, as the "fantasy spun on, richly and rapidly," (98) she completely reverses herself and sees him as "a pillar of society" (99). Reality is constantly manipulated in the story to fit Mrs. Placer's beliefs. Even her name reflects the children's being placed with her as, according to various critics, Jerry's and Peter's names reflect their parts in the play.

The most obvious connection between the two narratives, however, is the central position occupied in each by the dog.[4] In the story, Caesar, who was originally named Laddie and belonged to the girls, has been taken over by Mrs. Placer and turned into a vicious brute who attacks the milkman, the paperboy, the meter man, and even a salesman, whose wound required stitches. He is lustrous black, sleeps in Mrs. Placer's bedroom, and "gulped down a whole pound of hamburger" (110) that Mr. Murphy had poisoned. The dog in The Zoo Story is also black, he attacks Jerry when his territory is intruded upon, and he "gobbled" down a hamburger that Jerry had filled with rat poison. The only significant difference between the two dogs is that Caesar dies from the poison and the other dog, after suffering, recovers.

Other details in the story parallel those in the play. Mr. Murphy plays solitaire with cards that anticipate the regular decks in Jerry's box; the fire chief in Stafford's story, like Jerry, visits prostitutes; on the day of Caesar's death, the narrator announces, "Oh, it was hot that day!" (108), while on the critical day of the play, Jerry says, "It's a hot day" (40); and Mrs. Placer's phrase, "I just have to laugh," repeated by the narrator at the end of Stafford's story, anticipates Peter's uncontrollable hysteria when Jerry tickles him.[5]

Less obvious but more important, however, are the motivational parallels in the two stories. Near the end of Stafford's story, the narrator acknowledges, "You may be sure we did not unlearn those years as soon as we put her [Mrs. Placer] out of sight in the cemetery" (113), and the rest of the narrator's behavior in the story, to the concluding hysterical laughter, bears out her statement: the behavior they were forced to follow has imposed a pattern on their young lives and motivates their adult actions. In her concluding comments on the train, she describes the marijuana she thinks she sees in the fields outside the windows and spins an elaborate fantasy about a priest riding with her on the train. Jerry in *The Zoo Story* also follows patterns of behavior he learned as he grew up, and these account for much of his motivation.

His philosophy, however, seems taken over almost directly from a character in Carson McCullers's story "A Tree, a Rock, a Cloud," published in 1955, two years after "In the Zoo" and three years before *The Zoo Story*. This story also has circumstantial parallels with Albee's play. As Peter is accosted in a public park by Jerry, who tells him his life story, so here a young newsboy stops at a diner, a public place, for a cup of coffee, where he is accosted by an old man who describes how his wife had run away ten years before. The old man sought her in "Tulsa, Atlanta, Mobile, Chicago, Cheehaw, Memphis" (101), just as Jerry's mother had left his father for an adulterous trip through the southern states. Both Jerry and the old man act as teachers; and while Leo, the diner owner, refers to the old man as a "prominent transient" (99), Jerry refers to himself as a *"permanent transient"* (37).

Yet these patterns of similarity are less important than the thematic one, the nature of love. Like Jerry, the old man attempts to impose his view of life upon an unresponsive audience, and he anticipates Jerry's philosophical statement on how one should learn to love. The old man tells the boy that at first he wanted only to find his wife but, as time went on, he forgot what she looked like. He learned to love objects he found in the road, then a goldfish, a street full of people, a bird in the sky, a tree, a rock, a cloud, or the newsboy that he is now addressing. Jerry also believes that he must learn to deal "with a bed, with a cockroach, . . . some day, with people" (34–35). Each character states that the ability to love must be learned in a gradual ascension from simple inanimate objects to human beings. Each main character ends by declaring his love; the old man for the newsboy, and Jerry, in his perverse fantasy, for Peter.

These two stories, together with the embedded narratives in Albee's play, suggest answers to some questions that, within the explicit structure of the play, remain unanswered. The play describes four periods in Jerry's life: his childhood and adolescence, including the death of his family and his first sexual experiences; the recent conflict at his rooming house, known in the play as "The Story of Jerry and the Dog"; his experience at the zoo earlier in the day during which the play takes place; and finally, the central event of the play, his encounter with Peter in the park. Each section is clearly delineated except for the third, the experience at the zoo. The importance of this section, however, is emphasized by the play's title and Jerry's opening line, "I've been to the zoo. . . . I said, I've been to the zoo. MISTER, I'VE BEEN TO THE ZOO!" Throughout the play, Jerry reminds Peter and the audience of this event's significance with lines such as, "Do you want to know what happened at the zoo or not?" (39). This motif sets the audience up for a climactic description, but it is one that never appears in the play. Jerry begins to tell the zoo story, but then abruptly starts the fight with Peter. The four narratives of the play parallel each other so carefully, however, that by examining the other three, together with the short stories described earlier, we can extrapolate and determine what happened at the zoo and why Jerry's ideas of love are so intertwined with death. The four narratives reinforce each other through four major themes: love, death, territorial conflicts, and past conditioning that leads to fantasy.

Jerry presents his narratives quite carefully, and although he begins with the incident at the zoo, he quickly shifts to questions about his location; later he starts again to tell of the zoo but veers away: "let me tell you some other things" (27). The implication is that these "other things" will illuminate the incident at the zoo to the extent that it will not need to be explicitly recounted.

Among these "other things" which Jerry will tell are his first experiences with physical love and death. His most extensive physical relationship, he tells us, occurred when he was fifteen; for eleven days, he had a homosexual relationship with a park superintendent's son (25).[6] Jerry tells nothing about why the relationship ended after eleven days. Did the boy move away? Were they discovered and forbidden to meet again? Or did the superintendent's son, like so many other boys in Albee's plays, die—literally, like the mistreated twin in *American Dream*, or figuratively, like the imaginary son or the boy who drank "bergin" in *Who's Afraid of Virginia Woolf?* Whatever his fate, he simply disappears from the account.

Such disappearances and deaths were common in Jerry's early life. When he was ten, his mother ran away, and after a year-long absence, she died in Alabama (24). His father brought the body home in late December, and after a two-week drinking binge, his father was killed by a city bus. Jerry moved in with his mother's sister for seven or eight years, and then she died on the afternoon of his high school graduation. With the possible exception of his affair with the Greek boy, every relationship Jerry has experienced has ended in death.

Nor is Jerry's concern with territory, which culminates in his takeover of the park bench, surprising. Homeless, obligated to see his aunt's home first as "her apartment" and then as "my apartment" (24), he now has no turf to call his own. Further, each family member died out of home territory—the mother in

Alabama, the father in a city street, and the aunt on the stairs to her apartment. None of the characters die in their own houses or beds. The pattern seems clear, and Jerry learns it: venturing out of one's territory is dangerous and perhaps deadly. This pattern will be repeated when Jerry ventures into the dog's domain at the boarding house and when he tries to take over Peter's bench in the park. Like the girls of "In the Zoo," events in Jerry's childhood are shaping him to react in a predictable way.

After Jerry describes his early life, he assures Peter that despite his youthful homosexual experience, he now loves "the little ladies" (25). Yet, other lines of dialogue indicate Jerry's continued interest in men. He tells Peter he doesn't talk to many people except in phrases such as "keep your hands to yourself, buddy" (17). He also admits his women "aren't pretty little ladies" (34–35). Does this mean that his women are fat and ugly, probably whores? Their reluctance to be photographed (25) seems to fit such an interpretation; yet he is filled with fury over this fact, and his comment on the deck of pornographic playing cards, that fantasy becomes a substitute for real life, may mean that these little ladies are men whom he sees once and then, in guilt and anger, never sees again. The next phrase in this particular speech, which begins an attempt to show how a man must learn to deal with things, speaks of "making money with your body which is an act of love" (35). Jerry seems to be denying, except for an early experience, his homosexual desires and is having compulsive one-night stands with either prostitutes or men who he pretends to himself are women. He also denies his own prostitution. Despite his comment that people must know the effects of their actions (33), Jerry cannot face himself or his actions: a relationship with a mirror is "too hard, that's one of the last steps. With . . . toilet paper . . . that's a mirror, too; always check bleeding" (34). He cannot accept his own image, his homosexuality, or even his animalistic nature, which manifests itself in the blood on the toilet paper, so he maintains his distance from everyone, including himself.

Jerry cannot avoid his landlady, however, in the next section, the story of Jerry and the dog; she presses her body against him and Jerry resorts to fantasy, perhaps of the type he is even now telling Peter. When the landlady attempts to seduce him, he lies to her about what they had done in her room in earlier meetings and she is satisfied. His use here of fantasy is the reverse of his earlier statement about the pornographic playing cards, which for boys are "a substitute for a real experience," but adults "use real experience as a substitute for the fantasy" (27). His statement criticizes a world that cannot live up to his fantasy expectations and indicates a desire for another relationship as valid as that with the Greek boy. His later sexual relationships seem to be merely experiences through which he can recapture, in fantasy, the ecstasy of this earlier love. The comment about the pornographic playing cards functions as a metaphor for Jerry's entire outlook on life. Unable to face the life he lives, Jerry shapes reality into something more meaningful; he constantly reevaluates the past, turning it into a pattern that he only now perceives. For example, only *after* Jerry has tried to kill the dog and failed does he begin to rationalize, telling Peter that he really wanted the dog to live and that the experience was a learning process. After Peter expresses horror, Jerry acknowledges, in an echo of his statement about the pornographic cards, that such real-life experiences make good fantasies to read about (29).

More significant, however, than the landlady is her dog, and Jerry reminds us that the story of the dog is associated with his visit to the zoo and the park (30). The landlady's large, black dog, all black except for bloodshot eyes and a red sore on its forepaw, "almost always has an erection. . . . That's red, too" (31). The dog with his aggression and his erection is a masculine image who contrasts with cats, a feminine image: the man selling hamburgers asks if the meat is for his pussycat, but Jerry denies pussycats, which earlier he had identified with wives and daughters. Yet the dog, like the little ladies, appears as a dual sexual image, for as he eats the hamburger that Jerry offers, he makes "sounds in his throat like a woman" (31). The dog's color, black with some red, is the color of death.

Jerry's relationship with the dog parallels his attitude toward himself. He remarks to Peter, "*Her* dog? I thought it was my . . . No. No. You're right. It *is* her dog." If this dog, "Malevolence with an erection," is seen as Jerry's sexual drive, *his* dog, then his initial love for it parallels his early love affair, and his attempt to kill the dog is a metaphor for his attempt to destroy his sexuality, an attempt to deny his homosexuality. But he cannot destroy his sexual side, and the dog survives, albeit somewhat weakened: "I had tried to love and I had tried to kill, and both had been unsuccessful by themselves." (34). This failed attempt at destroying the animalistic side of his nature anticipates the successful and final attempt at death in the park.

Jerry's monologue following this story of the dog is virtually a gloss on the old man's "science" of love in the McCullers's story (103–4). When the boy asks the old man, "Have you fallen in love with a woman again?" the old man replies, "I am not quite ready yet." Jerry apparently *is* ready, for after the speech about love, he compliments Peter, says he's not leaving, and begins to tickle Peter.

The territorial concerns in the dog story are fairly obvious. Jerry ventures into what he thinks is neutral territory in the rooming house, but the dog regards the hall as his territory, and the conflict leads to violence and then attempted murder as Jerry fights for the right to reach the stairs to his room.

Jerry has promised Peter to tell next about what happened at the zoo (29), and now he begins. The zoo experience has traumatized Jerry, for in his first conversation with Peter, after commenting on the weather, he returns to his original subject, saying "I've been to the zoo" (15). Jerry carefully orchestrates his account, telling Peter, "I went to the zoo to find out more about the way people exist with animals" (40).

Jerry's motivation reminds us of his attempt to establish contact with the dog, and his account of the zoo recalls many of the earlier themes. The animals and people remind us of the landlady's dog, Peter's parakeets and cats, and all the people enclosed in the boarding house where Jerry lives; the children remind us of Peter's two daughters and no sons and of Jerry's orphaned childhood; the animal stench brings to mind the landlady; the vendors selling balloons and ice cream call to mind the man from whom Jerry bought the hamburger; and the barking seals and screaming birds echo the masculine/feminine dichotomy that runs throughout the play: the seals, barking, are doglike and masculine; the birds, slang for women in England and associated with daughters and disease, are feminine. The last description of the zoo in this section is, "the lion keeper comes into the lion cage . . . to feed one of the lions" (40). Then Jerry begins harassing Peter into the fight that ends the play. But Jerry had earlier stated what happened when a person ventured into territory not his own; his mother died, his father died, his aunt died, and he was attacked by a dog. Thus, when the lion keeper goes into the cage to feed the lion, the pattern of Jerry feeding the dog will be repeated: it will eat the food and then go for him. The lion was evidently successful in its surprise attack on the keeper because Jerry has said, "Wait until you see the expression on his face" (19). It is the attack on the zoo keeper and his face that will be seen on TV that night and read about in the paper the next day. It is also the event that reinforces all of Jerry's earlier beliefs and starts him walking northerly to the park where he suicidally invades Peter's territory.

Each of the directions mentioned in the play has symbolic significance and is associated with a character. Because Peter lives between Lexington and Third Avenue on 74th Street, in the east 70's, he embodies the East, with culture, sophistication, and the other characteristics of the eastern seaboard. Jerry, in contrast, lives in a rooming house "on the upper west side . . . Central Park West; I live on the top floor; rear; west." By associating himself with the West, Jerry links himself with the more masculine western image. Jerry states early in the play, "I don't like the West side of the park that much." When Peter asks, "Why?" Jerry replies, "I don't know" (14). The reason is given obliquely later in the play. Peter threatens to call a policeman, but Jerry says, "They're all over on the west side of the park chasing fairies" (43). Jerry's repression of his homosexuality is disturbed by the blatant displays so obvious in the west side of the park. If he had accepted his sexuality, Jerry would have accepted the west side of the park as his home turf, just as his boarding house is on the upper west side (22), but he has suppressed his feelings so much he no longer knows why he dislikes that side of the park.

South is associated with Jerry's mother, for her journey after abandoning the boy and his father was through the southern states, until her death. North is associated with cold, detachment, frozen bodies and minds, and ultimately death. Jerry emphasizes his mother being a "northern stiff," and he describes how "I've been walking north . . . but not due north." He is moving toward death, but circuitously, just as he slowly leads up to the story of the zoo. As the boy said about the old man in "A Tree, A Rock, A Cloud," "He sure has done a lot of traveling" (105).

Jerry is now in a foreign environment: like his mother, he has gone "a long distance out of the way to come back a short distance correctly." He had made a journey south that morning to the village in order to walk back north, pausing at the zoo, but he has not yet reached the safety of his area of town. His mother's return north as a corpse anticipates his own journey north to death. Out of his home territory, as he tries to take over Peter's bench, Jerry sets the stage for disaster.

The last major section, the conflict in the park, ties together the strands that have been carefully developed. After dropping his account of what happened at the zoo, Jerry begins to tickle Peter in a displaced sexual advance: tickling is traditionally associated with sexuality because of the loss of control and the physical intimacy involved. Peter is nervous because tickling is looked upon with suspicion among adult members of the same sex. The advance is a part of Jerry's efforts to make Peter over into the kind of person he is looking for. Jerry has walked straight from the zoo "until I found you . . . or somebody" (48), but he has also ridiculed Peter for his lack of masculinity. Jerry is looking for a human equivalent of the dog and the lion, but Peter, on first impression, does not fit the image. Jerry has already ridiculed Peter's marriage, the daughters he has instead of sons, and the daughters' birds and cats. Peter's profession as a textbook editor and his decision to have no more children, implying emasculation, have allied him with the cultured, passive, scholarly, feminine point of view. Failing, as he knew he would, in his attempt to reach Peter through intimacy, Jerry now tries to reach him, as he did the dog, through violence.[7] Jerry shapes the reality he has found until it fulfills his death fantasy. Conditioned by experience to believe that love leads to pain and death, that sex is a one-time affair,[8] and that people who venture into alien territory are in grave danger, Jerry sets up Peter to act out a fantasy of love and death; in it he will kill the animalistic self that, symbolically, he failed to destroy when he poisoned the dog.

In the conflict that follows, he goads Peter to a fury in which Peter loses his temper, becomes revitalized, seizes the knife, and holds it in front of him. The phallic image is obvious. Jerry, however, has learned his lesson well: *he* is the outsider intruding into the alien territory; *he* has failed to accommodate himself to society's norms; and *he* is repelled by the sexual and physical sides of his nature that refuse to stay locked in cages. Therefore, *he* must die, and he rushes upon the knife. In the stage directions, Albee specifies for tableau of "Jerry impaled on the knife at the end of Peter's still firm arm" (47). The themes of perverse sexual love, of death, of reality shaped into fantasy, and of the price paid by the outsider are all embodied in this climactic image. Then the two men scream.

Jerry now explains to Peter, "Now you know all about what happened at the zoo . . . the face I told you about . . . my face, the face you see right now" (48). Some critics have interpreted this passage literally—that it is Jerry who will be featured in the TV story, but he is speaking metaphorically. He is in the park, several blocks from the zoo, and Peter's understanding of what happened at the zoo, if he does understand, comes from Jerry's parallel actions. Like the lion keeper, Jerry came into the lion's home area and, even though this lion had to be revitalized, Jerry directed the part and the actions as he felt they must inevitably go. And when he says "my face," he again is speaking metaphorically, indicating that the agony on the lion keeper's face and that on his face are identical, for earlier he had referred to "the expression on his face" (19).

Like the old man in the McCullers's story, Jerry wants to learn to love, but what he has learned about himself and love is unacceptable. Like the girls in the Stafford story who "lived in a mesh of lies and evasions, baffled and mean, like rats in a maze" (111), he is reduced to ritual fantasy. His final action is inevitable because it came from within: "Could I have planned all this? . . . I think I did" (48).

In conclusion, Mrs. Placers's fantasies enabled her, in Stafford's story, to deal with a world she would not accept, one that denied her the status she demanded. Unable to tolerate the rigidity she imposed on their childhoods, the girls also retreated into fantasy, a habit that continued into their adulthoods. Jerry also faced a world that rejected him, and he manipulated reality until it fit his destruction fantasy: he was unable to learn to love; he was unable to accept his own physical nature and his homosexuality; and failing, he chose death. He deliberately set up a pattern of destruction that imitated his mother's one-year destructive trip, for he went south and then came north to death; he orchestrated his own death as carefully as he planned the death of the dog; and he used his death as a method both of revitalizing Peter and symbolically restoring Peter's virility through violent action. But at the end of the play, the audience is left with the vision of the zoo, in which people are alienated from one another in rooms like cages, and in which a sexual caress has been displaced to a knife embedded in the chest. As Albee stated in more detail in *The Sandbox*, *The Death of Bessie Smith*, *The American Dream*, and *Who's Afraid of Virginia Woolf?*, American society has deteriorated into a vicious fantasy, a zoo in which human animals, some real and some imaginary, scream and fight and die.

Notes

1. William M. Force summarizes, somewhat cynically, the major critical positions on the play.

2. Dubler notes in Genet's *The Balcony* that "private fantasy is achieved only through the conscientious accumulation of realistic details" (54), details that Jerry generously supplies. In conversation, however, Albee stated to me that Jerry was a "liar."

3. Albee acknowledged knowing Stafford's work but refused to comment on the

connection between either of the stories and his play, a stand consistent with his public discussions of his writings.

4. Levine cites a parallel between Jerry's dog and a black dog in Thomas Mann's "Tobias Mindernickel," in which the main character stabs the dog to death, as Peter does Jerry. Albee's use of a character named Tobias in *A Delicate Balance* may tie in with the same story.

5. Albee also uses such uncontrollable laughter for the young man who kills his father in *Virginia Woolf*.

6. Making the boy "Greek" may be a homosexual pun.

7. No one has accepted Jerry's statement that Peter was expecting to meet another man in the park. Yet such an assignation, whether Peter was actually married or was lying, would explain his being in the park regularly ("I sit on this bench almost every Sunday afternoon, in good weather. It's secluded here . . . "[41]), his determination to protect his meeting place, and his reason for not leaving earlier, a passive stance that many critics see as unbelievable.

8. Brown (1969) accurately states, "Sex in Albee very rarely, if ever, is something done out of love; it is a weapon; it is a vile appetite" (49).

Works Cited

Albee, Edward. *"The American Dream" and "The Zoo Story."* New York: New American Library, 1961.

Brown, Daniel R. "Albee's Targets." *Satire Newsletter* (Spring 1969): 46–52.

Dubler, Walter. "O'Neill, Wilder, Albee: The Uses of Fantasy in Modern American Drama." Ph.D. diss., Harvard University, 1964.

Force, William M. "The *What* Story? or Who's Who at the Zoo?" *Studies in the Humanities* 1 (1969–70): 47–53.

Irwin, Robert. "The 'Teaching Emotion' in the Ending of *The Zoo Story*." 6 (1976): 6–8.

Levine, Mordecai H. "Albee's Liebestod." *College Language Association Journal* 10 (March 1967): 252–55.

McCullers, Carson. *Collected Short Stories and the Novel "The Ballad of the Sad Cafe."* Boston: Houghton Mifflin, 1955.

Ramsey, Roger. "Jerry's Northerly Madness." *Notes on Contemporary Literature* 1 (1971): 7–8.

Stafford, Jean. *Bad Characters.* New York: Farrar, Strauss & Giroux, 1964.

Woods, Linda. "Isolation and the Barriers of Language in *The Zoo Story*." (September 1968): 224–31.

Zindel, Paul, and Loree Yerby. "Interview with Edward Albee." *Wagner Literary Magazine* 3 (1962): 1–10.

Peter Malekin

The Self, the Referent, and the Real in Science Fiction and the Fantastic: Lem, Pynchon, Kubin, and Delany

> It is *we* alone who have fabricated causes, succession, reciprocity, relativity, compulsion, number, law, freedom, motive, purpose; and when we falsely introduce this world of symbols into things and mingle it with them as though this symbol-world were an "in itself," we once more behave as we have always behaved, namely *mythologically*.
>
> (Nietzsche 33)

> Why could the world *which is of any concern to us*—not be a fiction? And he who then objects: "but to the fiction there belongs an author?"—Could he not be met with the retort: *why*? Does this "belongs" perhaps not also belong to the fiction? Are we not permitted to be a little ironical now about the subject as we are about the predicate and the object? Ought the philosopher not to rise above the belief in grammar?
>
> (Nietzsche 47–48)

In these pronouncements from *Beyond Good and Evil*, Nietzsche had already raised the basic issues in postmodernist literature and poststructuralist criticism. The reality we discuss in language may in fact be language itself; the "we" that do the discussing may in our self-conception equally be aspects of the linguistic field. Fact and fiction cease to be opposites: to manipulate fiction is to transform fact, and to realize that this is so is to transform fiction.

Subsequent development of these ideas has, however, diverged. Three modern thinkers, all of them influential in poststructuralism, illustrate the range of possibilities. For Barthes, the language (*langage*) of a writer is a socioeconomic product, yet by rending apart the canonical codes of our culture, the modern writer can produce in the reader an erotic *jouissance* or *évanouissement*, an abandoned swoon of pleasure that Barthes also compares to Zen satori (Barthes *Le degré*, 42; *S/Z*, 37; *Le plaisir*, 15, 33–38, 57–58). For Heidegger, language is the essence of the interrelation of subject and object: "language speaks" and humans become human while the earth becomes a world (*Poetry, Language, Thought,* 189–210). For Derrida, language is instead *écriture,* writing, bearing the indelible "trace" (*trace*) of a primal division. Meaning resides in the play of language, in which all is at risk, for the play has no fixed center, the center being functional, not ontological (Derrída *De la grammatologie,* 68–69, 88–92; *Of Grammatology,* 46–47, 60–63; "Structure," 248–71).

The mind-language-object or ("reality") triad that interests the three thinkers has always been a concern of the literature of the fantastic, and it has become an explicit theme in modern science fiction, especially in the work of Delany. Alfred Kubin, the earliest of the writers to be briefly considered, was interested in reality and the mind rather than the status of language, and did not indulge in deconstructive devices or self-reflexive narratives. Nor was his novel of 1909, *The Other Side,* marked by a multiplicity of codes. Nevertheless, in theme, symbol, and the ambiguity of its close, it is subversive of conventional reality. It is an anti-science fiction in that Patera, the founder of the Dream Kingdom, "has a profound aversion to all forms of progress . . . especially in the domain of science" (Kubin 13).

However, Patera becomes a demiurge that contains its own opposite in the form of Hercules Bell, the American, the embodiment of applied science, resourcefulness, and the urge for progress. Hercules Bell and Patera eventually merge as a single body struggling with itself. The struggles of this hybrid demiurge are rendered with an obscene vividness as the bodies change shape and size, absorb seas and mountain ranges, or wither to drop like a dead wart off a giant distended phallus and testicles. In the Dream Kingdom, our subjectivity becomes the demiurge's objectivity, and our objectivity becomes the demiurge's subjectivity. Our "reality," the world of money and social structures, is experienced as a figment of the imagination. While there is no technical sleight of hand in the narrative form, realist incident, metaphysical speculation, cosmic symbolism, vision, and surrealist detail are all placed on one level. At the end, the forces of the Dream Kingdom burst into ordinary life. The barriers between so-called dream and so-called reality are down.

In contrast to Kubin, Delany's imaginative structures seem hard and factual. In *Babel–17* and *Stars in My Pocket,* there is no doubt about what is subject and what is object, and the narratives have a clear story line with a definite beginning, middle, and end. Nonetheless, in addition to his tremendous imaginative energy, Delany has the self-conscious sophistication of the modern intellectual in his handling of the idea of language. Babel–17 is described as highly analytical and precise, objective in the sense that it contains no sign for "I" or "you," "mine" or "yours." It precludes any distinction between symbol and objective reality and any possibility of self-criticism by its user. It also contains none of the semantic ambiguities of ordinary language. As a weapon, it is effective in controlling subjects whose synapses have been so mutilated that a sense of "I" cannot surge through and break up the self-enclosed linguistic structure. Moreover, naming can be programmed as a tautological definition in the manner of Newspeak or the language of Stalinism as commented on by Barthes (Barthes *Le degré*). The language of Babel–17, plus the mutilation of synapses, thus becomes a means of shifting a subject's psychological balance so that the ego becomes unconscious and neurotically out of contact with the objectively conscious mind. The language of Babel–17 is then the sole reality of the person who has been subjected to it. The Nietzschean trap of language has been closed and locked. This trap is, however, presented as an idea rather than projected in the language and narrative technique of *Babel–17* itself.

In *Stars in My Pocket*, Delany makes play with the illusion of language in a much wider context. The evelm "v'ea'd" points out to Mary Dyeth that:

> the real affinity between us is that all our myriad cultures, and all yours, are founded on love of illusion. It is not that we both talk, but that we both talk endlessly of persons, places, things, and ideas that are not currently before us to taste. It is not that we both build home-caves, construct travel-guiders that stretch for thousands of kilometers over the land, lay out social grounds, or put together musical compositions and complex combinations of food and flavoured stone, but that we both build, construct, lay out, and put together these things according to plans, visions, imaginative schemes that until we have realized them, have no real existence. . . . As I went down, seeking Korga, how many worlds, I wondered, how many ways of life had suddenly made the transition to illusion, to mere memory, to meaning without referent. (Delany *Stars*, 231–32)

The passage is interesting in that it creates a moment of reader self-consciousness, highlighting the nature of the book itself as a language structure without a referent. It also instances in "to taste" a shifting of the semantic implications of ordinary words that forces the reader's emotional and social presuppositions into consciousness. (The most striking example is the use of "she" to refer to a rational being of any sex, and "he" to refer to an object of sexual desire, whether male, female, or neuter.) Elsewhere, the arbitrariness of signifiers and language patterns is also highlighted in the variations in gesture language, in the discussions of phonetic symbolism, ideographs and shift runes, and in Mary Dyeth's assertion that the "infinite spaces between [the] referential shards [of language] are more opaque to direct human apprehension than all the star-flooded vacuum" (Delany *Stars*, 364). Nevertheless, the quoted passage concerning the evelm is traditional, "classic" in Barthes's sense of the term. The antitheses, parallelisms, and lucidity are part of a rhetoric of persuasion, and while what we are being persuaded of is recognizably modern, the parameters of persuasion are conventional. In this respect, *Babel–17* and *Stars in My Pocket*, despite Delany's exhilarating imaginative fecundity, remain closed texts.

Lem, in *Solaris*, also retains the conventional narrative form with a beginning, middle, and end, though the note of the ending is one of open interrogation rather than resolution. While the technological world of *Solaris* is much nearer our own technology than anything in Delany, nevertheless *Solaris* is an open text as Delany's are not. It has plurality of cultural codes, in the sense in which the term is used by Barthes in *S/Z*, and ultimately none of them is privileged.

These cultural codes emerge in relation to the questions of reality, the validity of scientific knowledge, the nature of personal identity, and the limitations to communication. The exploration of these questions focuses on humanity's relation with the ocean on Solaris and Kelvin's relationship to his "visitor," the reconstituted Rheya, apparently occasioned by the ocean. Rheya as reconstituted is virtually identical with the original Rheya except for certain absences of memory, preeminently the memory of the conclusion of the earlier Rheya's relationship with Kelvin in her suicide after a quarrel. Like an ordinary human being, the reconstituted Rheya can and does question her own reality: her parting note before her second suicide is even signed Rheya with the name Rheya crossed through. We are in the area where the meaning of words is and is not valid, as in Heidegger's use of "Being" (Cited in Derrida *Of Grammatology*, 80–81, 82–83).

How can Kelvin decide whether the new Rheya is "real," or indeed whether all that he seems to be experiencing on Solaris is "real"? The physical tests on the new Rheya show her to be identical with the old except on the subtlest of material levels. Is, then, mind and consciousness merely a by-product of biochemistry, and does the "person" become somebody else if the physiological basis shifts? Moreover, is the person as a center of free activity simply another illusion? The new Rheya is tied to Kelvin, following him everywhere until she decides to kill herself, but the same syndrome could occur in ordinary life. The question reflects back on ordinary, everyday identity, as is made explicit in Kelvin's dream of the dead Gibarian, who is warning Kelvin of the forthcoming death of the new Rheya:

> "You are not Gibarian."
> "No? Then who am I? A dream?"
> "No, you are only a puppet. But you don't realize that you are."
> "And how do you know what *you* are?" (Lem 131)

The "*you*" applies to the reader just as much as it does to Kelvin. Meanwhile, within the house, Kelvin's investigation short-circuits because it is always conducted in terms of the continuum whose reality it seeks to disprove or establish; similarly with Kelvin's attempts to decide whether he is hallucinating the whole Solaris sequence. All tests, including the last, which he tends to regard as final, could be part of the hallucination. All that is established is that the hallucination is consistent. In a tortuous tautology, reality is assumed to be conformity with a systematic logic that is taken to be real.

Hence, also, the awareness in *Solaris* of the limitations to the validity of science itself. As Snow remarks, "You must know that science is concerned with phenomena rather than causes" (Lem 77). The causative structure is simply a schema for predicting phenomena: what the phenomena are in themselves is another issue. Moreover, scientific formulation is in terms of our minds and consciousness, and in addition, scientific prediction becomes less certain as it moves away from inanimate matter. When faced with the nonhuman phenomenon of the ocean, the categories of the human sciences, biology, and psychology do not fit. It is impossible to decide whether the ocean is animate or inanimate, whether concepts like "purpose" can apply to it, and what any supposed purposes might be. Hence the careful balancing in the account of the history of Solaristics between orthodox scientific thought, "cranky" explanations, and all-out logical attacks on science as anthropomorphism and a form of religion. The preclosed nature of science and human morality, and the difficulty of communicating at all with nonhuman consciousness, are focused in the isolated human beings shut in with their "visitors," and faced by an enigmatically responsive ocean.

Solaris is "modern" in Barthes's sense in that there is no dominance by a single authoritarian code; rather, multiple codes qualify and criticize one another within the text. There is no answer, no solution, and the terms of all possible questions are undercut.

Of all the texts under consideration, it is Gravity's Rainbow that is the most decidedly "modern," or in the technical literary sense, postmodern. Through the book, there runs a series of contradictions: materialistic determinism versus chance; religious predestination versus free will; design versus random configuration; rational predictability working in terms of statistical and general formulations, not individual instances, versus irrational and inexplicable prediction in individual cases. The Poisson distribution of the falling rockets conforms to statistical models, but Roger Mexico cannot foretell where the next rocket will land. Slothrop's amorous encounters, or at least the stars on his map, do, however, indicate where the rockets will fall. These contradictions evoke but do not answer questions of relationship of mind to matter and the validity of the concept of the causation, even of time. The rocket arrives before it is heard approaching, reversing the "normal" sequence of events: similarly, effect may precede cause, or cause and effect may be a misconception. The various intellectual conceptualizations, religious, political, or scientific, are not right or wrong, they are simply functional within their own terms of reference, and there is always a point where they cease to function.

Human minds, however, tend to seek closed structures, the designed and unrandom, the controlled. Humans invent the long molecular chains of the plastics, closed chains that do not react with natural substances. Frans Van de Groov and the other Dutch settlers on Mauritius hunt to extinction the dodo, with its alarming lack of obvious design, plan, purpose, rational closure. The characters project or react to the sense of design as myth, whether it be the churchgoers at Christmas responding to the faded magic of Christian myth or Slothrop merging into Rocketman. Saviors and scapegoats proliferate: Slothrop is dressed as a savior pig, Marvy takes over the costume and is with black humor castrated in Slothrop's place, Gottfried and presumably Enzian end up as sacrificial victims in rockets, Bianca is neurotically strangled. Yet the myth of *Gravity's Rainbow* itself contains all these other myths and remains open-ended: inconclusive as a narrative, multilayered as a structure, and subversive of the oppositions of formal categorization.

In this context, the question of control becomes an illusion. As Slothrop becomes paranoid, he sees that everything fits, that he has been manipulated by Jamf and General Electric and IG Farben and the rocket and plastics cartel. He has been controlled by one aspect of the ubiquitous market, the market in which everything—sex, human life, the Jews, information—has its price. Yet, as the spirit of Roland Feldspath says through the medium Carroll Eventyr in the first séance scene in the book:

> A market need no longer be run by the Invisible Hand, but now could *create itself*—its own logic, momentum, style, from *inside*. Putting the control inside was ratifying what de facto had happened—that you had dispensed with God. But you had taken on a greater, and more harmful, illusion. The illusion of control. That A could do B. But that was false. Completely. No one can *do*. Things only happen. A and B are unreal, are names for parts that ought to be inseparable. (Pynchon 30)

Beyond the market, including the IG Farben hierarchy discovered by Bland among the dead, lies the "outer radiance" that Pan can carry Geli to. This radiance recurs in the book as Nora Dodson Truck's zero and final indifference of the outer radiance, the "amazing perfect whiteness" that Slothrop glimpses when he is running for his life from Marvy's Mothers, the Kirghiz light beyond Allah at the edge of the world, and the "radiance of what we would become" mentioned by Blicero to Gottfried, the rocket victim (130, 357–58, 720, 724). This outer radiance can be regarded as either positive or negative, or it may be illusion: polarity and interpretation belong to the field of the viewer.

As the novel moves toward its end, the reader is left with the audience in the Orpheus Cinema, the film stopped, the screen blank without the show of phenomena, revealing the hidden known face (our own and death's, possibly) while the rocket poises above us. We are encouraged, ironically or otherwise, to sing while there is still time. The ending is again ambiguous. Those seeking rational closure will find it negative. A Buddhist like Mondongen would think differently.

The multiple frames of reference explicitly invoked or implied by the ambiguous symbolism are paralleled by the narrative structure and syntax of the text. The main character disintegrates, characters overlap and merge, and the audience is sporadically brought into the text, while many of the "sentences" work by an agglomeration and ramification that violates the traditional clause with subject, verb, and object.

Gravity's Rainbow is what Barthes would call a "writerly" text. The book subverts distinctions between subject and object, reality and fantasy, the living and the dead, the reader and the text. The configuration of the mandala-text is the process by which a reader writes the book and herself.

None of the texts considered has the full panoply of postmodernism in the manner, for instance, of Calvino's *If, on a Winter's Night, a Traveller*, with its endless play on texts as texts. All, however, bear on the question of the self, the referent, and the real, and shed reciprocal light on the basic tenets of modern critical theory. The novels may not have referents, but they do have reference, in that the mental sets of the texts are part of the intextuality of modern culture, and text and intertextuality do partially define a reader's "I." Yet the "I" is not totally defined by text and intertextuality. Even the opening paragraphs from Nietzsche imply that the mind is potentially, and to some extent in actuality, free from language and intertextuality, and Barthes implies the same of the reader-critic, even though he confuses the ultimate clarity of satori with the encroaching unconsciousness of a swoon. Heidegger goes further, generating an explicit sense of the "region" beyond the horizon of awareness, and therefore beyond the bounds of the subject-object dichotomy (Heidegger *Discourse*, 64–65, 83).

Here lies the crux. A freedom from codes is not another code, just as the "I" consciousness is not an object. The "I" that is defined by the objective must ultimately be illusion in the sense of being an impermanent aspect of changing codes. Delany's novels discuss and project this kind of "reality." Kubin, Lem, and Pynchon are aware of possible alternatives. Pynchon uses a conflict of codes to disestablish codal autonomy. From one point of view, *Gravity's Rainbow* is Derrida's game without a center, where all is at risk. If, however, the mind does indeed extend beyond language structures and even beyond the subject-object dichotomy, then *Gravity's Rainbow* could equally be an enactment of freedom within the text and within all intertextuality. In that case the technique is the message, and freedom or bondage lies in the "I" of the reader.

Works Cited

Barthes, Roland. *Le degré zéro de l'écriture suivi de Nouveaux essais critiques*. Paris: Seuil, 1922.
———. *Le plaisir du texte*. Paris: Seuil, 1973.
———. *S/Z*. Paris: Seuil, 1970.
Delany, Samuel R. *Babel-17*. New York: Bantam, 1982.
———. *Stars in My Pocket Like Grains of Sand*. New York: Bantam Spectra, 1985.
Derrida, Jacques. *De la grammatologie*. Paris: Editions de Minuit, 1967.
———. *Of Grammatology*. Trans. Gayatri Spivak, Baltimore: Johns Hopkins, 1976.
———. "Structure, Sign, and Play in the Discourse of the Human Sciences." *The Structuralist Controversy: The Language of Criticism and the Sciences of Man*. Ed. Richard Macksey and Eugenie Donato. Baltimore: Johns Hopkins, 1972. 248–71.

Heidegger, Martin. *Discourse on Thinking: A Translation of Gelassenheit.* Trans. John M. Anderson and E. Hans Freund. New York: Harper Torchbooks, 1966.
———. *Poetry, Language, Thought.* Trans. Albert Hofstadter. New York: Harper Colophon, 1975.
Kubin, Alfred. *The Other Side.* Trans. Denver Lindley. Harmondsworth: Penguin, 1973.
Lem, Stanislaw. *Solaris: The Chain of Chance, Perfect Vacuum.* Trans. Joanna Kilmartin, Steve Cox, Louis Iribarne, and Michael Kandel. Harmondsworth: Penguin, 1981.
Nietzsche, Friedrich. *Beyond Good and Evil: Prelude to a Philosophy of the Future.* Trans. R. J. Hollingdale. Harmondsworth: Penguin, 1973.
Pynchon, Thomas. *Gravity's Rainbow.* London: Pan Picador, 1975.

II

Theory of National Fantasy—
Tradition and Invention

Brian Stableford

The British and American Traditions of Speculative Fiction*

What I want to do in this essay is compare and contrast the development of speculative fiction in two nations that share a common language. I have two purposes in mind in doing this. First, I want to dramatize the sharp differences that existed at one time between the traditions of speculative fiction in Britain and in America, but which have been partly obscured in much historical writing that lumps them together as aspects of a single story. Second, I want to suggest some explanations that help to account for these sharp differences.

It is perhaps surprising that early twentieth-century British speculative fiction, which I shall call for the sake of convenience "scientific romance," and early twentieth-century American speculative fiction, which I shall call "science fiction," were so strikingly different.[1] After all, many texts were published and read on both sides of the Atlantic, and the science fiction magazines edited by Hugo Gernsback reprinted a good deal of work by the key figure in the British tradition, H. G. Wells. Despite this degree of shared access to one another's traditions, British writers and American writers were for several decades engaged in distinctly different projects, until scientific romance was engulfed by the tide of cultural "coca-colonization" that followed the end of World War II and was displaced by British science fiction.

Scientific romance became established as an identifiable popular genre during a boom in periodical publishing at the beginning of the 1890s. It had numerous historical connections with previously existing genres, including utopian fan-

*This essay was presented by Brian Stableford, guest scholar, as a featured luncheon address.

tasies and imaginary voyages, but two of these associations were of cardinal importance.

Scientific romance really grew out of the genre of future war stories that had been established in Britain in the wake of George Chesney's classic exercise in propaganda *The Battle of Dorking* (1871). Two of the most important early writers of scientific romance, George Griffith and M. P. Shiel, achieved their first significant literary successes with future war stories, Griffith with *The Angel of the Revolution* and Shiel with *The Yellow Danger*. Many of the minor contributors to the genre came into it by this route. H. G. Wells, the central figure of the tradition, wrote several important future war stories, including *The War in the Air* and "The Land Ironclads." Future war stories were to remain a vital component of scientific romance throughout its history, and might easily be regarded as the hard core of the genre.

In addition, the new genre was much enlivened by input drawn from the popular scientific journalism of the day, which abounded in speculative essays celebrating new discoveries in science and their possible implications. H. G. Wells began his literary career with such exercises in scientific journalism, and the imaginative premises used in his most famous scientific romances all emerged from flights of fantasy first couched in the form of essays—the gradual evolution of *The Time Machine* from an essaylike form to the story with which we are now familiar has been well documented. Charles Howard Hinton, who published two volumes entitled *Scientific Romances*, mingled therein essays and stories, while the French astronomer Camille Flammarion—a prolific writer of articles for the popular magazines—was one of the major influences on catastrophic fantasies of the day. This connection between scientific romance and speculative essays was also retained throughout the history of the genre.

The preoccupation with war exhibited by British speculative fiction of this period is easy to understand. As a tiny nation with a large worldwide empire inexorably in decline, Britain harbored a strong sense of threat, especially with respect to the imperialistic ambitions of the newly consolidated German nation. Britons knew that they would eventually have to fight for their foreign possessions against other European nations, and the Great War was visible on the imaginative horizon for many years before it actually came. This anxiety was mixed with a determination to triumph, a desire to make permanently secure that which was under threat. Much future war fiction before 1914 was therefore belligerent and bloodthirsty. When the war did come, it arrived having been advertised for many years as a war that would end war, and Britons were all the more eager to fight it because of this preestablished mythology. The actual experience of the war, though, betrayed these expectations in no uncertain terms. It turned out to be the vilest of wars, horrific in its cost in human lives, a war that achieved nothing save the destruction of Europe as the economic heart of the world.

The writers of postwar scientific romance had to live with this betrayal of their hopes and dreams, and it is entirely understandable that their futuristic imagination thereafter focused in large measure on what they considered to be the historical lesson of the Great War: the belief that a new war, fought by air fleets that would bomb defenseless cities with high explosives and poison gas, would wreak destruction of a more horrific kind and on a more terrible scale than was readily imaginable. Imagery of this kind features extensively in books like Edward Shanks's *People of the Ruins*, Cicely Hamilton's *Theodore Savage*, Neil Bell's *Gas War of 1940*, John Gloag's *Winter's Youth*, and S. Fowler Wright's trilogy *Prelude in Prague*, *Four Days War* and *Megiddo's Ridge*.

Americans, by contrast, felt themselves under no particular threat of invasion or involvement in war before 1914, and did not immediately involve themselves in the war in Europe. The historical situation of the United States was very different from Britain—it had, indeed, been the first great defector from the declining empire. Its geographical situation was just as obviously in complete contrast. The sheer size of the United States, and the relative weakness of its neighboring nations, made the idea that it might be invaded and overrun patently ridiculous.

Thus the handful of future war stories produced in America before 1914 show not a trace of that desperate anxiety that fired the British genre. Because America came into the Great War late and because it was so far away from the arenas of conflict, the effects of the war on the noncombatants at home were small by comparison with the effects on noncombatants in Europe. In effect, America became the only real winner of the war, when economic hegemony within the community of nations was shifted dramatically from devastated Europe to New York. The United States did suffer depression after the crash of 1929, but at that time Europe had still not recovered from 1918, and its plight was compounded by the depression, becoming so much worse that the way was paved for the growth of fascism, which ultimately precipitated the war of 1939.

Americans between the wars were largely, and understandably, untouched by the apocalyptic anxieties that fed and generated so much scientific romance: the fear of enemy air fleets obliterating civilization with poison gas simply did not seem applicable to the American situation. In consequence, American speculative fiction developed very differently. The American futuristic imagination was not constrained by that looming specter of future war that kept its British counterpart in virtual captivity. Unfettered, American speculative writers took conspicuous advantage of certain opportunities almost entirely neglected by British writers. In particular, they became fascinated by interplanetary fantasies. A key figure in the development of the exotic romance that was eventually fed by pulp editors and writers into Hugo Gernsback's gadget-ridden "scientifiction" was Edgar Rice Burroughs, who used Mars and Venus as settings for marvelous adventurous odysseys which were, in essence, the ultimate daydreams.

This spirit of imaginative indulgence, though not at all consistent with Gernsback's manifesto for a futurological science fiction that would celebrate the liberating power of technological invention, infected science fiction to such a degree that hypothetical explorers were soon hurled beyond the bounds of the solar system in search of an infinite array of worlds where *anything* might exist and *anything* might happen. While scientific romance remained preoccupied with the swindling and possible destruction of worldly empire, science fiction became entranced with the grandiose possibilities of galactic empire.

• • • • •

Scientific romance was continually enlivened, and thereby saved from being dour or imaginatively unambitious, by input from essays in speculative science. Wells, in his work in this vein, was carrying forward and strengthening a tradition that was as much intellectual play as anything else—a toying with ideas that was largely abstracted and amused; a variety of armchair philosophizing. After the Great War it extended through the works of such writers as J. B. S. Haldane and Julian Huxley and spawned the extensive series of "Today & Tomorrow" pamphlets. Such cerebral ideative play fitted in well with the British *Weltanschauung.*

In America, where ideative play was much more pragmatic and much more purposive, popular science writing tended to have a rather different emphasis, much more orientated toward tinkering with hardware. Where England prided itself on producing explorers, America was delighted to be the home of inventors, and the character of American speculative thought was geared to building gadgets rather than castles in the air. Thus the way in which Hugo Gernsback asked his writers to borrow from science and tried to derive scientifiction from the popular science journalism in which he had previously specialized was different from the way science and scientific romance met and mingled. Gernsback's approval of and admiration for Wells should not blind us to the fact that the two men followed different imaginative procedures in quite distinctive styles.

The most imaginatively adventurous scientific romances—John Beresford's *The Hampdenshire Wonder,* E. V. Odle's *The Clockwork Man,* John Gloag's *Tomorrow's Yesterday,* and Murray Constantine's[2] *Proud Man* among them—tend to be rather *dreamy* works even when they are not, like Olaf Stapledon's *Star Maker* or John Beresford and Esme Wynee-Tyson's *The Riddle of the Tower,* actual visionary fantasies. They frequently begin in country villages, and very often return full circle, with the initial circumstances restored, so that the world remains essentially undisturbed by the flight of fantasy. Science fiction novels very rarely do this: they often begin and almost always end with worlds radically transformed, altered out of all recognition, because here flights of fancy are very definitely *incarnate,* solidified in machinery and put into practice.

The pragmatism of American speculative thought, contrasted with the abstractness of British speculative thought, is not too difficult to understand when the historical situation of each nation is again considered. At the turn of the century the United States was a political and cultural entity still in the making, a civilization that was literally being built, raised out of the wilderness. Every new symbol of technological advance—the railroad, the oil well, the radio station—was contributing to a process of *creation,* and was seen in that light.

Britain, on the other hand, was a political and cultural entity based on long traditions, a country where change tended to be seen not in terms of creation, but in terms of disturbance and disruption. Its aristocracy had never been swept away, like the ancien régime in France, by a revolution: instead the traditional ruling class retained its prestige and cultural hegemony even though it was being gradually absorbed and usurped by the bourgeoisie and its nouveau riche. The writers of scientific romance were, almost without exception, champions of progress and apologists for new technology, but they had a thorough understanding of the fear of change and disruption that was part of their cultural heritage, and they fully appreciated how enormously difficult it would be to persuade their fellow Britons to accept change. H. G. Wells, perhaps the most eloquent and insistent propagandist for progress the nation produced, was continually forced, in both his fictional and his nonfictional accounts of the shape of things to come, to suppose that the old order would have to be literally torn down or blasted apart before it could yield to a new.

America was freer than any other nation from the ideological legacy of an old order—freer even than revolutionary nations like France or Russia—because America had no traditional aristocracy that had owned its lands since the Middle Ages. Much of its territory, in fact, was effectively up for grabs. It was therefore wide open to American speculative writers to envisage the building of a radically new world, different from anything that had gone before. Britain, perhaps the least free of the developed nations from the burden of its past and the narcotization of conservatism, was at the opposite end of the ideological spectrum, despite its historical connections with the United States and their common language.

H. G. Wells dubbed the period following the end of the Great War "The Age of Frustration," and scientific romance between the wars can be regarded as an extraordinary elaboration of that spirit of frustration. It shows up not merely in the pessimistic fantasies of destruction by war and in such cynical analyses of perverted utopian dreams as Muriel Jaeger's The Question Mark and Aldous Huxley's Brave New World, but also in the supposedly optimistic works of the period. When hope for the future is offered in postwar scientific romance, it is usually tied to the idea that there might be some kind of miraculous transcendence of the human condition—that a new race might appear free from the awful psychological hang-ups which prevent ordinary men from creating a just and satisfactory social order. Images of these "superior beings" can be found in the Amphibians of S. Fowler Wright's The World Below, the catpeople in John Gloag's Tomorrow's Yesterday, the utopian supermen of John Beresford's "What Dreams May Come . . . ?", the "Young Men" whose coming was celebrated in M. P. Shiel's last novel, the "elevator man" of Gerald Heard's Doppelgängers, and many of the future species in Olaf Stapledon's Last and First Men. Such superhumans are always contrasted with our own kind, and the reader of such books is invited—indeed, commanded—to feel humiliated and debased by comparison.

This quasi-nostalgic yearning to be replaced by something better, which reaches a literally hysterical pitch in Claude Houghton's *This Was Ivor Trent* and becomes the object of cunning black comedy in Andrew Marvell's *Minimum* scientific romance lasted only as long as the experimental phase of the middlebrow popular fiction magazines—they had virtually abandoned their enthusiastic championship of outré material as early as 1905. From then on scientific romance was considered esoteric and was effectively forced to seek a place in more rarefied strata of the market: it filled a spectrum extending from the cheerfully middlebrow to the earnestly highbrow; its imaginatively adventurous works became increasingly heavy in their philosophical pretensions, to the point where the paperback reprint of *Last and First Men* was a Pelican book packaged as though it were nonfiction.

In America, by contrast, science fiction was caught up in a kind of fictional brand warfare when the popular pulp magazines began genre specialization as a marketing tactic. Speculative fiction was gradually squeezed out of the middlebrow magazines as they began to cultivate different images in consequence of the kind of advertising they were carrying. The spectrum of American science fiction thus extended from precariously middlebrow outlets like John Campbell's *Astounding*, to unashamedly lowbrow pulps featuring costume drama and adventure stories of a kind relegated in Britain to the boys' papers.

Because of these contrasting developments in the fiction markets in Britain and the United States, scientific romance remained much more closely in touch with customary criteria of literary merit than science fiction did until the end of World War II, when science fiction's rapid sophistication coincided with its massive penetration of the British popular fiction market. Ironically, it was in the same postwar decade that a good deal of British speculative fiction began to appear in the lowbrow regions of the market via cheap paperback books (though by that time the "science fiction" label had *Man; or, Time to be Gone,* contrasts very strongly with the use of superhumans in science fiction.

Early pulp supermen, like the one in John Taine's *Seeds of Life,* were usually menaces to be destroyed in the interests of preserving humanity. Later, science fiction writers followed the lead of A. E. van Vogt's *Slan* in seizing upon a notion popularized by J. B. Rhine's researches in extrasensory perception, that we all might be harboring latent superhuman powers just waiting for the right moment to come into bloom. Thus, while scientific romance was replete with images of exhausted, effete, and decrepit humanity waiting to be overtaken, science fiction could present images of active, enthusiastic humanity equipped with new powers within as well as without—technological mastery combining with mental evolution to make certain that there could be no limits to human achievement. Very often in science fiction the reader is invited—indeed, commanded—to identify with the superman and feel proud of the identification.

Thus, in scientific romance of the 1930s, neither the future nor the stars could possibly belong to *us,* but only to those who might come after, while in science fiction of that era all of space and time was ours, to claim if we would.

There is a sharp contrast between the future of Olaf Stapledon's *Last and First Men* and the future of Laurence Manning's *The Man Who Awoke,* or between the universe of Stapledon's *Star Maker* and the universe of Isaac Asimov's *Foundation* series. In the scientific romances, the vast panorama of time and space is outside of the limited scope of our kind; in the science fiction stories, we are *there*: we come, we see, we conquer.

• • • • •

These ideological contrasts between scientific romance and science fiction are, of course, further complicated by contrasts in the relative stations of the two genres in the literary marketplace. The true fashionability of scientific romance lasted only as long as the experimental phase of the middlebrow popular fiction magazines—they had virtually abandoned their enthusiastic championship of outré material as early as 1905. From then on scientific romance was considered esoteric and was effectively forced to seek a place in more rarefied strata of the market: it filled a spectrum extending from the cheerfully middlebrow to the earnestly highbrow; its imaginatively adventurous works became increasingly heavy in their philosophical pretensions, to the point where the paperback reprint of *Last and First Men* was a Pelican book packaged as though it were nonfiction.

In America, by contrast, science fiction was caught up in a kind of fictional warfare when the popular pulp magazines began genre brand specialization as a marketing tactic. Speculative fiction was gradually squeezed out of the middlebrow magazines as they began to cultivate different images in consequence of the kind of advertising they were carrying. The spectrum of American science fiction thus extended from precariously middlebrow outlets like John Campbell's *Astounding,* to unashamedly lowbrow pulps featuring costume drama and adventure stories of a kind relegated in Britain to the boys' papers.

Because of these contrasting developments in the fiction markets in Britain and the United States, scientific romance remained much more closely in touch with customary criteria of literary merit than science fiction did until the end of World War II, when science fiction's rapid sophistication coincided with its massive penetration of the British popular fiction market. Ironically, it was in the same postwar decade that a good deal of British speculative fiction began to appear in the lowbrow regions of the market via cheap paperback books (though by that time the "science fiction" label had been imported and much of the fiction was produced in imitation of American pulp science fiction.)

The relative literary sophistication of much scientific romance will inevitably encourage literary critics to see it as a superior genre to contemporary pulp science fiction, and perhaps to regret its absorption, in the 1950s, into a generalized Anglo-American popular culture. This should not allow us, however, to overlook the fact that both genres had their particular merits and virtues.

The virtues of scientific romance were its moral earnestness, its anxious concern with possible abuses of technology, its scrupulous skepticism regarding the mythology of progress, and its corollary analyses of the many ways in which ideals of freedom and justice might be subverted.

The virtues of early science fiction were its imaginative ambition and enthusiasm, its prolific inventiveness and melodramatic grandiosity, its hunger for ingenious novelties, and its corollary fecundity of images and ideas.

There is an ironic sense in which what each genre tended to lack was exactly what the other had in abundance, and the rapid convergent evolution of the two genres after World War II can thus be seen as a kind of productive cross-fertilization and as an advantageous blending of interests. The revitalized post–World War II science fiction of America and Britain is a healthier and more admirable genre than its pulp predecessor or scientific romance.

I think, however, that we should be prepared to see more in the merging of science fiction and scientific romance than simply a fusion of marketplaces. We should also recognize that the elements of contrast between the cultural backgrounds that generated such different species of speculative fiction have to some extent been overtaken by events.

The sense of threat and apocalyptic anxiety, which generated so many fantasies of world destruction in Britain while America remained complacent, is now no longer confined to Europe. America is no longer beyond the potential reach of the forces of destruction. Although World War II did not, as so many British speculators feared, obliterate civilization in Europe—largely because the Geneva Convention held up far better than anyone expected it to—it did, in the manner of its closure, introduce the world to a new apocalyptic threat: the atom bomb. When Russia began testing nuclear weapons, America was infected for the first time with a kind of fear and a sense of threat that had been endemic in Europe for decades. The anxiety level of American science fiction was thus stepped up by an important order of magnitude, which brought its worldview much more closely into line with that of scientific romance.

In addition to this, the expansive phase of American development was slowly petering out. The United States stopped importing legions of European immigrants and began instead to consolidate. The western frontier disappeared, swallowed up by the sheer munificence of the success of its pioneers. New transport and communications systems contributed to a metaphorical shrinking of the vast nation. America had inherited a kind of ideological empire by virtue of its exploits in World War II, but then saw that empire go into the kind of rebellious decline that had earlier overtaken the British Empire. Inevitably, America saw in the decades following World War II the growth of exactly that kind of conservative spirit that Britain had inherited from its historical tradition, and American speculative writers quickly came to understand, even if they did not sympathize with, the characterization of change as disturbance and disruption rather than progress and opportunity.

In the 1950s, therefore, American science fiction had little option but to take on board many of the features of scientific romance, and by so doing make the continuance of an independent tradition of scientific romance redundant. After World War II, Britain and America have come to share in very large measure a commonality of outlook, experience, and anxiety that makes the speculative fiction produced in the two nations much more similar in its tone and concerns than could have been the case between 1890 and 1945.

In spite of this conflation of the two traditions, though, I think it is still possible to find in British science fiction a distinctive kind of flavor. Much of it still retains a kind of cool sobriety that can be contrasted with the heat and hyperactivity of much American science fiction. When British science fiction is nostalgic, as it often is, it is nostalgic in a rather pastoral vein. Some American science fiction is nostalgic like that, too, but much of it is nostalgic in a very different way, looking backward precisely when it pretends to be most forward-looking, hoping to rediscover somewhere outside the earth a new frontier where all the old pulpish dreams will once more become meaningful. The assertive pragmatism of old is still retained by much American science fiction, often becoming more propagandist in the face of assumed unfashionability. In contrast, that fanciful abstracted pipe-dreaming that played so large a part in inspiring scientific romance still lies at the root of much British science fiction, which tends to view assertive pragmatism as a kind of vulgar clowning. The champions of change in British science fiction still tend to stand back from their images of evolutionary transcendence, while much American science fiction still yearns for the incipient superhumanity of the man in the street. In these respects there is still a sense in which British and American speculative fiction are divided within their commonality, using the same vocabulary of ideas but speaking with distinctive accents.

Notes

1. A more detailed analysis of the term *scientific romance* and its application can be found in Brian Stableford, *Scientific Romance in Britain, 1890–1950*, London: Fourth Estate, 1985.

2. "Murray Constantine" is a pen name used by Katharine Burdekin, who also published some scientific romance under her own name.

Joseph Andriano

"Our Dual Existence": Archetypes of Love and Death in Le Fanu's "Carmilla"

The Irish author Joseph Sheridan Le Fanu (1814–1873) is known today primarily for his Gothic tales—especially "Green Tea" (1869), which has been called "the archetypal ghost story" (Sullivan 11)—and "Carmilla," which first appeared in the collection *In a Glass Darkly* in 1872. Throughout his career as a writer of ghostly fiction, Le Fanu wrote of everything from dead lovers to demonic monkeys, but not until the last year of his life did he tackle the female vampire. "Carmilla" is about a lesbian revenant who vamps an adolescent girl, Le Fanu's narrator.

James Twitchell claims that "Carmilla" is "a conscious attempt to render Coleridge's *Christabel* into prose" (129). But the text is much more than a mere "rendering" of Coleridge. Many of the similarities between the two works may be due to their authors' mutually independent manipulation of the same folklore motifs about the lamia figure. Le Fanu's anxiety is not merely one of influence.

In any case, the most important similarity between the two works is what distinguishes them from all other lamia tales—lesbianism. Why do Geraldine and Carmilla seek female lovers? It is, I think, *not* because the male writers wanted to explore "the psychodynamics of perversion" (Twitchell, 129). Lesbianism is not the issue; gender signification is. We have male writers identifying with female characters. Coleridge reveals that Christabel is his persona when he has her carry Geraldine across the threshold—a male role, after which Christabel/Coleridge assumes a "feminine" role. Likewise, in "Carmilla," Le Fanu deliberately avoids mentioning the narrator's name for the first forty pages, inviting confusion between female narrator and male-implied author. Since the lamia's victim (usually male) is in a submissive, even masochistic role, which is socioculturally defined as feminine, he may as well have a female name. He is then revealed as "Laura." But why are Carmilla and Geraldine not signified in turn by masculine names to correspond to their dominating sadistic roles? A

Jungian reading suggests that they are dominating mother figures, icons of the terrible mother archetype, who is always a dominatrix.

The gender reversals in the vampire tale, moreover, reflect the confusion caused by a tension between archetypal androgyny—the instinctive tendency to fuse the opposites—and stereotypical dualism, the sociocultural tendency to polarize them. If feminine aggressiveness is denied (if woman's role is reduced to one of submission, of suffering and being still), it will reassert itself with the fury of a "writing fiend"—as Carmilla does.[1] So terrifying is this return of the repressed that the man succumbs and submits, ironically becoming feminine himself. The result is a frightening travesty of androgyny. "Carmilla" is more than just a tale of terror, however; it is also a love story in which the instincts of both love and death are subliminally viewed in a positive light.

The work begins with a prologue in which the author cites one Doctor Hesselius (a "psychic doctor") who considers Carmilla's story "as involving . . . some of the profoundest arcana of our dual existence" (222).[2] How this phrase is meant exactly we are invited to conjecture after we have read the tale. But we know at the outset from this announcement of deliberate ambiguity that "Carmilla" is not going to be another *Varney the Vampire*.

The narrator is an Austrian girl whose father is English but whose mother's lineage is mysterious. All we know of her at first is that she was an Austrian lady who died in Laura's infancy. Laura lives with her father in a *schloss*, and she has been brought up by a benign governess "whose care and good nature *in part* supplied to me the loss of my mother" (244—emphasis added). But only in part—that phrase is crucial, as Laura unconsciously reveals when she describes her "early fright":

> I can't have been more than six years old, when one night I awoke, and looking round the room from my bed, failed to see the nursery-maid. Neither was my nurse there. . . . I was vexed and insulted at finding myself, as I conceived, neglected, and I began to whimper . . . when to my surprise, I saw a solemn, but very pretty face looking at me from the side of the bed. (225)

The apparition is a young woman whose presence causes the child to stop whimpering. "Delightfully soothed" as the lady lies beside her, Laura falls asleep again, only to be "awakened by a sensation as if two needles ran into my breast very deep at the same moment" (225).[3] She cries out, causing the lady to slip down to the floor and hide under the bed. Finally, the child is frightened (anything that hides under the bed must be scary) and screams.

The first vampiric visitation of Carmilla is remarkable for several reasons. She comes when the child feels neglected and anxious, needing a mother to soothe her to sleep. The cherishing, nourishing, positive role of the mother archetype is conjured, but she suddenly turns into her opposite, the antimother, she who takes life *from* the breast. She is the mother in her terrible aspect, who withdraws the breast as punishment. So traumatic, in other words, is the loss or withdrawal of the mother, that her absence becomes a demonic presence: a devouring antimother. Both the soothing presence and the punishing absence of the mother comprise Carmilla's character. Thus when she reappears, she will be not only a pleasure-giving lover-friend but also a "writhing fiend."

Laura insists that this "early fright" was not a dream; but in true ambiguous Gothic form, Le Fanu has given the vampire a hypnagogic origin. We are not surprised, however, when Laura finally meets her dream-mother in waking life. Laura is nineteen now, awaiting the arrival of a prospective friend, whose visit, and the new acquaintance had furnished her day dream for weeks (227). But the girl, she learns, is dead. She was the ward of Laura's father's friend General Spielsdorf, who has written in a letter that she was killed by a "friend who betrayed our infatuated hospitality" and whom he now is hunting (228). Deprived of a new friend, Laura once again needs soothing. She finds a friend to fulfill those daydreams: the very fiend Spielsdorf hunts.

The scene describing Carmilla's reappearance (229–32) is one of the triumphs of late Gothic fiction. The carriage accident on the horror-story level is a sham designed to dupe the unsuspecting mortals into inviting the demon into their house. But the incident is given mythic dimensions when the carriage swerves "to bring the wheel over the projection roots of . . . a magnificent lime-tree." In Germanic mythology, the lime or linden is sacred to Minne, the goddess of love, and to the Great Goddess (De Vries 299) who appears in this violent eruption from the unconscious. At first, she is manifest only in the persons of Carmilla and her mother, but Le Fanu seems to have intuited that this vision of archetypal femininity was somehow incomplete. As Blake and De Quincey knew, it is threefold, not twofold. And as Jung explained, her three aspects, corresponding to heaven, earth and the underworld, evince respectively "cherishing and nourishing goodness," "emotionality and passion," and the "Stygian depths" (Jung 9.1: 82). Carmilla's mother, Mrs. Karnstein, at least in appearance, is the good mother, her daughter is the love-goddess, but where is the missing lady to complete the trinity—Hekate? We only learn later that she was in the carriage all the time. Le Fanu seems to have understood that although Mrs. Karnstein and Carmilla were the only ones necessary to the narrative's surface structure as a horror story, its deep structure as myth demanded the third figure. One of Laura's companions, Mademoiselle De La Fontaine, claims that she saw

a hideous black woman with a sort of colored turban on her head . . . who was gazing all the time from the carriage window, nodding and grinning derisively towards the ladies, with gleaming eyes and large white eye-balls, and her teeth set as if in fury. (234)

Her teeth suggest vampirism, but more important is her terrible aspect—hideous, derisive, angry. She plays no other part in the story but to complete the Unholy

Trinity, integral to the conflict that later develops between patriarchal and matriarchal forces.

The apparently injured Carmilla is escorted into the *schloss*, while her mother goes off on what she calls a mission of life and death. When Carmilla regains consciousness, she asks where "mamma" and "Matska" are (232–33). (The latter name means "mud.") She is informed that her mother has had to leave while she convalesces at the *schloss* for three months. But no one asks her who Matska is. She remains the mysterious hag in the carriage. Her only other manifestation seems to be in the anecdote Mademoiselle De La Fontaine tells about the full moon's effect on the sailor-cousin of hers: one night he fell asleep,

> with his face full in the light of the moon. . . . awakened after a dream of an old woman clawing him by the cheek, with his features horribly drawn to one side; and his countenance had never quite recovered its equilibrium. (229)

This passage symbolizes what William Veeder has shown to be one of the major themes of "Carmilla": the vicious return of repressed femininity in a patriarchal society (198).

The mysterious hag, associated with the moon and with earth ("Matska"), is the first of several indications that the demonic feminine in the tale is closely associated with nature. Although "mamma" and Matska appear to leave Carmilla, they really do not—they are a part of her. We have already seen how Carmilla is herself a mother figure. Her aspect as nature-death goddess becomes more apparent later when she begins her gruesome depredations on Laura.

Laura eventually discovers that Carmilla is the same woman who had appeared to her when she was six (236). Carmilla claims that she had a similar dream, and Le Fanu begins a breakdown of boundaries between the two ("I you and you me"), as Laura becomes inexplicably attracted to and repelled by Carmilla (237). The "ambiguous alternations" (Le Fanu 237) of attraction and repulsion have been adequately explained by Veeder and Day in sexual terms. Carmilla is the sexual element Laura has had to repress. But there is a dimension to Carmilla that leads us "beyond the pleasure principle": Carmilla is the "suggestress of suicide" (Cf. McCormack 191: "vampirism seen as a projection of this kind is suicidal in structure"). She is De Quincey's *Mater Tenebrarum*, who makes the grave seem sweet by creating a languor "which, from its very sweetness . . . is fancied to be health":

> There was an unaccountable fascination in its [the languor's] earlier symptoms. . . . Dim thoughts of death began to open, and an idea that I was slowly sinking took gentle, and somehow, not unwelcome possession of me. (255)

The passages evincing Carmilla's sultry sexuality have been quoted by practically every commentator on the tale. Less emphasis has been given to the Carmilla who says "everyone must die; and all are happier when they do. Come home" (242). This death-goddess, whose "home lay in the direction of the west," cannot be completely explained in sexual terms. The tapestry opposite the foot of her bed "representing Cleopatra" shows the queen not in the act of vamping, but "with the asps to her bosom"—killing herself (235). Sex is important to Carmilla because it produces a "little death":

> "You are afraid to die?" [Carmilla asks Laura.]
> "Yes, everyone is."
> "But to die as lovers may—to die together, so that they may live together. . . . " (246)

She sounds like Gottfried von Strassberg in *Tristan;* her vision is that of *Lie-bestod*—she seeks a dialectic of love and death. "I live in you; and you would die for me, I love you so" (248). The first clause is a vivid reminder that she is daimon, not demon—an inner spirit. But she is not the transformative anima, an energy source. She is the static, languid spirit of dissolution, whose element is not air but earth.

What makes her so frightening is not only her attractiveness but her ardor. She loves Laura passionately because Laura cannot admit to herself that *she* loves death. Much easier to accept is the notion that *death* loves her. Her repression, then, is not only of the sex instinct but of the death instinct. She cannot admit the truth about herself—that she finds death romantic (248), and inwardly longs for it. Her longing for the dead mother becomes a longing for death itself, personified as a vampiric reincarnation of the dead mother. Carmilla's identity as an image of the dead mother becomes even more obvious when she and Laura are looking at the portrait of Mircalla of Karnstein, a seventeenth-century countess (obviously Carmilla herself). Laura reveals, out of nowhere, that she is maternally descended from the Karnsteins. "Ah!" replies Carmilla languidly, "so am I" (248).

Laura and Carmilla are related through the mother, then. Laura's father later reemphasizes that his daughters' Karnstein connection is purely matrilineal (267); his family is free of vampiric pollution—that is, of suicidal tendencies.[4] Again, the parental archetype is vividly polarized: the patriarchal Logos is the Lord of Light and Spirit, while the matriarchal Eros is the Lady of Darkness and moribund flesh (*Karn*-stein; *Car*-milla). Is it possible to destroy the polarization so that the two contrary systems can interact progressively in Blake's and De Quincey's sense? To view Carmilla only as a horror to be eradicated by General Spielsdorf and his crew is to keep the contraries apart, maintaining "male hegemony" (Veeder 205; Day 88). Laura never wholly subscribes to the masculine view of Carmilla as a monster. Unconsciously, even after the vampire is dispatched, she still listens for Carmilla's "light step . . . at the drawing-room door" (228). Archetypes do not die. Although repulsed by the men's revelation to her of Carmilla's vampirism, Laura is *still* attracted to Carmilla's beauty, to the beauty of death. Throughout the story, she oscillates through "ambiguous alternation" (228), vividly realized in Carmilla's transformations from beautiful woman to a black catlike beast (252) to a "black palpitating mass" (281).

She is the animal and the muddy earth, reminding us of our tie with nature. Thus she coldly rejects Spirit. When Laura's father says, "We are in God's hands. Nothing can happen without his permission . . . [for] He is our faithful creator; he has made us all, and will take care of us," Carmilla scoffs vehemently:

> "Creator! Nature! . . . And this disease that invades the country is natural. Nature. All things proceed from Nature. . . . All things *in the heavens, in the earth, and under the earth,* act and live as Nature ordains." (245— emphasis added)

At a funeral, the religious hymns make her ill (242–43), and Laura has never seen her kneel and pray (252). Like Gautier's Clarimonde and DeQuincey's Lady of Darkness, she is the "defier of God." Notice that she is careful to place all three princes—heaven, earth, and the underworld—within the nature goddess's realm. She is the voice of the Unholy Trinity who claims that there is no resurrection of spirit after death. She wants Laura to rise again before she dies, to find regeneration rather than horror in the vision of death as nature's way of creating life.

The vampire in "Carmilla," then, does not represent, as Twitchell and the men in the text think, the unnatural, "sterile love of homosexuality" (*Twitchell* 129). She is the *natural* tendency that makes the snowy woods of death look "lovely, dark, and deep." The beauty of this death-goddess becomes the Gorgon's ugliness only when her promptings are ignored. Repressing her does no good; one must try to befriend her without letting her take complete possession. It is a delicate balance, which Laura is not able to achieve because the archetypal opposites remain hopelessly split; the sexes and what they represent maintain their "dual existence." A dialectic is never achieved.

In Jungian terms, it now becomes clearer why Sheridan Le Fanu chose to make his haunted protagonist a girl. In most Gothic tales involving a female demon, she haunts a *man*—as temptress, succubus, or vampire. Le Fanu followed Coleridge's exception to the rule not because he was fascinated by lesbianism, but because he was concerned about his own death. Shortly before writing the tale, he made out his will, feeling the end to be near. He died only a few months after "Carmilla" was published.[5] When a man needs to come to terms with death, the anima must participate. In taking the first-person point of view of a fascinated girl, Le Fanu identifies with her; that is, he signifies his own anima as "Laura." She becomes the mediator between the man and the frightening mystery of death, which is signified by "Carmilla," the mother archetype in her aspect as *Mater Tenebrarum*. The writer makes his mediatrix suffer, purging himself, at least while he writes, of the painful anticipation of his own death.

For Le Fanu, to write "Carmilla" was to practice the art of dying.

Notes

1. This psychodynamic has been explored fully by William Veeder and William Patrick Day (86–90).

2. All page references to "Carmilla" are to *In a Glass Darkly* 228–88.

3. The vampire did not originally go for the jugular vein. In folklore, it often attacked "the chest near the heart," as Ollier (939) puts it euphemistically, like a good Victorian. There were even some kinky vampires who went for the toes.

4. In folklore, the vampire was often imagined as the animated corpse of a suicide; vampirism was thought to be the direct result of—the punishment for—suicide (Twitchell 7–9).

5. This interpretation of "Carmilla" is not meant to reduce the text to a mere attempt by Le Fanu to deal with his approaching death. Rather the extratextual information that the author was worried about dying when he created the text (see McCormack 268–70) sheds light on the signification of the text's symbols and helps explain the "femininity" of Le Fanu's persona.

Works Cited

Day, William Patrick. *In the Circles of Fear and Desire: A Study of Gothic Fantasy.* Chicago: University of Chicago Press, 1985.

De Quincey, Thomas. "Levana and Our Ladies of Sorrow." *Suspiria De Profundis: Confessions of an English Opium Eater and Other Writings.* New York: New American Library, 1966. 113–223.

De Vries, Ad. *Dictionary of Symbols and Imagery.* Amsterdam: North Holland Publications, 1974.

Jung, Carl Gustav. *The Collected Works of C. G. Jung.* Trans. R. F. C. Hull. 20 vols. Princeton: Princeton University Press, 1953–79.

Le Fanu, Joseph Sheridan. "Carmilla." *In a Glass Darkly.* London: John Lehmann, 1947. 228–88.

McCormack, W. J. *Sheridan Le Fanu and Victorian Ireland.* Oxford: Clarendon Press, 1980.

Ollier, Emand. "Vampyres." *Household Words* 11, no. 255 (February 10, 1855): 39–43.

Sullivan, Jack. *Elegant Nightmares: The English Ghost Story from Le Fanu to Blackwood.* Athens: Ohio University Press, 1978.

Twitchell, James B. *The Living Dead: A Study of the Vampire in Romantic Literature.* Durham, N.C.: Duke University Press, 1981.

Veeder, William. "*Carmilla*: The Arts of Repression." *Texas Studies in Literature and Language* 22 (1980): 197–223.

Bud Foote

The Panchronicon: A New Hampshire Yankee in Queen Elizabeth's Court

In spite of the fact that time travel savors more of fantasy than of scientific plausibility, it has been, as we know well, a staple of science fiction since L. Sprague deCamp's *Lest Darkness Fall,* just as it has been a common theme in myth and legend for centuries. Travel to the future, Rip van Winkle–fashion, goes back at least to the story of the "Seven Sleepers of Ephesus," recounted by Gibbon (1,052–53) but dating, in its earliest versions, back to the sixth century; similar travel reulting from the passage of time at a different rate— such as might be found in modern science fiction dealing with nearly as-fast-as-light travel (LeGuin's "Semley's Necklace," for example)—is found in such legends as the story of True Thomas (Child 317–329), who spent an apparent three days with the Queen of Faerie only to find that ten years had passed in the outside world.

Travel to the past, however, is a somewhat more recent notion. To be sure, such magicians as Faust were able to conjure up visions of the past, and such victims as Scrooge were treated to apparent travel to their own pasts; but in none of these earlier cases were the travelers given the option of altering those pasts.

Apparently, the first time traveler in literature to profit by his travel is Hank Morgan in Twain's *Connecticut Yankee.* Like many a figure of our youthful fantasies, he makes use of his knowledge of what is going to happen; like many a figure of our middle-aged fantasies, he uses his later experience to optimum advantage; like many a European imperialist, he utilizes his more advanced technology to amaze the indigenous yokels and carry his profits to the bank in wheelbarrows.

Since deCamp, such figures have become standard in science fiction; and though few later heroes behave with the greed of the Connecticut Yankee, we can all call his descendants to mind by the dozens: those who, like Poul Anderson's Havig in *There Will Be Time,* travel to the past to frustrate enemies in the present; those who, like Dean McLaughlin's Farman in "Hawk Among the Sparrows," use contemporary technology to triumph over the armies of the past; and those who, like Heinlein's Lazarus Long in *Time Enough for Love,* find time travel the ideal way to get a girl just like the girl that married Dear Old Dad.

Curiously enough, however, figures like this are few and far between in the fifty years between Twain's *Yankee* and deCamp's *Lest Darkness Fall.* One of these rare descendants of the Yankee does, however, appear in 1904 in a little-known novel by Harold Steele MacKaye called *The Panchronicon;* and it is this novel, the extent to which it seems indebted to Twain's book, and the new ideas that appear in it, which I should like to discuss.

Unlike Hank Morgan, MacKaye's time traveler, who rejoices in the name of Copernicus Droop, departs from his present (1898) quite deliberately, with the intention of making a profit, and in a machine, rather like Wells's time-traveler of a decade before. Unlike Wells's machine, however, which seems more like a bicycle than anything else, Droop's device bears more than a passing resemblance to Captain Nemo's *Nautilus*—which had appeared in Boston in translation by 1873—being equipped with staterooms, beds, carpets, wooden paneling, electric chandeliers, and a player piano.

Again unlike the Connecticut Yankee, Copernicus Droop, a native to Pentonville Center, New Hampshire, does not go without company. He needs his cousin, Rebecca Wise, a forty-year-old spinster—and, perforce, as chaperone, her much younger sister Phoebe. They will, as he plans, return to 1876, during which year Rebecca rejected a promising suitor with lots of money. Droop's plan is that Rebecca will marry the unsuspecting victim, and that with his new cousin-in-law's capital to back him, Droop will then invent " 'the graphophone, the kodak, the vitascope, an' Milliken's cough syrup an' a lot of other big modern inventions' " (20) and all three travelers will end up with a million apiece.

Droop is not, like Hank Morgan, a man accomplished in the engineering of his time; he is, in fact, the town drunk. Nor is the time machine—the Panchronicon—his invention; he has inherited it from a traveler from the twenty-sixth century, unfortunately dead of pneumonia in Droop's present. The principle on which the device works is, as far as I can tell, unique to this book. Time passes, Droop tells Rebecca and Phoebe, as a result of

"the sun cuttin' meridians. . . . An' you know's well's I do, Miss Phoebe, that ef a man travels round the world the same way's the sun, he ketches up on time a whole day when he gets all the way round. . . . Ef a feller was to whirl clear round the world an' cut all the meridians in the same direction as the sun, an' he made the whole trip around jest as quick as the sun did—time wouldn't change a mite for him, would it? . . . Follow out that same reasonin' to the bitter end! . . . an' what will happen ef that traveller whirls round, cuttin' meridians jest twice as fast as the sun—

goin' the same way? . . . Why, as sure as shootin, I tell ye, that feller will get just one day younger fer every two whirls round!" (14–16)

And just how, one may ask, is this to be accomplished? The traveler from the future has implanted an iron pole precisely at the North Pole, to which one may attach a ring and a rope:

> "ain't it clear that ef a feller'll just take a grip on the North Pole an' go whirlin' round it, he'll be cuttin' meridians as fast as a hay-chopper? Won't he see the sun gettin' left behind an' whirlin' the other way from what it does in nature? An' ef the sun goes the other way round, ain't it sure to unwind all the time thet it's ben a-rollin' up?" (16–17)

Droop's logic is irresistible; indeed, says Phoebe, that must be the reason so many folks have been trying to reach the North Pole. (Peary had begun his attempts in 1886, twelve years before the putative date of the action of the novel in 1898.) But how is Droop to get to the Pole? It turns out that the Panchronicon is not only a time machine but also an airplane. As we have noted, it is, in its interior appointments, a vast advance on the open-air kite of the Wright brothers' first powered flight in 1903. It boasts similar advances in propulsion: jets raise the Panchronicon off the ground, a propeller at the rear drives the machine forward, and the angle of the attack of the wings can be changed to raise or lower the ship in flight (63).

On their trip to the Pole, the travelers achieve an altitude of five miles, moving along at 130 miles an hour. The velocity, Droop explains, keeps them warm from "the sides o' the machine rubbin' on the air" (64). Rebecca, however, always the proper New England spinster, finds the speed annoying because it prevents her opening the windows to air out the bedclothes.

Rebecca and her sister Phoebe, in fact, are much better New Englanders than was Twain's Connecticut Yankee; or perhaps it is simply that they come from farther north. As soon as Droop proposes his scheme, they begin to see the moral objections: it would be, they say, just like stealing to market Milliken's syrup as Droop's (42). But Droop responds that stealing something before it has been invented, or for that matter, even thought of, is not stealing at all.

Rebecca is not convinced: if Milliken is making money out of it *now*, and Droop invents it *then*, then when the time comes for Milliken to invent his syrup it won't be there for him to invent—and that, she says, is as bad as robbing him.

For Hank Morgan, the Connecticut Yankee, such moral questions would simply not exist. Indeed, the moral and economic questions raised by Twain in *Connecticut Yankee* are not those peculiar to time travel, but those always involved in the imposition of new technology and ideas on an unsophisticated public, in the morality of revolution, and in the uses of power.

MacKaye also allows his travelers to open up some of the paradoxes of time

travel, an area barely hinted at in *Yankee*: when Droop attempts to soothe
Rebecca's qualms by pointing out that Milliken isn't going back with them, but
will go on living in the "present," just as he has done, Rebecca nearly catches
sight of the hitherto unexplored theme of parallel worlds: " 'What! . . . Will he
be livin' in one time an' we be livin' in another—both at the same—' " (43)
In his attempt to clear up the matter, Droop confuses things in a way that
anticipates the later remarks of Larry Niven: " 'No—no! . . . He'll go on livin'.
That's what he *will* do. We'll go on havin' lived. Or to put it different—we
have gone on livin' after we get back six years—to 1892.' " (43)

You will have noted that the proposed destination has been changed from
1876 to 1892; and the reason for that change is another question which arises
in this book but not in *Yankee*. Will Phoebe get younger as she goes back in
time? If so, then in 1876 she will be only two years old; and she is not about
to put up with being spanked. The question arises later, when by accident the
Panchronicon has been sent even further back, when Phoebe, even though by
now she knows she will not get any younger, views her approaching date of
birth with considerable apprehension in the fear that when she reaches that
date she will wink out of existence (114).

The Panchronicon's motor gets stuck, the centrifugal force holds the travelers
to the side of the cabin and prevents their doing anything about it. Eventually
the rope holding the craft to the Pole breaks, and by miraculous chance, the
Panchronicon lands in a suburb of London in the year 1598.

Phoebe is delighted; in her own time and place she was a student of Shakespeare, a tentative adherent of the Baconian theory, and a romantic dreamer
over certain letters from Elizabethan time which had come down in her family.
Here MacKaye opens up a line of thought only hinted at in *Yankee*: the discontent
with the present that spurs the traveler into the past. I say "hinted at" because
we see little of Morgan's life in the 1880s, but he does remark after he gets to
the past that

> "I was just as much at home in that century as I could have been in any
> other; and as for preference, I wouldn't have traded it for the twentieth.
> Look at the opportunities. . . . What would I amount to in the twentieth
> century? I should be foreman of a factory, that is about all; and could drag
> a seine down street any day and catch a hundred better men than myself."
> (viii)

(The twentieth century, of course, is not Morgan's natal century: but is *is* a
century into which he could have reasonably expected to live.)

Droop, of course, is delighted with 1598, because he can set up as a photographer and make a fortune. Phoebe can find out whether Bacon really wrote
the words of Shakespeare; also, as it turns out, her true love turns out to be
resident in Elizabeth's England.

Here again, *The Panchronicon* introduces a concept that will become more important in later science fiction. If a time traveler is to be happy in the past, it will be because he or she is rewarded there is one of four ways unavailable or unattained in his or her own present:

1. political and/or economic power,
2. fulfillment in sexual love,
3. the opportunity to do firsthand research into the past, or
4. the perception that the past is simpler, more genuine, more heroic, or more colorful than the traveler's own time.

Political and economic power, primarily, and secondarily, his marriage to Sandy, and, to a small extent, the color and dash of Malory's version of the sixth century, are the things that settle the Connecticut Yankee down in Camelot; research never occurs to him—he is, after all, as Twain wrote to Dan Beard, " 'a perfect ignoramus [with] . . . neither the refinement nor the weakness of a college education.' " (*Examiner* 16) Now, these three rewards continue to be available to the time traveler in subsequent science fiction: travelers rise to wealth and power, find amatory fulfillment, and return to ages for which they have felt nostalgia from *Lest Darkness Fall* down to the present day. But the scholarly urge to find out what really happened is everywhere, as it is not in *Yankee*—in Silverberg's *Up the Line,* in Anderson's *Dancer from Atlantis,* in Finney's *Time and Again,* and, perhaps most strikingly and beautifully, in LeGuin's "April in Paris." And it is *The Panchronicon* that introduces this theme to modern science fiction.

Droop and Phoebe, then, are well set in the English Renaissance; but Rebecca, totally the creature of her own time and place, unmotivated by politics, economics, amorousness, or nostalgia, is miserable. Like the Yankee in his first reactions to King Arthur's time, she feels that she has wandered into a circus or a madhouse. She behaves there just as she would behave at home, and in a fine twist of humor, MacKaye allows Queen Elizabeth to interpret her Yankee egalitarianism not as a lack of respect for royalty, but as an indication that this strange American lady must be royalty in her own country.

Furthermore, MacKaye allows the notion of reincarnation to creep into the book; Phoebe has often felt drawn to her Elizabethan ancestor, and on her arrival in 1598 she becomes, in some sense, that very woman. Part of her remembers her native dialect and home; but part of her drops into MacKaye's version of Elizabethan English and inhabits the body of her ancestress.

In later time-travel fiction, the closed circle, in which what the traveler does in the past does not change the present but is already part of the past of that present, is to appear again and again (the most noted example being perhaps that in Heinlein's "All You Zombies"). Twain, to be sure, had made the Yankee introduce the expression "paying the shot" into the English language of the sixth century, but the idea is casually tossed aside; MacKaye seems to be the first writer to make significant use of this theme in time-travel literature, and he does it in a way that is, at this state of science fiction development, most beautifully complex. Phoebe meets Shakespeare as he is mulling over the "all the world's a stage" speech and offers to complete it for him. "As you like it," he says and she suggests the remark as a title for the play. She completes not only that speech, but the "to be or not to be" soliloquy of Hamlet, and therefore becomes a part of her own past.

Furthermore, on their own departure from 1598, the travelers take Francis Bacon with them; on the run, and arrogantly scornful of the idea that he could have been responsible for the productions of a mere play-actor, he discovers in the nineteenth century that the works of Shakespeare are valued far above his own. He therefore writes—under that pseudonym of *Delia* Bacon—the book that will encourage many folk to give him the credit for Shakespeare's plays. He is later returned, of course, to his own time.

In spite of the fact that MacKaye has seen many implications in the time travel that Twain, inventing the whole subgenre fifteen years before, did not—implications that were to be rediscovered and used again and again in later science fiction—the book remains essentially a light comic work, *Connecticut Yankee* out of *David Harum*. Consequently, of course, the terrible bitterness and isolation of Twain's work never appear, nor does the holocaust-like impact of the present on the past. Droop, profiting by Morgan's example, takes care not to be taken for a witch; Rebecca, reminding the reader of Morgan's terrifying use of fireworks, scares the whey out of pursuers by igniting lucifer matches; but everyone, of course, lives happily ever after, with minimal damage both to the past and to the present. Phoebe finds in 1598 Guy Fenton, the swain who had written the love notes to her ancestress and alter ego; he returns with her to 1898 and New Hampshire, where they marry and happily raise a child named for the father of Phoebe's ancestress. Hank Morgan, returned to the present, is more fearfully isolated; but if Guy Fenton suffers any temporal shock as a result of being plunged into Pentonville—which town, in a typical time-travel use of paradox, seems to have been named for him—the record sayeth naught of it.

The final reminder of Twain's *Yankee* comes at the very end of the book. Hank Morgan's story, you will remember, is recounted to "M. T.," Twain's narrator, when Morgan is not only on the brink of death but has had several whiskies; and thus a Jamesian ambiguity is cast over the truth of the whole story. Similarly, MacKaye vouches for the truth of his story by sending the reader to ask Mr. and Mrs. Guy Fenton of Pentonville to recount the stories of which they are so fond; and gives further ostensible proof and submerged doubt by noting that in the Fenton woodpile are several bottles of the ale so beloved of the Elizabethans and so condemned by the good folk of Pentonville, New Hampshire, 1898.

The only thing rarer than first editions of *The Panchronicon* would appear to be second editions: it is, after all, a whimsical and trivial entertainment, owing as much to stock regional humor as to Mark Twain's *Yankee*. I would argue, however, that because of its use of themes derived from the *Yankee*, and, more importantly, because of its early perception of moral and philosophical questions later to be found throughout the literature but largely ignored by Twain, it deserves at least a minor niche in the canon of time-travel fiction.

Works Cited

Anderson, Poul. *The Dancer from Atlantis*. New York: Signet/New American Library, 1972.

———. *There Will Be Time*. New York: Signet, 1973.

De Camp, L. Sprague. *Lest Darkness Fall*. New York: Pyramid Books, 1963. Original and shorter version. *Unknown*, December 1939.

Child, Francis James. *The English and Scottish Popular Ballads*. New York: Dover Books, 1965.

Finney, Jack. *Time and Again*. New York: Simon and Schuster, 1970.

Gibbon, Edward. *The Decline and Fall of the Roman Empire*. New York: Heritage Press, 1946.

Heinlein, Robert A. "All You Zombies." *The Unpleasant Profession of Jonathan Hoag*. New York: Pyramid, 1961, 126–137.

———. *Time Enough for Love*. New York: Berkley, 1974.

LeGuin, Ursula K. "April in Paris." In *The Wind's Twelve Quarters*. New York: Bantam, 1976, 23–36.

———. "Semley's Necklace." *The Wind's Twelve Quarters*. New York: Bantam Books, 1976. First published as "The Dowry of the Agnar." *Amazing* (1964). Later as the prologue of *Rocannon's World*. New York: Ace Books, 1966.

MacKaye, Harold Steele. *The Panchronicon*. New York: Scribner's, 1904.

McLaughlin, Dean. "Hawk Among the Sparrows." *Analog* (July 1968), 8–53.

Niven, Larry. "The Theory and Practice of Time Travel." *All the Myriad Ways*. New York: Ballantine, 1971, 110–123.

San Francisco *Examiner*. "Mark Twain, the Man, as Dan Beard Knew [Him?]." (April 25, 1910). Cited in the Norton Critical Edition of the *Connecticut Yankee*. Allison R. Ensor, editor. New York: Norton, 1982.

Silverberg, Robert. *Up the Line*. New York: Ballantine, 1969.

Twain, Mark. *A Connecticut Yankee in King Arthur's Court*. New York: C. L. Webster, 1889.

Verne, Jules. *Twenty Thousand Leagues under the Sea*. Boston: G. M. Smith, 1873.

Wells, H. G. "The Chronic Argonauts." *Science Schools Journal* (April 1888). Revised as "The Time Traveller's Story." *The New Review* (1895). Further revision in *The Time Machine and Other Stories*. New York: Holt, 1895.

Joyce Watford

Techniques of the Fantastic in Two West African Novels

Doris Lessing wrote that Africa represents the exotic and the marvelous—the legitimate "otherness"—as *The Palm-Wine Drinkard*, by Amos Tutuola, and *Things Fall Apart*, by Chinua Achebe, illustrate.

Amos Tutuola and Chinua Achebe, guardians of a rich and proud culture, are great Nigerian storytellers who weave into their art traditional sources and genres to recreate the magic that their writings so frequently exemplify. Both Tutuola and Achebe draw upon the fantastic to dramatize answers to real-world questions, to make sense of real-world phenomena, and to handle real-world fears. Tutuola and Achebe are contemporary writers.

Tutuola grew to fame in 1952 with his book *The Palm-Wine Drinkard*. Almost immediately, *The Palm-Wine Drinkard* was translated into three European languages and was praised as a tall devilish story. *The Palm-Wine Drinkard* has been likened to *Pilgrim's Progress* and Tutuola to John Bunyan, to William Blake, and even to Dante. Like John Bunyan, Tutuola is a man of little formal education, but he instinctively knows, with supreme artistic and imaginative skill, how to cram a basic adventure tale with significant happenings that will hold audiences or readers spellbound (More, *Seven African Writers* 42–43).

In *The Palm-Wine Drinkard*, the Drinkard, who seeks his Palm-Wine Tapster through Unreturnable Heaven's Town to Deads' Town, becomes a pilgrim, on one level, and invites comparison with Bunyan's pilgrim, Everyman. Both *The Palm-Wine Drinkard* and *Pilgrim's Progress* are in the time-honored art form of a great quest; however, after general comparisons the parallels between *The Palm-Wine Drinkard* and *Pilgrim's Progress* begin to falter (Tibble 92). Tutuola tells of a quest that incorporates fantasies that most of us encountered as children in dreams, daydreams, legends, and myths (biblical, heroic, Greek, and Northern European). Mingled with these familiar myths are myths of a lurid Africa partly of Tutuola's fervent imagination and partly of his knowledge of Yoruba oral folktales. In *The Palm-Wine Drinkard*, Tutuola tells of the African bush of ancient days, before the coming of irksome, reasonable, European order (Tibble 96).

Tutuola's imaginative universe in *The Palm-Wine Drinkard* may be depicted in categories of myth operating on four levels of fantasy: daydreams or fantastic delusions of self-grandeur; magic; horrible, terrible monsters; and mystery reminiscent and symbolic of religious and spiritual views. As myth and fantasy come together to create Tutuola's imaginative universe in *The Palm-Wine Drinkard,* the first level of fantasy—daydreams or fantastic delusions of self-grandeur—springs forth and connects our childish sense of helplessness to the Drinkard's "being able to do anything in the world: "His biggest *juju* is to become 'Father of the Gods' who knows the secret of all gods" (Tibble 97).

Magic, the second level of fantasy in Tutuola's imaginative universe, is revealed through the Drinkard's control over events, which illustrates power we humans must have longed for throughout the ages: to change ourselves into birds, squirrels, creatures that airily leave the hard earth, mice that disappear into convenient small holes, fish that swim into the deep—far out of danger—pebbles that can be conveniently and easily lost sight of by enemies, or better still, creatures that can become quite invisible. All of this magic makes for a hero's escape when he gets into any of his inevitable tight corners as a result of his adventurous daring (Tibble 97).

The third level of fantasy in Tutuola's imaginative universe is that of monsters and horrors. Tutuola's monsters are terrible reptiles that live in haunted spots, in underground caverns, in fearful forests, or on bare mountains. His monsters are horrible and have varying numbers of claws, eyes, tentacle-arms, legs, or horns. His monsters are also giants of imponderable size and incomprehensible terror. To this category, too, belongs the "complete, full-bodied gentleman" whom the strong-willed, but beautiful, lady follows into the dangerous forest: "This gentleman has the parts of his body on hire." At night he has to return his parts to the lenders before he becomes only a skull and retires to the skull family's house below the ground (Tibble 97).

The lady herself parallels the Beatrice of Dante, the Ariadne of European myth, the Umnandi or Nandi of Plaatje and Mofolo of African myths. She becomes the Drinkard's wife and follows him loyally to the end of his journey and home again. She shares all of his perils and never once fails to comfort or encourage. To African myth, as well as to European myth, belong the Drinkard's encounters with Death in Death's yam garden and with that terrible half-child, Zurrjir, who emerges from the Drinkard's wife's swollen left thumb, and who, from the first, talks with a lower voice like a telephone, fights grown men, and eats so much he causes famine. Anne Tibble, in *African-English Literature,* reminds us that Zurrjir clearly has affinity with the English Tom Thumb. His life is in folk stories of many European nations. However, in Yoruba myth or African myth, Zurrjir is the child who knows more than his parents; and in Tutuola's story, he becomes so frightful that his parents are forced to kill him. Killing Zurrjir brings shock and dismay just as those unchildlike children—the swarms of hostile, frightening "dead babies" who infest with other deads the one road to and from Deads' Town—shock and dismay as they psychologically symbolize the helpless rebellion of *all* young people, African and others (Tibble 97).

The three good creatures in the story (Drum, Song, and Dance) introduce the fourth and final level of fantasy in Tutuola's imaginative universe. Drum, Song, and Dance are the wholesome three-in-one of music, of poetry said or sung, and of dance-mime. These three characters belong together and represent the legendary blessings of time to restore spiritual oneness and to celebrate life. Also at this level of fantasy is Tutuola's Faithful Mother who lived in the White Tree. The Drinkard and his wife stayed with the Faithful Mother for a customary one year and a few days before they were fortified with roast-meat, cigarettes, and drinks, and were told by Faithful Mother that she could not keep them any longer and that they must continue their journey. Faithful Mother, having counterparts in Asian, African, and European cultures, is comparable to the White Goddess, the earth-mother of northern myth; to the Mother Goddess of Hindu villages; and to many other cultural and religious myths. Her White Tree is comparable to the Bo Tree, the Igdrazil, the Druid's Oak, the Tree of Knowledge, and the Tree of Life. The swallowing of the Drinkard and his wife by the Hungry Creature and the Drinkard's hacking his way out of the Hungry Creature's stomach also remind us of Jonah and the Whale (Tibble 98).

At this final level of myth and fantasy—mystery—is also the well-known golden egg. After indomitable perseverance, the Drinkard at last finds his dead Tapster, who sadly explains that deads can never again live with the living because the deads do everything backwards, even to walking. The Tapster, however, gives his master a miraculous egg that will produce food for whoever asks for it (Tibble 98). Finally, the Drinkard and his wife leave Deads' Town and return to their homeland to find a famine.

The egg comes in handy and gains the Drinkard popularity and prominent status until, amidst reckless merrymaking, the guests smash the egg, the "source of beneficence"; but the Drinkard is wiser after his initiation by perilous travel to Deads' Town. Now he knows what life and people are like and what popularity and social status are worth. He also knows that gifts like the egg can be abused. The Drinkard sticks the egg back together, and the egg, thereafter, is able to produce only whips instead of its usual varieties of food and kegs of palm-wine. Equally pleased with the egg's new capability, the Drinkard re-invites to his house the merrymakers who broke the egg; he commands the egg to produce whips, which begin to flog the irresponsible merrymaking food demanders. Tibble reminds us that this second deed is reminiscent of the money-changers whipped from the temple in the Bible.

The final chapter of *The Palm-Wine Drinkard* shows Tutuola blending African and European myth. Most African cultures, as part of their explanation of life's mysteries, believe in a High God (a Creator) and a Great Mother. In some myths, the High One is connected with the sun and is male, while the Great

Mother is connected with the fruitful earth and is female. However, the Famine in the Drinkard's home town is discovered to be the result of a quarrel for seniority between a *male* Heaven and a *male* Land, once "tight friends." Tutuola's variation of African culture portrays the supreme deity as the male sky God (and not the old female earth goddess) when the Drinkard becomes the people's savior and tells them how to stop the famine. The people are to send to Heaven a sacrifice of two fowls, six kolas, one bottle of palm oil, and six bitter kolas. The only person who can be made to carry this sacrifice to Heaven is a slave. Heaven gladly accepts the "sacrifice" and *male* Land agrees to be Heaven's junior. When the people send a human sacrifice along with fowls and kolas to Heaven, Tutuola reveals that he is making visionary use of many ancient and almost infinitely mutable myths. After the Drinkard's plan to end the famine has been carried out, rain falls for three months, and in the Drinkard's home town, there was "no famine again." Here, the allusion is reminiscent of the story of Sodom and Gomorrah and the Flood, in reverse, however (Tibble 99). Thus, Tutuola's tale ends, but not before the universal role of the Drinkard has been made clear.

Gerald Moore, in *Seven African Writers*, sees the Drinkard as a hero who is linked with the restoration of harmony between man and his gods, for it is the Drinkard's new understanding, won by the hard way of adventure, that enables him to settle the cosmic quarrel through which man is suffering (49).

Thus ends the symbolic journey of the Drinkard in quest of full understanding—a journey that led him, like Gilgamesh, Orpheus, Heracles, or Aeneas before him, into the underworld, there to confront death itself and attempt to carry off some trophy to the world of the living as a symbol of his mastery over the two worlds. The Drinkard's trophy is finally symbolized by the Drinkard's full understanding of his universe and his role in it: to acknowledge, to restore, and to reconcile.

Tutuola's style (so closely related to talk) and his content compounded of fantasy and variations of African-religious-heroic myth, illustrate superb fantastic treatment of a visionary plot, of symbols, of theme, and of imagery throughout *The Palm-Wine Drinkard*.

Chinua Achebe, a younger man than Amos Tutuola, and an Ibo man, comes next to Tutuola in importance as a prose African writer. Achebe, as a novelist, works not in imaginative fantasy but on the opposing basis of realism; but even the most realistic narratives must be fantastic to some extent, since the fantastic makes reversals on ground rules of reality. If there were no ground rules of reality, there could be no reversals. Eric Rabkin, in *The Fantastic in Literature*, reminds us that the fantastic has a place in any narrative genre, but that genre to which the fantastic is exhaustively central is the class of narratives called *Fantasy*. Amos Tutuola's *The Palm-Wine Drinkard* is a *Fantasy*, with a capital F; but Chinua Achebe's *Things Fall Apart* is a *fantasy*, with a small ƒ (29–30).

Chinua Achebe's *Things Fall Apart* is a classic of modern Africa, a moving story of one overproud Ibo man trying to resist culture shock and failing as the stable and supportive world of the Ibos is threatened by the increasing proximity of the white man. To illustrate how Achebe draws upon the fantastic to reveal the inevitably tragic disjunction between the Ibos and the white Europeans, note the following passage. (The white man is not yet perceived as a threat. The men of the tribe are discussing the nature of the world, a world large enough to contain even the fantastic.) Rabkin calls our attention to the diametric up-down and black-white reversals in the passage where Obierika talks of white men, white like a piece of chalk:

"And these white men, they say, have no toes."
"And have you ever seen them?" asked Machi.
"Have you?" asked Obierika.
"One of them passes here frequently," said Machi.
"His name is Amadi." Those who knew Amadi laughed. He was a leper,
and the polite name for leprosy was "the white skin." (29)

Rabkin notes that there is a very gentle use of the fantastic here. The *unbelief* of Obierika tells us that the white man is an *anti-expected* phenomenon in the world of these Ibo men. "The disjunction between covert and overt ground rules that produces the conflict related in the laughter at Machi's joke is the disjunction between taking a phenomenon as anti-expected and taking it as dis-expected" (Rabkin, *The Fantastic in Literature* 30).

The *dis-expected* refers to those elements that the text has diverted one from thinking about, but which, it later turns out, are in perfect keeping with the ground rules of the narrative. The *anti-expected* refers to those elements that defy our preconceptions, such as when the unexpected is truly fantastic, and it is the anti-expected that prevails in the Ibos' laughter and thinking about white men who can be white without being diseased (30).

Rabkin goes on to point out, in this key passage, that what is at first fantastic to the Ibos makes its first step toward becoming all too possible. At this early point in the novel, the association of white men with disease is satiric; by the end of the novel, however, after the demoralizing of these individual Ibos and the total eradication of their tribal social structure, the disease image can be seen as prophetic. "Although *Things Fall Apart* is not very fantastic, it does use the fantastic to make its point" (30). Achebe's use of techniques of the fantastic can be seen in other places throughout the novel.

Jonathan Peters in *Dance of Mask: Senghor, Achebe, Soyinka*, sees a vision of cultural and political history pre-dating imperialism and Eurocentrism in Africa. The title and epigraph of *Things Fall Apart* are taken from William Butler Yeats's poem "The Second Coming": "Things fall apart; the centre cannot hold." Yeats reminds us that mere anarchy is loosed upon the world, as the blood-dimmed tide is loosed and as the ceremony of innocence is drowned everywhere. He tells us that the best lack all conviction, while the worst are full of passionate intensity.

According to Peters, Yeats saw in "The Second Coming" imminent anarchy marked by sinister transformation of values, as the formless chaos from outside challenged the forces of civilization with its own antithetical values. The above paraphrased passage from "The Second Coming" states that in the flux of conflicting forces, the "ceremony of innocence" is drowned in a tide of anarchy. At this very moment in history, force and passion are manifest not in the best but in the worst of the conflicting events. Yeats in 1921 had seen the cataclysmic events at the beginning of the twentieth century as the outward manifestations of a revelation like the birth of Christ some two thousand years before. Peters tells the reader that Achebe, in 1958, viewed the coming of the white man to Umuofia at the turn of the century as a comparable phenomenon that would prove to be a mixed blessing. Peters believes that in *Things Fall Apart*, Achebe has brought together the story of Okonkwo and the cultural history of an imaginary society at a critical moment in time. Through a finely etched symbolism achieved by careful ordering of imagery and allegoric or symbolic episodes, Achebe is able to recapture the order, harmony, and peace in Umuofia before the forces of anarchy swiftly take over, bringing about a breakdown of order as the title of the book suggests, and the time that Achebe is depicting the viable society that Umuofia represented, he is also foreshadowing its doom through symbolic legends and anecdotes, such as the gathering of locusts; the stories of the Albino, the leper, and the white man on an iron horse; and the fable of the Vulture and Rain. These anecdotes, as told in the novel, produce antiexpected and dis-expected phenomena. For example, the locust-gathering episode appears as an unobtrusive anecdote about the rich variety of life in Umuofia. The legend of the locusts is first told to the reader as Nwoye's favorite story told to him by his mother. The legendary account of the locusts is placed between the brief story of Ikemefuna's coming to Umuofia and joining Okonkwo's household in chapter 7 and the announcement and fulfillment of his sacrificial slaying in that same chapter. The reader learns first of Ikemefuna and his positive influence on Nwoye and then is given an example of Nwoye's favorite story balanced against a brief outline of Okonkwo's manly tales of intertribal wars. The story of the locusts is recounted in the same legendary style that Achebe uses to tell the reader the story about Ikemefuna. The elders said that the Locust appeared once in a generation, then: "They went back to their caves in a distant land, where they were guarded by a race of stunted men. And then after another lifetime these men opened the caves and the locusts came to Umuofia" (Achebe 53). This dis-expected is revealed as the legend becomes reality when the locusts actually appear in Umuofia to find Okonkwo, Ikemefuna, and Nwoye repairing the walls of their compound. The arrival of the locusts brings joy to the villagers, for the locusts will be gathered and savored as a delicacy by all, including Okonkwo, Ikemefuna, and Nwoye. Then, suddenly and shockingly, in a happy, after-harvest setting, the announcement of Ikemefuna's imminent death is made. The story of the locusts and that of Ikemefuna have figurative import with political and religious overtones, which becomes clear as the novel progresses (Peters 100). Achebe uses the locusts to symbolize the dis-expected slaying of Ikemefuna that is connected to an Oracle that

Okonkwo disobeys and that swiftly paves the way for Okonkwo's seven-year exile from his homeland. Secondly, Achebe uses the descent of the locusts of Umuofia to symbolize and foreshadow the advent of the white man, Okonkwo's slaying of him, and Okonkwo's own death.

However, the anti-expected and the dis-expected are used to establish the link between the locust symbolism and the advent of the white man in Africa. Obierika's description of the white man on an iron horse deserves quoting for its symbolic treatment of the first contact between blacks and whites in Africa (Peters 100):

> "He was not an albino. He was quite different." He [Obierika] "was riding an iron horse. The first people who saw him ran away. . . . In the end the fearless ones went near and touched him. The elders consulted their Oracle and it told them that the strange man would break their clan and spread destruction among them."

Drinking a little of his wine, Obierika went on to describe how the fearless ones had killed the white man and tied his iron horse to their sacred tree because the iron horse had looked as if it would run away to call the man's friends. Obierika remembered that the Oracle had said that other white men were in their way and that they were locusts. The first white man was simply their harbinger sent to explore the terrain, and so the fearless ones killed him. (Achebe 128).

The white man is a strange phenomenon to the Abame villagers, and they run away from him, for the only phenomenon in their reality to liken the white man to is disease—sickness. However, when the few fearless ones approach and touch the white man, little do they think about their own contamination by doing so (they receive the taint of the leper). Afterward, though, acting out of the instinct for self-preservation, the clansmen decide to kill the lone white man and thus preserve their clan. Although the villagers hope to subvert it, the message of the Oracle is clear: This is the first of many white men and whether they kill him or not, as the forerunner of many more, the white man will break up their clan (Peters 101).

Like locusts, the white men will spread destruction over a people's harvest of tradition and order. When the people of Abame see their Harbinger, they eliminate him quickly without waiting to see the size of the swarm. Thus they leave themselves open to the destruction that comes to them, unlike the people of Umuofia in the actual locust episode referred to earlier. The people of Umuofia, following the advice of their elders, patiently wait for nightfall when the wings of the locusts will be wet with dew. Since the locusts also arrive in Umuofia after the harvest season, they do not destroy crops, thus making their appearance a joyful one, full of power and beauty (Peters 101).

According to Peters, there is some ambivalence about the shod white man who, described in legend, has no toes.

Just as locusts, hungry for food, "settled on every tree . . . breaking mighty tree branches with their sheer weight, so too the white man's all-pervasive influence crumbles existing structures. But as Peters points out, the locusts are also edible and the Umuofians are able to savor them as rare delicacy; likewise, the white man who destroys the old order with his power also brings many benefits never before enjoyed by the villagers. (Peters 101)

Achebe has used the images of the leper and the locusts to emphasize the predatory and insidious nature of the colonial administration—ironic phenomena that are fantastic to the Umuofians but that become too soon their stark reality (Peters 102).

The reader also notes that when Achebe draws upon fable, idioms, and proverbs, he further makes use of fantastic elements to reveal those dynamic socioeconomic, political, and religious aspects of a people's reality that form interesting dimensions of their psyche. Among the Ibo, the art of conversation is held very highly, and proverbs and idioms are the palm oil with which words are eaten (Achebe 10). Often, the idioms and proverbs contain bits of the anti-expected. The following passage illustrates Achebe's use of proverbial material:

"The lizard . . . said he would praise himself if no one else did. I began to fend for myself when most people still suck at their mother's breasts." Nwakibie cleared his throat. . . . "Eneke the bird says that since men have learned to shoot without missing, he has learned to fly without perching. I have learned to be stingy with yams. But I trust you." (Achebe 24)

Life in Umuofia is dominated by religious or spiritual elements. Thus, the Umuofians' belief system is one dominated by fantastic elements. Achebe aptly reveals that Umuofians are a deeply religious, superstitious people who believe in magic. Through a patina of idioms, images, and fable, Achebe again draws upon the anti-expected to symbolize the destructive consequences that are played out in the second and third parts of the novel and that eventually cause the old religious belief system to fall apart. Using idioms suggesting the anti-expected, Achebe reveals that the Umuofians believe in the dominance of a female spirit principle, *Ani*, the earth goddess and the most important deity; in other gods and spirits capricious or benevolent; in the individual's *chi*, or personal god; in the *ikenga*, which stands for the strength of an individual; in the power of Oracles, priests, and priestesses; in *Agbala*, the Oracle of the Hills and Caves; in *ogbanje*, a child who repeatedly dies and returns to its mother to be reborn; in reincarnation; in *egwugwu*, a masquerader who impersonates one of the ancestral spirits of the village; in the role of the ancestors as knowledgable beings and intercessors on behalf of the living in the immensely powerful otherworld; and in the evil of darkness and the birth of twins, to cite a few examples. Achebe, using the fantastic as a tool, symbolizes and summarizes the ambivalence of the destructive and regenerative forces that grow out of the clashes between the African and European belief systems and cultures. "The harmonious Ibo culture is consequently 'primitive' and, to justify the colonial occupation, the sedate peoples of the Lower Niger become warring 'tribes' which must be 'pacified.' As Achebe demonstrates, the same shortsightedness afflicts both administrators and missionaries in their reaction to traditional African culture" (Peters 113). In the story of the quarrel between Earth and Sky (Achebe 52), Sky's withholding rain from Earth causes famine until Vulture is sent to plead with Sky. Vulture wins from Sky a concession that produces a flood. Peters concluded that, similarly, the education and many other gifts brought by missionaries will improve the material well-being of the society. Also, the religion can bring relief to a thirsty soul like Nwoye's, but the insidious element found in the tactics and attitudes of colonialism, especially the total rejection of a people's cultural heritage as worthless and depraved, can only inflict severe wounds on their dignity and sense of history (Peters 114).

Finally, in their quests to give meaning to that perennial instinct in man that longs to justify and explain his circumstances and the complex world he lives in and his place in it, Amos Tutuola and Chinua Achebe, two Nigerian writers, have succeeded in calling forth their rich, varied worldviews to create remarkable pieces of literature, superbly endowed with fantastic elements. Both writers, relying on their African heritage to provide a common culture through content that includes concepts about time, death, and communal imperatives, bring news of values and attitudes of a strange part of the world and of people who have only recently gained prominence in world affairs. Because the colonial experience created ambiguities for Africans and African cultures, modern African writing has been concerned exclusively with the reality of African life, and modern African writers see it as their social and literary duty to recreate reality, to educate—to make people know. The fantastic represents a basic mode of human "knowing" of reality, a theory that holds true in *The Palm-Wine Drinkard,* by Amos Tutuola, and in *Things Fall Apart,* by Chinua Achebe.

Works Cited

Achebe, Chinua. *Things Fall Apart.* New York: Fawcett Crest, 1969.

Killam, G. D. *The Novels of Chinua Achebe.* New York: African Publishing Corporation, 1969.

———, ed. *African Writers on African Writing.* Evanston: Northwestern University Press, 1973.

Moore, Gerald. *Seven African Writers.* New York: Oxford University Press, 1962.

———. *Things Fall Apart: Chinua Achebe.* London: Morrison & Gibb, 1974.

Peters, Jonathan A. *Dance of Masks: Senghor, Achebe, Soyinka.* Washington, D.C.: Three Continents Press, 1978.

Rabkin, Eric S. *The Fantastic in Literature.* Princeton: Princeton University Press, 1976.

———, ed. *Fantastic Worlds: Myths, Tales, and Stories.* New York: Oxford University Press, 1979.

Tibble, Anne, ed. *African-English Literature*. New York: October House, 1965.
Todorov, Tzvetan. *The Fantastic: A Structural Approach to a Literary Genre*. Ithaca, N.Y.: Cornell University Press, 1973.
Tutuola, Amos. *The Palm-Wine Drinkard*. New York: Grove Press, 1953.

III

Fantastic Vision in Children's Literature

*Nancy Willard**

Making the Dreamed Earth

The woman who taught me the most about writing fantasy did not read fairy tales and she would not have understood science fiction. She liked the gossip and weather of this world; the *Farmer's Almanac* and the newspaper were her favorite reading. I have found inspiration for fantasy in both of these publications, but my grandmother read for the facts.

When she opened the Sunday paper, she headed for the women's page and checked out the column called "Alice Greer's Sewing Club." Every Sunday it offered a free pattern, and my grandmother clipped and saved them and seldom used them. Though she did not read fairy tales, she sewed them. My grandmother made quilts.

She stitched green chapels and plaid lilies, gryphons and angels. But no matter how fantastic her subject, she never bought the fabric to make it. Her creatures were always made of what she called odds and ends—the hem of her old winter coat, the sleeve of my mother's jacket, the lace from my aunt's party dress. When you drew one of her quilts over you and spied an angel pieced on the corner, you felt a sense of déjà vu. The angel was both fantastic and familiar; its wings were made of something you had worn and discarded. My grandmother knew that clothes wear out but angels, never. Fantasy, she taught me, is rooted in the familiar. And what has stayed with me from the fantasies I read when I was growing up—the Alice books, the Chronicles of Narnia, and all the George MacDonald books I could lay hands on—was the moment when the ordinary became fantastic: Alice standing on the other side of the mirror, gazing back at her own living room; Lucy standing in the snowy woods of Narnia, looking through the magic wardrobe at the ordinary house she has left behind.

We all know that what one person calls supernatural may be as natural as breathing to another. When reviewers called my novel *Things Invisible to See* a

*This essay was presented by Nancy Willard, guest speaker, as a featured luncheon address.

fantasy, I was surprised, because the dreams and spirits in that book were based on the experiences of several women in our family, whose stories I heard as a child. One of my aunts would describe her trips to heaven as matter-of-factly as a trip to the post office. After the novel was published, her daughter said, "I recognized my mother's vision in your book." Then she added, as an afterthought, "Did she ever tell you about the time she woke up and found twelve angels standing around her bed?"

The writer of fantasy learns to walk with heaven on one side and a sink full of dirty dishes on the other. Like my grandmother, I save a scrap here, a remark there, and try to work it into something richer and stranger than the place from which it came. After my father died, I was reading through his diaries and came across the mention of a native American healer who was summoned to cure his dying mother after the doctor could do no more. My father's mother died long before I was born, but I've seen her house, with its widow's walk and wrought iron fence, its carved woodwork and spiral staircase and servant's quarters, its oriental rugs and Victorian bric-a-brac. Into this house moved the healer for the last month of my grandmother's life, and from this odd meeting of two very different cultures came one of the characters in my novel *Cold Friday*.

The Uitoto Indians of Columbia tell a story about how the world was made from a dream that I think describes very well how writers of fantasy work:

A phantasm, nothing else existed in the beginning: the Father touched an illusion, he grasped something mysterious. . . .

Nothing existed, not even a stick to support the vision. Our Father attached the illusion to the thread of a dream and kept it by the aid of his breath. . . . He tied the empty illusion to the dream thread and pressed the magical substance upon it. Then by the aid of his dream he held it like a wisp of raw cotton.

Then he seized the mirage bottom and stamped upon it repeatedly, sitting down at last on his dreamed earth. (Coxhill 3)

The dreamed earth. Making something out of nothing. I suppose no two writers go about this in the same way. Like doubting Thomas, I like fantasy that is so vivid I can touch it, and I often make a model of the people or place I'm writing about to help me. The story that connects the poems in *A Visit to William Blake's Inn* is a waking dream—the poet William Blake keeps an inn, where he plays host to cats, angels, dragons, cows, rabbits, and tigers. But there is nothing dreamlike about the six-foot model of the inn which stands in my dining room, complete with a sun and moon circus, electric lights, and dining room chairs upholstered in cotton clouds.

Several years ago I was a visiting poet at a prison in Alaska, and I brought with me the only book that had not disappeared with my luggage somewhere between Minneapolis and Chicago, *A Visit to William Blake's Inn*. Stepping into the Fairbanks maximum security jail, I felt as if I'd entered the twilight zone.

Door after door after door clanged behind me, and the guard locked them carefully, as we walked to the windowless classroom deep in the center of the building. The prisoners, he explained, were color coded. The violent ones wore bright orange. The ones who had a record of good behavior wore blue. I entered the classroom and met my students: three Anglo-Americans from the lower forty-nine and six Native Americans—three Tlingits, one Athabascan, and two Inuits, who soon let me know that I should not call them Eskimos. Every fifteen minutes the guard arrived and counted us.

I looked at these men and all my remarks on the writing of poetry went clean out of my head. I talked about Blake and hoped they couldn't see my hands shaking. Blake, I thought, will mean nothing to them.

But I was wrong. During the discussion, one of the students remarked that he had been raised by his grandfather, who was a shaman. Surely this Blake was a shaman? Blake's visions were different from his grandfather's, but for the shaman, truth wears many faces. I thought of the visions my grandmother stitched, the angel and gryphons and green chapels, not removed from ordinary life but shining through it. I thought of what Blake says about visions: "When the doors of perception are cleansed, everything appears to us as it is, infinite."

Work Cited

Coxhill, David, and Susan Hiller. *Dreams.* New York: Crossroad, 1976.

Jules Zanger

Dorothy and Tarzan: Notes toward a Theory of National Fantasy

Appearing, respectively, eighty-seven and seventy-two years ago, Dorothy of Oz and Tarzan of the Apes remain two of the most familiar American fantasy characters ever created. Hardly any literate, or movie-going, or television-watching young American needs to be reminded of how Dorothy and Toto were transported from Kansas to Oz by a cyclone or how Tarzan was raised in darkest Africa by a tribe of great apes. The books and moving pictures and stage plays and comic strips which chronicled the adventures of these two very different characters have made them part of American folklore.

Frank Baum's book *The Wonderful Wizard of Oz,* in which Dorothy first appeared, was published in 1900 and became an immediate success, going into repeated editions; from it spun off the Oz series containing finally a full forty volumes.[1] It has been called "the first indigenous American fairy tale." Edgar Rice Burrough's *Tarzan of the Apes,* published fifteen years later, had similar popular success. Over twenty-five million copies of *Tarzan* books have been sold since the first appearance of the Lord of the Jungle, and the moving pictures, comic strips, and blatant imitations of Burroughs's fantasy are innumerable.[2]

It is conceivable that Dorothy and Tarzan are the most popular fictional characters for young readers ever created in the United States; they represent the emergence of a native American tradition of popular fantasy-adventure, and, whatever their possible indebtedness to such British models as Lewis Carroll's *Alice in Wonderland* and Rudyard Kipling's *Jungle Books,* they reveal a shared set of values grounded in the native American experience and distinctive from that found in English fantasy.

The presence of such a shared value structure seems to me to be particularly significant in the face of the extraordinary differences that distinguish Oz books from the Tarzan series. On one level, these works appear to have nothing in common beyond their popular success and that disregard for realistic probability appropriate to all fantasy. The differences in language, in tone, in subject matter, in moral atmosphere, and in intended audience that distinguish them from each other all are extensive; it is the extent of these differences that makes those characteristics they have in common the more remarkable.

The differences stem basically from the fact that the books were directed at quite distinct audiences. Baum explicitly intended his books to be read by children, an audience which, until he began to write, was reading or being read the fairy tales of Grimm or Anderson or the collections of Andrew Lang. Though his work was occasionally enriched by an ironic and veiled political allusion to reward the discerning adult, his primary audience was the preadolescent for whom the books had to be purchased; consequently, his books required (and achieved) parental approval. In his preface to *The Wonderful Wizard of Oz*, Baum promised the parents of his readers "a modernized fairy tale, in which the wonderment and joy are retained and the heartaches and nightmares are left out."[3] His stories were frequently advertised as American fairy tales, and the combination of modern and American apparently appealed to the parents of the brand new century.

Burroughs's intended audience, on the other hand, was clearly that of adolescent and adult readers. His first stories appeared in pulp magazines, a literary form which, like its predecessor, the dime novels, had a kind of fragile, subrosa legitimacy; they were certainly not pornography, but not literature either—"a waste of time and money." The pulps were purchased by their young readers themselves, frequently against their parents' wishes, or by adults as the sheerest escapism. When *Tarzan* was published in book form in 1914, it retained many of the characteristics of Burroughs's earlier pulp fiction.

Baum's language was, appropriately, relatively simple and familiar, though an occasional long word might appear, especially in the mouth of some comic, vaguely academic character. In the main, he wrote in easily accessible diction, using short sentences and a great deal of dialogue whose language corresponded to the homely American origins of Dorothy herself.

Burroughs's language in the Tarzan series was much more elaborate, pretentious, and elevated than Baum's. He used longer, more consciously rhythmical sentences, and a vocabulary laced with occasional mild archaisms to create a suitably epic tone: "Even the haunting mystery of the long tunnel failed to overcome the monotony of its unchanging walls that slipped silently into the torch's dim ken for a brief instant and as silently back into the cimmerian oblivion behind to make place for more wall unvaryingly identical" (*Tarzan, Lord of the Jungle* 120).

The proportion of description to dialogue in the Tarzan books was much greater than in Baum's work, as might be expected in a series whose hero was laconic if not inarticulate, and whose other major actors were frequently wild beasts.

Baum's audience was not only younger than Burroughs's, but also, it would appear, much more strongly feminine. We must distinguish here the audience who purchased it from that for whom it was intended. In all the forty Oz books, only five have boy heroes, and of those, one is revealed at the end to be a girl. Otherwise, Dorothy and General Jinjur and Ozma and Glinda dominate Baum's fiction. Tarzan's world, on the other hand, is a totally masculine adolescent fantasy in which women exist to be defended, rescued, desired, and fought for by men, but otherwise have little to do.

This difference in audience also explains the difference in tone and moral atmosphere of the two series. In line with Baum's stated intention to leave out "the heartaches and nightmares" of traditional fairy tales, there is little violence in the world of Oz. It is true that Baum included hairbreadth escapes and exciting moments and that a sensitive child might very well have an occasional heartache or nightmare from an Oz book, but generally conflicts in Oz were resolved without blood or death or pain. When Oz was besieged by the Nome King, Queen Ozma announced, " 'I do not wish to fight. No one has the right to destroy any living creatures, however evil they may be, or hurt them, or make them unhappy. I will not fight, even to save my kingdom ' " (Baum). Tarzan's Africa, of course, is filled with bloody, mortal violence between men and beasts, and men and men. It is a Darwinian garden in which Tarzan survives only by virtue of his continuous willingness and ability to kill.

Finally, for the purpose of this comparison, there are consciously erotic and sadistic elements in the Tarzan books that are completely absent from the preadolescent Oz series.

These extensive differences would appear to place Oz and Tarzan in quite different literary categories. Nevertheless, beyond these differences there are to be found a number of shared characteristics that make my linking them not altogether capricious.

One obvious characteristic these two share is that both in their own particular terms are heroic works involving the overcoming of danger in order to achieve a triumph of virtue over villainy. This characteristic, however, in no way distinguishes these American fantasies from their British counterparts.

On the other hand, these American fantasies have in common a number of patterns and emphases that are not usually apparent in the great models of English fantasy. To begin with, Oz and Tarzan are set in worlds in which the fantastic is continually mingled with the ordinary, with the "real" world. Tarzan's Africa juxtaposes the familiar material of the geography primer and of contemporary technology and events with lost colonies of sunken Atlantis, hidden cities peopled by thirteenth-century crusaders, and mysterious races of giants and liliputians. In *Tarzan, Lord of the Jungle*, Jimmy Blake shoots down a medieval, fully armored Knight of the Sepulchre with his forty-five automatic, recalling to the reader a similar if less bloody confrontation in Twain's *Connecticut Yankee in King Arthur's Court*. In Oz, when the Scarecrow, Jack Pumpkinhead, and Tip are trapped in the Emerald City, they escape on the back of a magically animated carpenter's sawhorse to which they tie themselves with a length of familiar clothesline. On differing levels of appeal and with differing degrees of realism, we have in Africa and in Oz "magic countries" whose fantasy employs the familiar American device of incongruity.

Much of this incongruity stems from the fact that these seminal American fantasy-adventures are contemporary in their settings, while British fantasies frequently take place in some mythic or prehistoric past. British fantasies often take the form of unfamiliar histories set in familiar landscapes of the past and future: Camelot, Stonehenge, the Roman Wall become the loci for the fantastic adventure. Wells's Morlocks live in the ruined tunnels of future London's underground. If time is the stuff with which British fantasists work, space seems to be the American imaginative medium. British fantasy draws upon a rich historical, literary, and mythic past. American fantasists, lacking such a past, learned to rely on American distances, on empty places on the map for their fantastic milieux. The Seven Cities of Gold, Cibola, and El Dorado were all prefigures of Pym's Antarctic and Dorothy's Oz.

Both Baum's and Burroughs's books take place in distantly imagined, exotic lands, but both occur in a clearly recognizable present. Baum's Oz and Burroughs's Africa are continually grounded in present time by contemporary allusions and references to drought-stricken Kansas and modern Europe.

In British fantasy, the forces of evil are often depicted as emerging from below—goblins, weasels, orcs, morlocks—possessing a kind of intrinsic wickedness quite apart from any inspired organizing principle that leads them. (It is difficult to imagine a benign orc, even after the passing of Sauron—or even a trustworthy weasel!)

The forces of evil in Oz come from above, not below. Baum's lower classes are hardworking, virtuous, and kind—in line with Baum's populist sympathies—and even when they serve evil, they do so only under constraint. Where British evil frequently tends to be proletarian, the American vision of evil is autocratic.

In Tarzan's world, evil comes to his jungle from above in the form of British bankers slaughtering game, or Arab slavers, or German diamond hunters, or a variety of European types motivated uniformly by greed. The simple Waziri, Tarzan's munchkins, must be protected by him from the exploitative representatives of higher civilization. No white man's burden for Tarzan, however: he carries no torch of commercial civilization or Christianity to the savages.

The only concession to civilization that Tarzan does make is to farm. (I confess my own astonishment at learning this.) Tarzan, with the help of his Waziri, runs the Greystoke Farm until it is destroyed by invading German forces during World War I. It was to this farm that he returned after rejecting the role of Viscount, Lord Greystoke in England, precisely as Dorothy elected to return to the Kansas farm of Uncle Henry and Aunt Em rather than remain as ruler in Oz.

But English lord and jungle lord are quite different roles: the first is based upon a system of rank and privilege, which in turn is based upon birth; the second is pragmatic, individual, and continually subject to renegotiation. Tarzan remains lord of the jungle only as long as he can prove by his strength and skill his right to hold that position. In fact, the whole twenty-five Tarzan books might be seen as the chronicle of his aggressive defense of his claim against beasts, blacks, and Europeans who would challenge him. He is Lord Greystoke by right; he is lord of the jungle by achievement.

Tarzan chooses to be the Jeffersonian aristocrat of merit rather than the European aristocrat of caste. And Dorothy of Oz shares many of his characteristics. In both we discover what have been called the populist virtues—simplicity rather than sophistication, individualism, and self-reliance—virtues born in a rural America not many years distant from the American frontier. Both Dorothy and Tarzan, having been shown the riches of the world, go back to the farm, just as Jesus goes back to the desert.

Unlike such British heroes as Tolkien's Strider or C. S. Lewis's Rillian, or even young Arthur himself, who move from obscurity into the transcendent kingship that is their destiny, these American heroes move from private obscurity to greatness, then back to relative obscurity again. Hawthorne's Gray Champion and the Lone Ranger suggest the range of possibility implicit in the pattern. A model for this pattern, especially for Tarzan, may have been the mythic Daniel Boone, who silently emerged from the darkness of the forest to effectuate the rescue of the helpless—and then as silently disappeared. Another model might be found in the American presidential system with its representative oscillation from public light to private darkness. Jefferson retiring in honor to Monticello and Nixon in exile to San Clemente are only variations on a basic American political design that is echoed in Dorothy's return to Kansas and Tarzan's return to the jungle.

The earliest version of this pattern may have been the Society of Cincinnatus, created by former officers in the American Revolution honoring that legendary Roman general who in the time of Rome's need, left his plow in a half-tilled field to serve and save his city and then returned to complete his plowing. General Washington, we remember, rejected the crown the third time, as Caesar did not, to return to private life.

Generally, British fantasy, taking its representative shape at the height of British imperial expansion, moves toward the achievement of social integration, community, and order—and kingship and aristocracy, by extension, are the external signs of such a state. In a special sense, that imperial vision moves also toward a kind of deathless transcendence. Imperial fantasy is haunted by heroes and kings who will not die, who will merely sleep till their time shall come again, till their second coming as armed messiahs: Drake under the chalk cliffs waiting to repel the ultimate armada, Barbarossa in his cavern in the Hartz mountains, Arthur in Avalon.

That ancient royal formulation, "The king is dead; long live the king," elegantly elides those mortality-steeped modifiers, "*old* king," "*new* king," affirming in its deliberate imprecision the mystery of the immortality of kings.

In this sense we can suggest that what I have described as imperial fantasy is essentially eschatological, having as its wellspring and template and end nothing less than the vision of the coming of the Kingdom of God in the last days.

American fantasy reverses the royal formula, so that "The king is dead; long live the king" becomes "Long live the king," followed by "The king is dead," stripping kingship of its mystery and restoring it to the inexorable narrative forms of nature.

By comparison with imperial fantasy, the American fantasies seem anarchic. They consciously prize simplicity and rural isolation; they tend to be intensely pragmatic and self-reliant. When, in *The Wonderful Wizard of Oz,* the Scarecrow, the Tinman, and the Cowardly Lion move to take their respective kingdoms, we see a deliberate democratization of kingship—the king as agricultural worker, as mechanic, as politician. Kingship has become homely and familiar, based on common sense and kindness rather than on birthright or divine right. Oz's rulers are elected by acclamation in an atmosphere deliberately reminiscent of a mid-western political rally.

British fantasy's villains (morlocks, weasels, and goblins) suggest the British middle-class fear of chartist revolutionaries—underfed miners and operatives pouring forth from their hovels and holes to terrorize the countryside. Like British fantasy, American fantasy can be perceived as responsive to conditions of social and economic change. The United States in the decades bridging the turn of the century suffered extreme economic depressions. By the end of the nineties, nearly a third of the nation's farms were mortgaged. Corn was selling for ten cents a bushel in Dorothy's Kansas, and cotton was getting five cents a pound. Between two and a half and three million—one out of five—workers were unemployed. More than 660,000 men were thrown out of work by strikes and lockouts, and following the model of Coxey's army, no fewer than seventeen "industrial armies" of the unemployed marched on Washington. It is this social and economic context that shapes both Baum and Burroughs. Both men were accounted failures by the time they had reached middle age. Both failed repeatedly in business enterprises before they turned to writing fantasy. Like their British counterparts, they created fantastic alternatives to their experience, but instead of a hierarchical, conservative vision of social order, the vision that impels their work stems from an older, rural, even frontier, America. Baum's world is much gentler, kindlier, more innocent that Burroughs's, which is filled with violence and death, but together they share the values of self-reliance, simplicity, and independence—values grown increasingly difficult to maintain in a rapidly urbanizing and mechanizing society.

The models I have described are, of course, neither mutually exclusive nor absolute. This has become especially true since the extraordinary American success of Tolkien's Middle Earth fantasies, which have given the imperial model a tremendous popularity that American writers have been quick to pick up on: both McKillup's *Riddle Master* trilogy and Herbert's *Dune* series are cases in point, and Luke Skywalker seems to be moving inevitably toward his mystical kingship now that his royal lineage has been discovered.

There are exceptions, of course. Ursula Le Guin's Ged in the Earth-Sea trilogy comes to mind—but in the main, those individualistic, democratic heroes who followed Cincinnatus back into the obscurity of their private lives seem to be disappearing with the spacious world that created them.

Notes

1. For a complete publishing history of the Oz books, see Frank J. Baum, *To Please A Child*, Chicago: Reilly and Lee, 1961.

2. See R. A. Lupoff, *Edgar Rice Burroughs, Master of Adventure*, New York: Canaveral Press, 1965. 229ff.

3. See my "Goblins, Morlocks, and Weasels: Classical Fantasy and the Industrial Revolution," *Children's Literature in Education* 8, no. 4 (Winter, 1977), 154–62.

Works Cited

L. Frank Baum, *Ozma of Oz*, Chicago: Reilly and Lee Company, 1907.
Edgar Rice Burroughs, *Tarzan of the Apes*, New York: Grosset and Dunlap, 1915.
———, *Tarzan, Lord of the Jungle*, New York: Grosset and Dunlap, 1928.

Michael Clifton

The Glass around the Jewels: Baum's Ambivalent Vision

Perhaps more completely than any other writer, the person who hopes to write successful children's literature must become a child again, to write with that combination of seriousness, simplicity, and wonder children demand in their stories: they will read no others. Arguably, then—because his books *have* been read and reread by generations of children—L. Frank Baum possesses this quality, this child*like*ness, to a great degree. It is a crucial attribute for writers, one that Erich Neumann calls "a special animation of the unconscious" and defines as

> the creative man's special kind of alertness. He usually possesses it even as a child, but this alertness is not identical with the reflecting consciousness of a precocious intellect. The childhood state of the creative individual can be characterized no better than in Hölderlin's words: "*und schlummert wachenden Schlaf*" ("and slumbers in waking sleep"). In this state of alertness the child is open to a world, to an overwhelming unitary reality that surpasses and overpowers him on all sides. At once sheltered and exposed, this waking sleep, for which there is as yet no outside and no inside, is the unforgettable possession of the creative man.(180)

The special, creative state Neumann describes is functionally an altered state of consciousness, one achieved in a writer's case not by drugs, fasting, or meditation, but by simple concentration in a relaxed posture, the restriction of the mind to a blank piece of paper as the writer sits at his or her desk, waiting for whatever will come. Because it is a variety of altered state, because most of the major phenomena of such states overlap (Mogar 385), because one of these phenomena is a shift toward increased imagery, and because the images themselves follow a remarkably regular pattern, it is possible to construct from various sources a visionary schema that indicates just how a particular writer reacts to this heightened sense of unconscious—with a sense of joy, of fear, or of ambivalence.

The first of these sources is Aldous Huxley's *Heaven and Hell,* in which he identifies the major imagery of visionary states as a sense of light and color in intricate, geometric forms resembling jewels and/or flowers (103–04). This is true in both the positive and the negative visions Huxley identifies, though the jewels and flowers seem divine in the first case and demonic in the second. The latter, the terrible vision, is accompanied moreover by a sense of isolation, of helpless shrinking and dehydration that Huxley calls "inspissation" (136), and the key to both is the presence or absence of negative emotions (137–38).

Huxley's findings are supported by those of the Russian mathematician V. V. Nalimov, whose most recent study, *Realms of the Unconscious,* adds to Huxley's light and colors the subjective sense of *space* accompanying the visionary experience: if it is pleasant, the other perceptions are joined by a sense of endless space and a movement through it resembling flight (248); if, on the other hand, the experience is unpleasant, then the sense of space is severely restricted, even claustrophobic, and the light and color of the positive vision are replaced by a stifling darkness (190).

Together with one additional feature of altered states—that subjects of fearful, drug-induced experiences sometimes perceive a glass barrier between them and their surroundings, as in Pahnke and Richards's *"Implication of LSD and Experimental Mysticism"* (411)—these findings can be combined either to predict the features of a visionary landscape or to analyze those of one existent. If that landscape is perceived happily, for instance, it will be filled with light, flowers, and jewels; inhabitants and visitors will fly freely over and about such a place. Alternately, if the landscape—that is, the subjective sense of the unconscious— is perceived *un*happily, it will be filled with dark, constricted places in which characters tend to become caught, for example, the multiple dungeons and tunnels of Tolkien's hideous Mordor, the territory of Sauron.

If the visionary landscape reflects an ambivalent sense of the unconscious, however, these attributes will be mixed: such a vision will contain jewels, flowers, light, and bright colors, but all these will be associated with (perhaps surrounded by) something glass. Visitors and inhabitants will alternately fly over this place or fall helplessly into it, and they will sometimes find themselves trapped, often by malignant versions of the flowers or jewels. It is this vision, this highly mixed sense of the unconscious, that is reflected in various imagery in Oz.

In addition, because these visionary images often appear in concert with imagery Jung describes, one can even argue which elements of the unconscious are responsible for some of the glass and constriction in Baum's kingdom. Two Jungian images that appear in Oz—those of the child and the round thing— are themselves representations of the creative state in which a writer becomes aware of the unconscious. Both, that is, picture an ideal integration of conscious and unconscious elements of the personality, or an ideal altered state ("The Psychology of the Child Archetype" 164; "Concerning Rebirth" 142); reflecting this unitary awareness, the child is often hermaphroditic ("Child Archetype" 175).

The most important archetypal image in Baum, though, is that of the anima, around whom a variety of visionary images cluster, both jewels and glass. According to Jung, she is the hidden female element of the male personality. For any man, and particularly for a creative one, she is both highly attractive—in a peculiarly erotic way—and highly dangerous ("The Archetypes of the Collective Unconscious" 25, 28); she is likely to appear to her hapless suitor as a "lamia or succubus, who infatuates young men and sucks the life out of them" ("Archetypes" 25). When she seems too appallingly dangerous to be even semi-human, according to Jung, she appears in a variety of animal forms—that of a cat, a snake, a lizard, or a bear ("The Psychological Aspects of the Kore" 184).

Nearly as often as she appears as the vampire or the cat, however—and this last comes not from Jung but from my own research into literary manifestations of such imagery—the anima overlaps the image of the child to form a hybrid, that wondrously attractive female child whose charms have proven irresistible to many more than poor Humbert Humbert. If the anima's erotic qualities are expressed, this magical girl's allure in fact resembles that of Nabakov's Lolita; if her eroticism is implicit, though, she is Alice or, in our case, Ozma.

However, even Dorothy is a version of this hybrid child-and-anima, and visionary imagery and perceptions therefore tend to cluster around her. Her frightening return to Oz in *Dorothy and the Wizard in Oz* is a good example. Falling into a chasm that opens during a sudden earthquake, Dorothy and her companion, Zeb, approach a remarkable sight, a cluster of

six great glowing balls suspended in the air. The central and largest one was white and reminded her of the sun. Around it were arranged, like the five points of a star, the other five brilliant balls; one being rose colored, one violet, one yellow, one blue and one orange. This splendid group of colored suns sent rays darting in every direction, and as the horse and buggy—with Dorothy and Zeb—sank steadily downward and came nearer to the lights, the rays began to take on all the delicate tintings of a rainbow, growing more and more distinct every moment until all the space was brilliantly illuminated. (24–25)

This light and its accompanying color display are the hallmarks of a visionary experience, as is the sense of endless space appearing with them: all are attributes of the positive experience, an exhilarating state of mind appearing imagistically here as the Jungian round thing; accurately, it is from these globes that the light and bright colors emanate in the scene Baum presents. The experience is not altogether happy, though, since Dorothy and Zeb are falling rather than soaring, and the combination of perceptions from both visions typifies the writer's ambivalence.

Interestingly, the two children here present a splitting of the Jungian child's originally hermaphroditic nature—a state best figured in Baum's work by the enchanted Tip-who-is-really-Ozma in *The Marvelous Land of Oz*. In *Dorothy and the Wizard in Oz*, Dorothy, as the female, unconscious element of the writer's personality, is relatively unafraid facing these visionary phenomena: it is she who first looks over the buggy's side to glimpse the glowing balls. Zeb, however— that male, conscious side of the personality—is far more fearful. Rather than looking, he huddles in the buggy and "shiver[s]. All this was so terrible and unreal that he could not understand it at all, and so had good reason to be afraid" (27).

This fear appears imagistically in two ways as the scene develops. First is the children's concern that they will be burnt or blinded by the light shining from these colored globes: as they rush past the burning spheres, Baum writes, the light streaming from them "was then so bright that it dazzled their eyes, and they covered their faces with their hands to escape being blinded" (28); as it turns out, however, "there [is] no heat in the colored suns," so the two escape unharmed after all. The second image reflecting Zeb's fear is that sense of something glass, listed above as indicative of the negative visionary experience. In this scene, that fear surrounds—or actually embodies—the children's desti- nation, which turns out to be an entire city of glass.

After they pass the shining globes, the boy and girl discover that they seem "to be falling right into the middle of a big city which had many tall buildings with glass domes and sharp-pointed spires. These spires were like great spear- points, and if they tumbled upon one of them they were likely to suffer serious injury" (29). In spite of the apparent fearfulness of the place—echoed in Dor- othy's making out beneath the glass walls "a number of queer forms huddled in the corners of [the] rooms" (31)—it is beautiful, since the "rainbow tints from the colored suns fell upon the glass city softly and gave to the buildings many delicate, shifting hues which were very pretty to see" (31).

Here again, Baum is torn between images of both visionary experiences, and his hesitation continues as Dorothy and Zeb approach this place of mingled beauty and fear: as they fall nearer, their movement begins to slow until, Baum writes, "they were floating very, very slowly—so slowly that it could no longer be called a fall—and the children had ample time to take heart and look about them" (28). Once they arrive and leave the buggy, in fact, their movement becomes that floating sensation of the exhilarating experience: Dorothy takes Zeb's hand, and "soon they were both walking through the air, with the kitten frisking beside them" (37).

The appearance of the kitten in this cluster of visionary imagery is significant, since it is one of the more negative, that is, inhuman, forms the animal tends to take. This one, brought with the children, behaves so badly that she is put on trial near the end of the book for murder, apparently having eaten one of the Wizard's tiny piglets. Her lack of regard for ordinary moral behavior—her essential amorality—both lands her in the difficulty to begin with and forms an important tie to other manifestations of the anima in the series, ones that take more obviously visionary or even slightly erotic forms.

One of these more obviously visionary manifestations of the anima is a cat native to Oz, rather than a visitor to this world like the one in *Dorothy and the Wizard*. Created by a magician and first appearing in *The Patch-Work Girl of Oz*, it is

> made of glass, so clear and transparent that you could see through it as easily as through a window. In the top of its head, however, was a mass of delicate pink balls which looked like jewels, and it had a heart made of a blood-red ruby. The eyes were two large emeralds, but aside from these colors all the rest of the animal was clear glass, and it had a spun-glass tail that was really beautiful. (47)

This cat is the essence of Baum's ambivalent vision, mingling as it does jewels, round things—the "delicate pink balls"—and glass in one "really beautiful" package.

A positive visionary anima, on the other hand, appears at Ozma's unveiling, when the enchantment changing her to Tip is undone at the end of *The Marvelous Land of Oz*. At the finish of Glinda's magic, what rises from the couch to where Tip lay is no longer male but rather

> the form of a young girl, fresh and beautiful as a May morning. Her eyes sparkled as two diamonds, and her lips were tinted like a tourmaline. All adown her back floated tresses of ruddy gold, with a slender jeweled circlet confining them at the brow. Her robes of silken gauze floated around her like a cloud, and dainty satin slippers shod her feet. (276)

Though Ozma is neither literally crystalline nor actually floating here, Baum's description of her combines both these visionary elements in sufficient strength to make her seem the embodiment of the positive experience. Perhaps because of her recent incarnation as Tip—her not-so-latent hermaphroditism—Ozma, of all the children in Oz, most nearly represents that treasure of the unconscious the Jungian child tends to be, though her very clear femininity shows her to be at the same time a representation of the anima. She is Baum's Alice: the perfect female child.

Because she is part anima, however, the uncertainty with which Baum faces this element of his unconcious tends to gather around her. Given her often-expressed goodness, of course—her moral perfection—elements or images of fear tend not to touch her. But her relations are not so exempt. In *Tik-Tok of Oz*, for example, in a kingdom of Oz rightfully ruled by "Ozga," a "distant cousin" of Ozma, Betsy spies a "splendid big greenhouse, its thousands of crystal panes glittering in the sunlight" (30). The kingdom, in other words, is a place of both vision and fear, like the city of glass discussed above.

Baum's subsequent description confirms this identification, since the green-house is "filled with magnificent rosebushes, all growing in big pots. On the central stem of each bush bloomed a splendid Rose, gorgeously colored and deliciously fragrant, and in the center of each Rose was the face of a lovely girl" (31). Although this description of the anima (animas, actually) seems at first to reflect a positive perception of the archetype—since the "lovely" girls resemble visionary flowers—these roses are in fact nasty. Not only are they armed with the long, dangerous thorns recalling the wicked spires of the city, but they repeatedly demand their visitors' deaths, the traditional punishment for visiting the kingdom.

A less fearful instance of contact with such visionary but malicious flower-girls in *The Marvelous Land of Oz* illustrates more clearly their disorienting effect on those who approach them. As the party in that sequel walks along, they find themselves

> surrounded by a field of tall stalks, every stalk bearing at its top a gigantic sunflower. And not only were these flowers almost blinding in their vivid hues of red and gold, but each one whirled around upon its stalk like a miniature wind-mill, completely dazzling the vision of the beholders and so mystifying them that they knew not which way to turn.
>
> But now the sunflowers suddenly stopped their rapid whirling, and the travelers plainly saw a girl's face appear in the center of each flower. These lovely flowers looked upon the astonished band with mocking smiles, and then burst into a chorus of merry laughter at the dismay their appearance caused. (136–37)

Like that from the glowing balls discussed above, the light of these flowers is "almost blinding"; in this case, however, the visionary light and color display is augmented by a rapid, dizzying motion the passersby find both "dazzling" and "mystifying." Here, the effect of the flower-girls' near presence more obviously resembles the symptoms of an altered state. Significant, too, are the "mocking smiles" and "merry laughter" the flowers share at the travelers' discomfort. They are as unsympathetic to another's plight, as amoral, as Dorothy's kitten or the glass cat.

Such flowers can, in fact, be positively dangerous, as they become in *The Patch-Work Girl of Oz*. Like the party approaching the sunflowers above, the one in *Patch-Work Girl* discovers a stand of remarkable plants that are not only in continual motion—their leaves sway "continually from side to side, although no wind was blowing" (117)—and highly colorful ("the most curious things about the swaying leaves was their color, [for example,] gorgeous yellows, turning to pink, purple, orange, and scarlet"), but whose effect is also similar to that of the sunflowers. The "changeful coloring of the great leaves was very beautiful," Baum writes, "but it was bewildering, as well, as the novelty of the scene drew our travelers close to the line of plants, where they stood watching them with rapt interest" (117).

Unlike the sunflowers, though, these plants are giant—they tower "twice as high as the top of the Patch-Work Girl's head"—and as a result, are more effectively unpleasant. Without warning, they turn on everyone in the group, including Ojo, who suddenly sees that

> half a dozen of the great leaves were bending toward him from different directions and as he stood hesitating one of them clutched him in its embrace. In a flash he was in the dark. Then he felt himself gently lifted until he was swaying in the air, with the folds of the leaf hugging him on all sides. . . .
>
> The minutes passed and became hours. Ojo wondered how long one could live in such a condition and if the leaf would gradually sap his strength and even his life, in order to feed itself. (119–20)

The open space and color display of the positive experience here change dramatically to the cramped and claustrophobic darkness of the negative. The flower's femininity, moreover, implicit in this manifestation, surfaces in Ojo's fear that the plant will "gradually sap his strength and even his life, in order to feed itself"—a straightforward instance of the anima's draining of energy to which Jung alludes.

The same sort of thing happens in *The Magic of Oz* when Cap'n Bill and Trot go to find the "Enchanted Flower" as a present for Ozma. Led by the glass cat— an ominous guide, but the only one who knows the way, significantly enough— the two watch the essence of Ozian flowerness as it blooms: "The colors of the flowers . . . were strikingly bright and beautiful, and the shapes of the blossoms were varied and curious. Indeed, they did not resemble ordinary flowers at all" (90). Trot, in fact, observes both a kaleidoscopic color display and an interesting combination of the flowers and the Jungian round thing.

> Just now a lovely group of pink peonies budded and bloomed, but soon they faded away, and a mass of deep blue lilies took their place. Then some yellow chrysanthemums blossomed on the plant, and when they had opened all their petals and reached perfection, they gave way to a lot of white floral balls spotted with crimson—a flower Trot had never seen before. (143)

Unfortunately, though, the reason she is watching the magic flower blossom is that there is "nothing else to do": she and the captain are both trapped, stuck fast the instant they set foot on the Enchanted Flower's island, discovering to their great dismay that newly sprung roots of flesh attach them to the soil. Not only that, but they are also growing smaller. As a local inhabitant tells them, "You'll grow small. . . . You'll keep growing smaller every day, until by and by there'll be nothing left of you. That's the usual way, on the Magic Isle" (149). Their predicament is an interesting overlap of that draining of vitality Ojo fears—actual rather than merely feared in this case—and Huxley's inspissation, that sense of shrinking and dehydration identifying the terrible vision. In Trot and the Cap'n's case, although the shrinkage is slow and painless, the danger is very real. As Trot warns, "The Magic Flower is lovely and wonderful, but it's just a lure to catch folks on this dreadful island and then destroy them" (185–86).

Because this visionary flower's status as anima is only implied—in the previous femininity of the rose-girls and sunflowers, and in the glass cat's special knowledge of its location—the reason for the danger attached to it is unclear; in more obviously feminine examples of the anima, however, the reason for the menace becomes clearer. There is, for example, "Reera the Red," a character in *Glinda of Oz* who

> assumes all sorts of forms, sometimes changing her form several times a day, according to her fancy. What her real form may be we do not know. This strange creature cannot be bribed with treasure, or coaxed through friendship, or won by pity. She has never assisted anyone, or done wrong to anyone, that we know of. All her wonderful powers are used for her own selfish amusement. (186)

Her description here could as well be that of the Glass Cat, since it captures the essence of the anima.

Baum surrounds this version of her with the saurian imagery Jung predicts: sitting with Reera in her cottage are "a great crocodile, its red eyes gleaming wickedly and its wide open mouth displaying rows of sharp teeth," "horned toads," and a "red-and-green lizard" (187). Reera herself, though neither cat nor bear, appears at first to the shocked observer as "a huge gray ape" with absurdly feminine accoutrements—"a lace cap" and "little apron of lace"—and with eyes that resemble the crocodile's gleaming red ones (they look "as if coals were burning in them").

Failing to frighten her visitor, however, she eventually changes herself to a far more attractive appearance, transforming herself into "a young woman, whose face was quite attractive" (191). This hint of feminine allure becomes even more pronounced when Reera finally assumes her true form. Having changed three "Adepts" from fish to their own true forms as three more highly attractive younger women, Reera feels herself outshone and finally shows herself also to be, in fact,

> a young woman fully as lovely as the three Adepts. She was not quite so tall as they, but her form was more rounded and more handsomely clothed, with a wonderful jeweled girdle and a necklace of shining pearls. Her hair was a bright auburn red, and her eyes large and dark. (205)

Surrounded again by her visionary imagery—both jewels and multiple instances of the round thing (her pearls)—this most fully developed version of the anima in Baum's series reveals in two words (that Reera's figure is more sexually developed, "more rounded," than those of the Adepts) the reason for the danger surrounding her, and by extension, for the glass around the greenhouse: it is that whelming eroticism peculiar to this element of the unconscious. Almost completely unexpressed in these children's stories, it nevertheless surfaces here more or less in spite of Baum.

As Jung points out in "Archetypes," however, the anima is "only one archetype among many" and "not characteristic of the unconscious in its entirety" (27); so, while her eroticism helps to explain *some* of the fear surrounding Baum's sense of the unconscious, it fails to explain all of it: Why is the city toward which Dorothy and Zeb fall made of glass, for instance? Why is Ojo, in *The Patch-Work Girl of Oz*, imprisoned again after he is saved from that captivating flower, this time in a dome of "colored glass," a combination of round thing, visionary colors, and fear? (196). With its jeweled floor and soft carpets, is this prison indicative of the positive or of the negative vision? For me, at any rate, these are tantalizing questions.

Happily for Baum, though, it is not really necessary to understand these images to react to them. The accuracy with which he records the imagery and perceptions of altered states, together with the thoroughgoing ambivalence toward the unconscious they reveal, are a potent combination. Like Poe, Baum captures what may be Everyman's vision: a sense of mingled terror and delight, dimly remembered from dreams and called once more into the light by the chronicles of Oz. It is this vision that guarantees his readership, since each generation of children reads the books with the same rapt interest that the giant flowers kindle in Ojo and Patches; like them, these new readers, too, will be captivated by the things they discover.

Works Cited

Baum, L. Frank. *Dorothy and the Wizard in Oz*. 1908. Reprint. Mineola: Dover, 1984.

———. *Glinda of Oz*. 1920. Reprint. New York: Ballantine Del Rey, 1981.

———. *The Magic of Oz*. 1919. Reprint. New York: Ballantine Del Rey, 1981.

———. *The Marvelous Land of Oz*. 1904. Reprint. New York: Dover, 1969.

———. *The Patch-Work Girl of Oz*. Chicago: Reilly & Lee, 1913.

———. *Tik-Tok of Oz*. 1914. Reprint. New York: Ballantine Del Rey, 1980.

Huxley, Aldous. *The Doors of Perception and Heaven and Hell*. 1956. Reprint. New York: Harper Colophon, 1963.

Jung, Carl Gustav. "The Archetypes of the Collective Unconscious." *The Collected Works*. 2nd ed. Trans. R. F. C. Hull. Ed. Sir Herbert Read, et al. Vol. 9 of 20 vols. Bollingen Series. Princeton: Princeton University Press, 1968. 3–41.

———. "Concerning Rebirth." *The Collected Works*. Vol. 9, 113–15.

———. "The Psychological Aspects of the Kore." *The Collected Works*. Vol. 9, 182–203.

————. "The Psychology of the Child Archetype." *The Collected Works*. Vol. 9, 151–81.

Mogar, Robert E. "Current Status and Future Trends in Psychedelic (LSD) Research." *Journal of Human Psychology* 2 (1965): 147–66. Reprinted in *Altered States of Consciousness: A Book of Readings*. Ed. Charles T. Tart. New York: John Wiley, 1969. 381–97.

Nalimov, V. V. *Realms of the Unconscious: The Enchanted Frontier*. Philadelphia: ISI, 1982.

Neumann, Erich. "Creative Man and Transformation." *Art and the Creative Unconscious: Four Essays*. Trans. Ralph Manheim. Bollingen Series 61. New York: Pantheon, 1959. 149–205.

Pahnke, Walter, and William Richards. "Implication of LSD and Experimental Mysticism." *Journal of Religion and Health* 5 (1966): 175–208. Reprinted in *Altered States of Consciousness: A Book of Readings*. Ed. Charles T. Tart. New York: John Wiley, 1969. 399–428.

IV

Science Fiction and Fantasy Films

*Vivian Sobchack**

Terminal Culture: Science Fiction Cinema in the Age of the Microchip

Ten years ago, a renaissance in the popularity of the American science fiction film was marked by the 1977 release of both *Star Wars* and *Close Encounters of the Third Kind*—films radically different in tone, thematics, and aesthetic sensibility from any of their generic predecessors. It was also in the late 1970s that previously elite electronic forms of representation such as the digital watch, the video game, the video recorder, and the personal computer became truly popular commodities—consuming us to the vast degree that we consumed them. It would seem, then, that our understanding of the changed nature of the contemporary American science fiction film might depend upon our coincidental understanding of the ways in which our lived experience of time and space have radically changed in this last and most popularly electronic decade of American culture. That is, the "altered states" of our cultural representations and our spatial and temporal consciousness cannot be considered anything less than an alteration in the basic forms of our technology—but they also must be considered something a good deal *more*. As Martin Heidegger tells us: "the essence of technology is nothing technological" (Heidegger 317). Technology is always "lived"—always historically informed by political, economic, and social content, always an expression of aesthetic and ethical value. As might be expected, these new aesthetic and ethical values find no more profound and concrete representation than in the American science fiction film—first, because the American cinema has increasingly incorporated the new electronic technology into its very modes of production, distribution, and exhibition, and second, because no matter how sometimes superficially "silly," science fiction cinema has always had as its

*This essay was presented by Vivian Sobchack, guest speaker, as a featured luncheon address. It is in part derived from material appearing in *Screening Space: The American Science Fiction Film* by Vivian Sobchack. Copyright © 1980, 1987 by Vivian Sobchack. Reprinted by permission of Ungar Publishing Company, New York.

distinctive generic task the cognitive mapping and poetic figuration of social relations as they are constituted and changed by new technological modes of being-in-the-world.

Given the recent and pervasive transformation of popular culture by and through electronic technology, it is hardly surprising that from *Star Wars* and *Close Encounters* to *Repo Man* and *Uforia*, the last decade's worth of science fiction films are so different in sense and sensibility from their cinematic forebears. These differences go much further than a simple transformation of the manner of the genre's "special effects" (using new computer-generated imagery, for example), or of its visible and emblematic representations of current electronic technology (which is less exciting to look at than earlier mechanical technology with visible moving parts). Beyond these sorts of obvious differences (whether "mainstream" and big-budget or "marginal" and low-budget), it is the existential attitude of the contemporary science fiction film that is a great deal different now from what it was when the genre emerged in the 1950s.

For example, in the 1950s during the genre's first "Golden Age," cinematic space travel had an aggressive and three-dimensional "thrust" to it—this, whether it was narrativized in optimistic, colonial, and phallic dramas of conquest and penetration or in pessimistic and paranoid dramas of earthly and bodily invasion. Space in these early films was semantically inscribed as "deep" and time as "accelerating" and full of "urgency." However, between 1968 and 1977, the nature of science fiction film space changed. With the exception of the singular *2001: A Space Odyssey* (which, while articulating space as open and vast, nonetheless cinematically transformed temporal "progress" into eternal regress), space during this period of great social and political upheaval became semantically inscribed as inescapably domestic and crowded. Time lost its previous urgency and statistically stretched forward toward an impoverished and unwelcome future seen as worse than a bad present. Representing the dystopian despair of a country negatively involved in both domestic and international struggles, the science fiction cinema of the period was primarily earthbound—heavy with the gravity of problems that all the shiny new technology of the 1950s either helped to cause or could not help to resolve. As Joan Dean points out of the films: "The single theme . . . that dominated the science fiction imagination between 1970 and 1977 was overpopulation and its concomitant problems of food shortage and old age" (Dean 37). Hardly successful box-office, the films of this period are overtly despairing. Space is mapped as having no further frontiers and appears as dense, constraining, and as destructive of human existence as a concentration camp. (Just go back and look at the mise-en-scène of *Soylent Green*.) Correlatively, time is figured in terms of a future with no temporal grasp or reach beyond itself and it no longer thrillingly or even comfortably promises progress as leading to anything other than the negativity of decay and entropy. The films of this period dramatize, as well, disenchantment with a "new" technology which has become "old," whose hope has been both literally and metaphorically *exhausted*—in ecologically destructive narrative fumes, and in a relative cinematic lack of interest in the technological hyper-bolizations of celebratory special effects and displays of technical power.

Then, in 1977, came the Lucas and Spielberg films—indicating what seemed a sudden and radical shift in generic attitude and initiating a remarkable popular renaissance of the genre. Unlike their 50s and 60s predecessors, both films could hardly be described as cool and detached in their vision, or cautionary and pessimistic in their tone. Through some strange new transformation, space and time seemed to expand, their representation and narrative mappings becoming somehow "youthful." As well, the wonders of technology somehow seemed to evoke domestic hope. Thus, *Star Wars, Close Encounters,* and the films that followed to constitute what is now surely a second Golden Age of the genre bear little similarity in either attitude or style to those of the genre's first Golden Age or of its subsequent Dark Ages. Indeed, even the low-budget, marginalized science fiction films that emerged in the mid-eighties as a kind of countercultural response to the spatial simplicity, temporal regressiveness, and suburban nos-talgia initiated by Lucas and Spielberg were hardly pessimistic or paranoid. Rather, they celebrated contemporary existence as wonderfully estranged and alienated, and recognized decay and entropy more as aesthetic than as destructive processes. Films like *Liquid Sky, Strange Invaders, Repo Man, The Brother from Another Planet, Night of the Comet,* and *Uforia* accept or embrace trashed-out, crowded, and complex urban space, and appreciate the temporal closure of the future for all the surprising material juxtapositions such closure necessitates and contains.

Indeed, nearly all of today's science fiction films construct a generic field in which space is no longer semantically understood as either three-dimensional and deep, or destructively constraining. Instead, space is described as a field for play and dispersal, a surface across which existential objects kinetically displace and display their materiality rather than inscribe it. This transformation of deep space into shallow surface occurs not only through the punctuation of cinematic space by electronic space, but also through a change in mise-en-scène: the composition and direction of cinematic activity. Even in those films that don't use electronic imagery, characters and activities simultaneously and randomly seem to bounce off each other as if they were blips in a video game, and action tends to busily overload the screen and disperse itself toward the margins in trajectories leading away from what used to be the traditional "center" of interest.

As well, the urgently accelerating or hopelessly static temporality of the earlier films has given way to a new and erotic leisureliness—even in action-packed films. Time has decelerated, but is not represented as static. Rather, it is ab-sorbing, consuming—filled with curious and compelling things, and dynamized as a series of concatenated events that do not cohere according to a linear logic or fulfill the teleological momentum of traditional notions of plot. Today's science fiction film evidences a structural and visual willingness to linger on random details. It takes a certain pleasure in holding the moment to sensually engage its surfaces, to embrace its material collections as "happenings" and "collage." This playfulness and pleasure are cinematic qualities certainly new to the genre, and they replace the cool, detached, and pseudoscientific vision that authenticated the fictions of the earlier periods.

This changed sense of space and time we have experienced in the eighties has—with some few exceptions—also transformed the new science fiction film's representation of the "alien," science fiction's cultural Other. (*Alien*, the remake of *The Thing*, the unpopular *Life Force*, and *Aliens* stand as those few echoes of the earlier period in which space was deep and thus invasion still conceivable.) A space no longer perceived and inscribed as deep, but described as all surface no longer poses the possibility of invasion. And a time no longer represented in terms of "happenings" and eclectic "collages" can readily absorb any sort of material difference without any fear of that difference's effects being major ones. Thus, from 1977 on, mechanical and biological aliens return to the screen not as the xenophobic fixtures they once were, but as cuddly, if powerful, inno-cents—or as mere oddballs, no more or less dangerous and strange than anyone else we might meet in a 7–11 convenience store.

The title *Enemy Mine* only emphasizes this major shift in attitude toward the cultural (and biological/mechanical) Other. In part, of course, this shift owes much to the last decade's attempts at "recovery" from the upheavals of the late sixties. During the last ten years, the representations of both politics and popular culture have attempted to recuperate and re-vision America's visible (and elec-tronically televised) loss of face and imperialist power in Southeast Asia, and the failure of American patriarchal mythology—as it was confronted and chal-lenged by the civil rights, youth, and feminist movements of the late sixties. Most recently (and coincident with the science fiction film's most loving treat-ment of the alien), this "recovery" has been celebrated in self-congratulatory and electronically mediated acts of confession and redemption. (Here I'd point to the "Live Aid" concert—which occurred shortly after *E.T.* mediated popular emotional engagement with the alien, horrific, and anorexic figures of starving Ethiopian children—and to the media blitz surrounding the recording of "We are the world, we are the children," a moving, if dangerous, reduction of political power to the private sector and to an innocent and personal location, rather in the manner of *Close Encounters* or *Starman*.)

Indeed, it is no accident that two cinematic coincidences serve to mark both the mid-seventies renaissance of science fiction and its mid-eighties popularity as somehow entailed with the re-visioning of America's history of failure and guilt in Vietnam. *Star Wars* (with its inverted tale of an evil imperialism fought by "underdog" rebel heroes) and *Close Encounters* (with its scrawny, little, and powerful aliens and childlike and innocent human males) appeared just a year or two before the first films to directly address American involvement in South-east Asia were released. *The Deer Hunter*, *Apocalypse Now*, and *Coming Home* all represent American men as the naive and innocent victims of an incom-prehensible and amoral war. It is just as telling, however, to note that in 1984 (at the height of science fiction's new popularity), Academy Award consideration was given to two performers who represented two different but similarly sympathetic, sweet, powerful but victimized, yet forgiving and loving aliens—the one from "outer space" in *Starman* and the other (the winner in his category) from Cambodia in *The Killing Fields*. In effect (and counter to the further revisionist fantasies of *Rambo*), recent science fiction has figured its aliens as heartrendingly, emotionally empowered innocents—and its human protagonists as striving less toward an assumption of their power or power over them than toward the redemption of human care for Others or the equality of a "live and let live" benevolent indifference.

In large part, however, this shift in attitude toward the alien and, the Other seems also a function of that new technology that has so transformed the spatial and temporal shape of our world and our worldview. The popularization and pervasiveness of electronic technology in the last decade has reformulated the experience of space and time as both expansive and inclusive. It has recast human being into a myriad of visible and animate imitations of human being, and has generated a semantic equivalence among various formulations and representations of space, time, and being. A space perceived and represented as superficial and shallow, as all screen or surface, does not conceal things: it displays things. Things are what they appear to be—and the paranoia that informed the representations of the 1950s with a sense of the hidden, with conspiracy, is no longer possible. As well, the new superficial and electronic space we live and figure cannot be invaded. It is open only to pervasion—a condition of kinetic accommodation and dispersal associated with the experience and representations of television, video games, and computer terminals. Furthermore, in a culture where nearly everyone is regularly alienated from a direct sense of one's self (lived experience commonly mediated by an electronic technology that dominates both the domestic sphere and the private or personal imagery or imaginary of the unconscious), when everyone is less conscious of existence than of its image, the once-threatening science fiction alien and Other become our familiars—our close relations, if not ourselves.

As in the 1950s, contemporary science fiction cinema seems to divide into two groupings related, in great measure, to the conditions of their production. But the two groupings are no longer divided (as they were in the fifties) as a function of their big-budget optimism or low-budget pessimism. Rather, mainstream and marginal films differ in the way they *both* celebrate a thoroughly domestic space and domesticated technology, embrace the alien Other, and realize a temporal reformulation of the genre's earlier futurism. The dominant attitude of most mainstream science fiction has been marked by sentimentality and nostalgia—clearly evidenced by *Star Wars*'s shiny evocation of the future as "Long, long ago" by *Close Encounters*'s yearning for childhood rather than for its end, and by the blatant pronouncement of the very title of *Back to the Future*. More complimentary than contradictory, however, the dominant attitude of most marginal science fiction toward the genre's traditional futurism has been marked by a literal (rather than ideological) conservatism and by a valorization of pastiche—a nonhierarchical collection of heterogeneous objects, forms, and styles from a variety of heretofore distinguishable spaces and times. Indeed, the marginal nature of these often independently produced science fiction films goes far beyond their production budgets and distribution problems, for their playful erasure of the boundaries traditionally marked off between past, present, and future, between outer space and domestic space, between alien and human, between the factual and the fictional, locates them as liminal— both within and without the genre. Their very presence and claim upon science fiction interrogates the temporal and spatial premises upon which the genre has traditionally based its identity.

Whatever their apparent differences, however, the generally sanguine attitudes and spatial and temporal realizations of both mainstream and marginal science fiction are surprisingly coincident. Significantly opposed in mise-en-scène, *Starman* and *The Brother from Another Planet* nonetheless offer us similar protagonists—the same male being "born again" as both "more human than human" and in a state of wonderful and innocent alienation. *D.A.R.Y.L.* and *Android* are made of the same innocently self-conscious and sweet biotechnology. And, although their modes of sublimity resonate quite differently, the transcendent endings of both *Cocoon* and *Repo Man* have much in common with each other. In sum, whether mainstream or marginal, most of the new (and popular) science fiction films celebrate rather than decry an existence and world so utterly familiar and yet so technologically transformed that traditional categories of space, time, being, and even "science fiction" no longer quite apply.

At this point, I want to turn more specifically to how the last decade of "popular electronics" has altered those categories and their representation not only in the movies, but in our everyday lives. Certainly, those traditional systems by which we have long oriented ourselves in space and time have lost much of their constancy and relevance for us in a pervasively electronic culture. New spatial and temporal forms of being-in-the-world have emerged—and found their most poetic figuration, if not their proper names, in the science fiction film. For example, previous mention was made of the way space in the 1950s was experienced and represented as three-dimensional and deep. Today, however, the traditional perception of depth as a structure projecting possibly bodily movement in a materially habitable space has been challenged by our current and very real kinetic responses to—but immaterial habitation of—various forms of simulated space from flight training capsules to computer terminals and video games. As a function of this new "sense" of space, our depth perception has become less dominant in our mode of dealing with and representing the world. To a great degree, our perception has become flattened by its encounters with the superficial electronic dimensionality of movement experienced as occurring on—not in—the screens of computer terminals, video games, music videos, and science fiction movies using computer-generated imagery, like *Tron* and *The Last Starfighter*. It has also become flattened by an excess of activity and things to look at, which keeps our eyes and our values on and across the surface. The two-dimensionality of a digital electronic schematization is not the only denial of depth; if the eye is asked to track too many dimensions (like *Buckaroo Banzai's* "8"), the sense of depth dissipates and disperses across a multitude of flattened trajectories.

Our experience of spatial contiguity has also been radically altered by digital representation. Fragmented into discrete and self-contained units by both disco strobe lights and microchips, space has lost much of its contextual function as the ground for the figured continuities of time, movement, and event. Space is now more often figure; more often a "text" than a context. Absorbing time, incorporating movement, figuring as its own discrete event, contemporary space has come to be experienced as self-contained, convulsive, and discontiguous—a phenomenon most visibly articulated through the mise-en-scène and editorial practices of *Blade Runner* and *Repo Man*, and most audibly announced in *The Adventures of Buckaroo Banzai: Across the eighth Dimension*, when the king-of-all-trades hero philosophizes to his rock concert audience in the following advice: "Remember, wherever you go, there you are."

If the digital "bit" has fragmented our experience and representation of space, then the character of electronic dispersal has dislocated our experience and sense of place. We are culturally producing and electronically disseminating a new world geography which politically and economically defies traditional notions of spatial "location." As a system of orientation, traditional geography has served to represent relative spatial boundaries predicated by differences not only of latitude and longitude and "natural" geophysical punctuation, but also of national real estate. Conventional geography, however, cannot adequately describe where contemporary Palestine is located. Nor was it able to circumscribe the boundaries of a Vietnam that located itself both "inside" and "outside" the American living room—and Cambodia. Our new electronic technology has also spatially dispersed capital while consolidating and expanding its power to an "everywhere" that seems like "nowhere." Again, where traditional orientational systems fail to describe our current economic and political experience, the new science fiction film poetically figures and brings to visibility the apparent paradox of a simultaneous spatial dispersal and concentration of economic and political power. We see it in the "Empire" of the *Star Wars* trilogy, which literalizes both the "cosmic" technological expansion of that power and its simultaneously intense and implosive concentration in the "black star" that is the Death Star. And *Tron* casts its narrative in a blatantly electronic form—the evil "Master Control Program" both dispersing and yet concentrating corporate electronic power and militarism across a video game culture in which even the good guys are electronic simulacra, occupying a computed space that defies traditional geographic description. (Or value—since geographically defined space is not the prize in this battle, but free access to information.)

We now live in a culture that has become increasingly mediated, decentered, and dispersed—at the same time that it has become increasingly homogenized, replicated, and unified through the proliferation of electronic technology and commercial franchise. The global scope and paradoxical nature of this culture in which the universal language is McDonald's make it difficult to envision or comprehend. And yet *Repo Man* is able to give it significant figuration—in the metageneric commodities casually dispersed across the film's decentered mise-en-scène. Pervasively present and as completely undifferentiated and equivalent in value as all of Otto's experience, the white cans and boxes all metagenerically marked "FOOD" visibly represent a culture whose identical, homogenized, canned and boxed nourishment belies its cosmetic diversification and fragmentation.

Multinational corporation has increasingly concentrated and centralized control over the world as marketplace, but its center now appears decentered—occupying no one location, no easily discernable place, simultaneously "nowhere" and "everywhere." How do we geographically locate OPEC? AT&T? In 1975, *Rollerball* represented such global corporate power and presence as threatening and dangerous, but ten years later that concentrated power and its decentered nature are seen as merely normal. One of the teenage Valley Girl heroines of *Night of the Comet* whines to comic effect in a moment of crisis: " 'You're not going to blame me because the phone went dead. I'm not the phone company. Nobody's the phone company anymore.' " The multinationals seem to determine our lives from some sort of ethereal "other" or "outer" space—one that only the science fiction film has been able to adequately visualize. This is a space that finds its most explicit figuration in the impossible towering beauty of *Blade Runner*'s Tyrell Corporation Building—an awesome megastructure whose intricate facade aptly resembles a microchip. It is a space that finds its most alienated and inhuman articulation as the "Corporation" in *Alien*, and its most outlandish expansion in the mining complex on Jupiter's moon, Io, in *Outland*.

Our traditional orientation toward ourselves as singular and private individuals also has been severely challenged by recent technological change. So has our certainty about what it means to shape time through images supposedly generated in the private recesses of subjective memory and desire. Today, privately experienced interiority appears less and less a necessary condition of human being. Personal vision once invisible to others has become publicly visible and commodified in media imagery. Our private memory also has been increasingly constituted from previously mediated spectacles rather than from what we used to think of as direct experience. Indeed, *Brainstorm* and *Dreamscape* merely figure this change in our thinking about the supposed privacy of personal experience and make explicit contemporary culture's colonization of the unconscious, its transformation and commodification of our subjective visual experience to objective and visible products.

As a result of this new and concrete form of extroversion, our temporal sense also has been made visible to ourselves and others and has been transformed in the process. Challenging our traditional temporal orientation toward social and personal history as a linear and progressive movement, the nonchronological

Moebius strip of television allows us to see and recognize the complexity, thickness, and reversibility of temporal experience. Re-tension and pro-tension are personal structures suddenly made publicly visible in "instant replays," "previews," and "reruns" which subvert linearity and chronology. As well, the VCR has allowed us to stop time, to collect or save the past, and to deny the inexorable and linear temporal progress toward a future "end." Again, this new control over time is made concrete in the new science fiction film—we can see it in the various scenographic and narrative conservations of *Blade Runner, The Terminator*, and even *Star Trek: The Voyage Home.* Now we can even go *Back to the Future* in a regressive form of time travel that celebrates a pseudohistorical past (the television fifties of *Leave it to Beaver* or *Father Knows Best*) and now we can go forward to the pseudohistorical present (Marty's, and Michael J. Fox's, "return" to the television eighties of *Family Ties*). Electronic culture has given us the means to play visibly with the past, present, and future, to mix them up in our representations, to deny their power over us, to devalue their traditional distinction, connections, and meaning. The new science fiction film represents this temporal conflation and play—in excessive decor marked by an objective temporal pastiche, in reversible narratives that temporally turn back on themselves, and in scenarios like *Repo Man, Liquid Sky*, or *Buckaroo Banzai*, which refuse the temporally cumulative meaning of experience and offer the latter as a "series of pure and unrelated presents in time" (Jameson 72).

Our human bodies also have been transformed by their experience and representation in the last decade of electronic culture—becoming pervasively recognized as cultural, commodified, and technologized objects. This is a phenomenon women and advertising agencies have been long aware of, but it now more globally informs a society that is obsessed with physical fitness. In the last decade we have come to idealize the human organism as a "lean machine"—sometimes murderously "mean," sometimes aerobically "perfect," and nearly impervious to death, the living body's ultimate "terminator." Indeed, in a decade when organ transplants and remarkable prosthetic devices are common-place, we are (for better or worse) theorizing our bodies, ourselves, as cyborgs. We have become increasingly aware of ourselves as "constructed" and "replicated"—not only through our general knowledge of recombinant DNA, but also through our heightened reflexive experience of using an always acculturated (and therefore "artificial") intelligence, and of being a "self" always (re)produced and projected as an image available to others. In Walter Benjamin's "age of mechanical reproduction," the unique status of the work of art was challenged by the technological transformation of the social world. In an age of electronic simulation and replication, however, it is the unique status of the human being that is challenged.

In the context of our newly exteriorized self-consciousness, the contemporary science fiction film has emphatically figured the most reflexive of robots, computers, androids, and replicants—all seeking emotional as well as functional fulfillment. They evidence doubt and desire, a sense of negation and loss, a self-consciousness and sentimentality new to the genre. They are (as *Blade Runner* suggests) "more human than human." However prideful, Robby—a distinctly 1950s robot—displays none of the comical anxiety and continual self-interrogation of CP30, or the tenderness of Val and Alta in the robotic family romance of *Heartbeeps*. However intellectually powerful, the 70s computer of *Colossus: The Forbin Project* feels no need to seek the origins and meaning of its own existence as does V'ger in *Star Trek: The Movie*, nor, "watching" displays of human affection and sexuality, does it experience the love and jealousy "felt" by the small "PC" of *Electric Dreams*. There are no previous science fiction film counterparts to the prurient sexual curiosity and image consciousness of Max in *Android*, who, completely aware of his own existential status as an imitation, still strives to further model himself after images of images: the personae of Jimmy Stewart and Humphrey Bogart he has seen in old movies. And nowhere before in the science fiction film (if in Mary Shelley) has such a fully self-conscious rage to live and eloquently ferocious challenge to humanity been articulated as in *Blade Runner*. Its "replicants" not only have human "memories" (given to them as to ourselves in the documentation provided by photographic images), but supremely reflexive, "more human than human," they are capable of both irony and poetry.

In the time, then, between the first and second Golden Ages of the American science fiction film, our traditional systems for representing ourselves to ourselves have become no longer fully adequate to our experience. Hierarchical and binary oppositions between surface/depth, here/there, now/then, past/future, organic/inorganic, self/other, reality/imaginary, and even science/fiction are now commonly challenged by the experience of our daily lives. We now live in a totally transformed cultural world, in a new and reformulated electronic age called by some "postmodern." This is an age, Fredric Jameson tells us, marked by two major cultural themes, which we find blatantly foregrounded in contemporary science fiction cinema. The one is an "inverted millenarianism" that replaces "premonitions of the future, catastrophic or redemptive" with a heightened sense of "the end of this or that" (53). Here we can look to the many already cited science fiction films that create the future as instantly old (there is poetic truth in turning DeLorean into a "time machine"), that produce the future as already over or displace it (like *Star Wars*) in a mythical past and promise us an inverted chronology of "prequels" rather than sequels. The second major cultural theme is an "aesthetic populism" that embraces and incorporates the "whole 'degraded' landscape of schlock and kitsch, of TV series and *Readers' Digest* culture, of advertising and motels, of the late show and the grade-B Hollywood films, of so-called paraliterature with its airport paperback categories" (54–55). Here we can look to the new science fiction film as reveling in schlock culture, literally incorporating it like *Star Wars* (noted as "a compendium of American pop and pulp culture" [Gordon 319]), featuring it like *Close Encounters* or *Starman* with their McDonald's golden arches, Baskin Robbins trucks, Holiday

Inns, Las Vegas casinos, or foregrounding it—pointing to a culture whose ar-
tifacts and happenings are as strange and schlocky as those generically constructed in low-budget science fiction, but also as normal as the "Hawaiian
Days" and "Mexican Fiesta Days" promotionals and costumes found under the
fluorescent lighting of your local homogenized supermarket chain (see *Uforia*),
or in the pages of the *National Enquirer* (see *Strange Invaders*), or in the windows
of suburban shopping malls (see *Night of the Comet*).

The postmodern, Jameson tells us, is not merely a new cultural style, but
rather a radically new cultural logic emerging from the new relations that exist
between American capital, multinational corporatism, and electronic technology. This logic not only dramatizes itself in the major thematics of "inverted
millenarianism" and "aesthetic populism," but also informs the very structure
of our representations with new aesthetic features. As Jameson characterizes
them, these are a

> new depthlessness, which finds its prolongation . . . in a whole new culture
> of the image or the simulacrum; a consequent weakening of historicity,
> both in our relationship to public history and in the forms of our private
> temporality . . . ; a whole new type of emotional ground tone . . . which
> can best be grasped by a return to older theories of the sublime; the deep
> constitutive relationships of all this to a whole new technology, which is
> itself a figure for the whole new economic world system . . . the bewildering
> new world space of late multinational capital. (Jameson 58)

Surely, the contemporary American science fiction film makes concrete and
visible (as no other genre and medium can) not only the major themes of
postmodernism, but also its aesthetic representation of cultural values. We can
see the new depthlessness literalized in the deflated dimensionality but inflated
value of science fiction space from the obvious computed superficiality of *The
Last Starfighter* to the dispersed and disorienting busy-ness of *Buckaroo Banzai*.
The "weakening of historicity" is made concrete in the genre's recent and
pervasive conflations of time from the explicit film noir references of *Blade
Runner* and *The Terminator* (with its overt time-travel plot line) to the implicitly
pseudohistorical nostalgia of *Star Wars* and *Star Trek*. The "new emotional
ground tone" can be seen in the transformation of previously deep and private
special affect into the visible representation of special effects (now sublimely
emotional when once they were meant to seem sublimely rational)—whether
articulated as the "sky singing" in *Close Encounters, E.T.*'s "heartlight," or in
the blatant titular transformation of "euphoria" to *Uforia*. Finally, our new
familiar relationship to heterogeneity and cultural difference has been reformulated as the multinational wholeness and sameness of the "new world space"
in which we live, finding its socially symbolic representation in the genre's
concrete embrace of the alien, from *E.T.* to *Liquid Sky*, or its literal erasure of

alienation, from *Star Wars* to *The Brother from Another Planet*. In sum, the American science fiction film is both symptom and symbol of the lived reality of social existence and practice during this last and most electronic decade. It affords a place where the new cultural logic finds both its most concrete and its most poetic figuration. Indeed, the American science fiction film may well offer us the most comprehensible maps we have of the postmodern world in which we live.

Works Cited

Dean, Joan F. "Between *2001* and *Star Wars*." *Journal of Popular Film and Television* 7, no. 1 (1978): 32–41.

Gordon, Andrew. "*Star Wars*: A Myth for Our Time." *Literature/Film Quarterly* 6, no. 4 (Fall 1978): 314–325.

Heidegger, Martin. "The Question Concerning Technology." Trans. William Lovitt. *Martin Heidegger: Basic Writings*. Ed. David Farrell Krell. New York: Harper and Row, 1977. 287–317.

Jameson, Fredric. "Postmodernism, or the Cultural Logic of Late Capitalism." *New Left Review* 146 (July–August 1984): 53–94.

Lisa M. Heilbronn

Natural Man, Unnatural Science: Rejection of Science in Recent Science Fiction and Fantasy Film

Preoccupation with "science": by which I mean not only technique or technology, but more generally "the state of knowing, knowledge covering general truths or the operation of general laws," as in Webster, 1051 is a common element in science fiction, fantasy, and horror films. Characters in these films search for knowledge, are created through knowledge, and may be destroyed by knowledge. Knowledge, in short, is power. The figure of the scientist appears frequently in all three genres. Although sometimes portrayed as a savior, the scientist is more often portrayed as either (a) a rationalist who is helpless in the face of a supernatural power, or (b) the creator of the horror or force to be faced. We may think of the character as a midpoint along a continuum bounded on one side by the power of the uncanny or unnatural and on the other by the power of natural forces only partially understood.

These two themes: the helplessness of science in the face of supernatural forces, and the potential of science to go too far in its attempts to understand nature and become an instrument of destruction, date back to seminal works of the nineteenth century, such as Bram Stoker's *Dracula*, Mary Shelley's *Frankenstein*, and Robert Louis Stevenson's *Dr. Jekyll and Mr. Hyde*. The underlying theme is a sort of double dichotomy, with the rational approach to the domination of nature opposed on the one hand by "older" forces outside of the natural world delineated by science, and on the other by a nature whose forces begin within the scope of reason but when unleashed prove to be beyond its control. The two disparate forces are united in their opposition to pragmatic science and the technological industrial world it fosters. These themes have become more pressing in the nuclear age, as fears about mass destruction and doubts about the value of technology have become widespread.

In stories centering on the supernatural, the scientist is cast as the possessor of knowledge that is powerless against the threat. There is another, more ancient body of knowledge that is effective against the forces of a coexistent spiritual world. This body of knowledge is often possessed by marginal figures—peasants, members of more ancient and/or preindustrial cultures such as gypsies, Indians, or Africans, or members of the dominant group too young to have learned that the distinctions between reality and magic are not "real." In some cases these characters possess a lore of science that can answer and defeat the threat. In other cases the "knowledge" necessary may be described as the ability to make contact with the species-being, to revert to primitive instinct and reject civilization's answers. Men of science may be aware of and value this other knowledge (Van Helsing in *Dracula*, Shepard in *Ice Man*), but despite this appreciation, they are often still helpless (the psychic investigators in *Poltergeist*, for example).

Until recently, in stories where the scientist is the cause of evil, the fault generally lay not with the technology, but with "the errant will of a lone individual." (Sontag 223) Not infrequently danger is unleashed when science is misapplied for reasons such as jealousy and revenge. The scientist is often presented as either insane when he begins his research, or driven mad by the strain of his isolated work. Even when research is begun with good intentions, such as the search for an end to world hunger in *Tarantula*, it can lead to evil results. The scientist in these cases is generally a lone figure, acting as a sort of inventor-entrepreneur.

Although these two common plots express doubts about the course society is pursuing away from traditional beliefs and toward a rational domination of nature, until recently plot resolutions generally restored faith in science and rationalism. Whether the solution came from the metaphysical world, or the defeat of an alien enemy, or with the reversal of the effects of a scientific invention, order was restored. The viewer could be reassured that there was an explanation for the event and a way to deal with it. Society's overall progress toward a rational, scientific technological mastery of nature continued. The supernatural elements were often portrayed as vestigial, last remnants of an older order disappearing in the glare of the modern day. Scientific disaster, when the responsibility of a lone individual, could be rectified the second time around.

This is no longer the case. In place of the supernatural monsters who could be controlled once the correct talismans were used, there are new monsters who seem indestructible and operate under no known system. As Tania Modleski says, "the contemporary horror film—the so-called exploitation or slasher film . . . [is] engaged in an unprecedented assault on all that bourgeois culture is supposed to cherish—like the ideological apparatus of the family and the school." (158) Horror films have become increasingly open-ended, and recent films about such familiar beings as the werewolf and vampire ignore the old "rules" for their monsters (see, for example, *American Werewolf in London*, *The Howling*, *Wolfen*, and Frank Langellas's *Dracula*).

Recent films focusing on science have frequently presented it as a failure—not for attempting too much, but simply in terms of its own goals. The world has been stripped of the superstitious explanations of the past, and its inhabitants are asked to accept the new explanations of science. But our belief in these explanations has become weak. "We no longer grant, or take it for granted, that men doing the work of the world together are working for the world's good, or that if they are working for the world's harm they can be stopped." (Cavell 62) It is as if the natural world contains within it a latent power capable of destroying the world, which science no longer has the self-confidence to control. Or to put it another way, science has cast out a natural element without which its endeavors are lifeless and finally pointless. In *Altered States*, for example, William Hurt learns how to regress to a more primitive being from a traditional culture. When he "improves" on their rite, using modern pharmacology and techniques, he cannot control it because of his personal social isolation.

This opposition between science and nature has taken several forms in recent science fiction, horror, and fantasy films. One form is the story in which the average person, acting on feeling and instinctive love, surpasses scientists in communication with aliens. It is Richard Dreyfuss's repairman, not one of Francois Truffaut's scientists, who is ready to evolve in *Close Encounters of the Third Kind*. The scientific team is presented as a menace throughout much of *E.T.*, and even when its motives are revealed to be benign, it is still presented as violating the alien's dignity, and as being able to accomplish far less with all its equipment than can Eliot with simple love and understanding. Similar themes can be found in films such as *Starman* and *The Brother from Another Planet*. I would argue that part of this loss of faith involves the growing impersonality of modern life. As society becomes more fragmented, the community at risk becomes harder to define. The lone scientist is now often only the representative of a corporation or the government, and cannot personally control the situation.

Some films, particularly the Lucas *Star Wars* trilogy and Steven Spielberg's *Indiana Jones* films, seek to reunite mysticism and technology. *The Return of the Jedi* puts the Soul (Force) back in the machine, but it does not renounce it.

Another opposition is that between modern science and natural man. This opposition was clear in two 1984 films, *Iceman* and *Greystoke*. The natural man— paleolithic or primate—takes the place of the alien, but the interaction between science and its subject remains much the same. In *Iceman* the scientists' original intention is to dissect the man they find in the ice. When they accidentally revive him, they concentrate on testing him to replicate his survival because cryogenic preservation would be marketable. In *Greystoke* John is treated as a specimen by many of those around him. In a crucial scene, he attends the opening of the African Wing of the Museum of Natural History, a beautiful edifice that conceals behind itself a chamber of horrors in the form of a vivisection lab. There he finds and frees his ape-father, only to see him murdered minutes later. The two films share common themes: science is blind to the emotional and ethical demands of the beings it studies, and if made aware of them is helpless to respond. Their goal is taxonomy, not empathy. Charlie is the property of the oil company funding the scientific expedition that found him. Greystoke can find no place in English society, and retreats to the jungle. The lack of moral authority on the part of science directs the loyalty and sympathy of the audience to its "victims," the natural man whom we have abandoned for technical expertise.

Similar themes can be found in *The Emerald Forest,* in which a man who has lost his son to an Amazonian tribe decides to let him remain with the tribe and destroy a dam to delay the end of their way of life. A similar tension between societies appears in Phil Kaufman's *The Right Stuff.* In a film dedicated to comparing Sam Shephard, a man who dominated machines, and the first astronauts' struggle not to be guinea pigs at the mercy of machines, a significant moment appears during John Glenn's first orbital flight. One of the astronauts has been sent to an Australian field station to communicate with Glenn during his flight. He meets aborigines who claim their own knowledge of the stars. As Glenn's flight takes place, a connection is made between their campfire's sparks and the "fireflies" Glenn sees in orbit.

This preoccupation with the sacrifice of our humanity in the interests of progress is not a new one in science fiction. As Susan Sontag commented in the late sixties, "science fiction films may also be described as a popular mythology for the contemporary negative imagination about the impersonal." (220–21) Dehumanization has been a common theme in science fiction, but it is an increasingly central theme, as is evident if we examine two recent successful films, *Aliens* and the David Cronenberg 1986 remake of *The Fly* (1958). Both involve the loss of the body to an insect life form: as a host for the alien queen's young in *Aliens,* to the dominance of the fly's genetic material in *The Fly.* The significance of the insect figure will be discussed later.

The loss of the body is clearly a central element in Cronenberg's version of *The Fly.* In the earlier version, the scientist was a family man, with a wife and child, and a caring brother. Although he also struggled with a loss of humanity, his will enabled him to destroy himself without loss or damage to others, and his humanity was not lost, but transferred to (or shared with) the fly transported with him.

Cronenberg's scientist, on the other hand, is cut off from society when the film begins: living in an isolated industrial area, taking no interest in social display (same clothes all the time), eating a limited diet, cut off from social interaction of all kinds including sex. His distance from society is symbolized by the handicap that has motivated his attempt to create instantaneous travel: motion sickness in all modern forms of transportation. Seth "doesn't understand the flesh," and this lack has prevented him from being able to convey that understanding to his computer so that it can transmit living tissue. Although his love for and brief relationship with Veronica enables him to convey an understanding of the flesh to his computer, this understanding is so limited that when confronted with the flesh of both Seth and a fly, the computer cannot distinguish between them and binds them at the molecular level. It is interesting that despite Seth's initial interpretation of his condition as cancerous (the flesh's natural growth and replenishment gone wild) and his latter claims that he is not turning into an insect, but a hybrid "Brundlefly," he describes his nature as becoming insectlike and amoral, and the eventual creature that is destroyed seems to be totally an insect, contained and concealed by a useless sheath of flesh. Although presumably the initial split between their DNA was fifty-fifty, the fly's wins out, perhaps because of its stronger drives. Seth's downfall is his reliance on his computer. Despite his initial understanding that its abilities are limited by his ability to program it, he trusts its logic, and continues to work alone with it to seek a solution to his condition even after he discovers its original error. He shares its blindness, and is ultimately merged with the machine in the final transportation.

Several common elements unite this film with another popular 1986 film, *Aliens*. In *Alien* (1979) the heroic crew, manipulated into taking the alien on board by their corporate employer with the assistance of an android crew member (synthetic human), faced a single foe whose origin and society remained unknown. Like Seth Brundle, they are betrayed by their reliance on their computer, "Mother," whose secret orders from the corporation actually mandate their destruction in favor of the Alien's survival. In *Aliens*, Ripley, the sole survivor of the Nostromo, accompanies a military rescue mission to a colony on the Alien planet. Only a single child, a young girl called "Newt," has survived by reverting to a wild, semiaboriginal state. (Her initial appearance resembles that of the Feral Kid in *Road Warrior*.) The aliens are revealed to be an insect society, complete with egg-laying queen, hatchery, and faithful workers. The military unit sent by the corporation to investigate the sight proves unable to combat the aliens effectively. In the end, it is Sigourney Weaver's strong maternal attachment to the girl Newt and her reliance on instinct that empower her in her combat with the alien queen.

Two common images appear in Cronenberg's *The Fly*, *Alien*, *Aliens*, and James Cameron's intermediate film, *The Terminator*: a correspondence between the cold, collective intelligence of the insect colony (a silicon life-form) and computer intelligence (based on silicon chips), and the image of the enemy body concealed within the human form. When *Alien* and *Aliens* are compared, a striking parallel emerges: in the first film a climactic point is reached when Ripley fails in her attempt to reset the overload command: she screams, "You Bitch!" at Mother's calm voice continuing the countdown, and flails at the machinery with her weapon. In an almost identical moment in *Aliens*, she utters the same challenge to the Alien Queen before they engage in combat to the death. One of the few things we learn about the Alien in *Alien*, during a brief scene between Ash and Ripley, is that the creature replaces its cells with silicon—unlike carbon, a nondecaying substance, and one crucial to machine intelligence. A similar machine/insect link appears in *The Fly*. Given Seth's attachment to the computer and his dependence on it, it is not surprising that in the struggle between his human character and the ruthless insect nature imposed on him by the computer, the insect wins out, or that he succumbs to the machine's solution: the inclusion of more organisms in the process.

The theme of concealment of an enemy within is also a shared image. In

John Carpenter's *The Thing*, the shape-changing alien erupts from within its previous incarnation during metamorphosis. In *Alien*, Ash's android-machine identity is concealed from the crew, much as the alien's continued presence is concealed in Kane. In *The Terminator*, the skeleton of a machine is concealed within a flesh exterior to confuse human rebels. Seth's transformation into an insect is concealed within a similar, albeit less healthy mask of flesh. His lover, Veronica, has a nightmare image of an enormous maggot contained within her flesh. The eventual insect body revealed at the climax of *The Fly* resembles both the machine exposed following a car explosion in *Terminator* and the metallic exoskeleton of the mature Alien in both *Alien* and *Aliens*. Our humanity seems to have become little more than a hollow shell concealing an inhuman, metallic core.

It is striking how little is learned in either film. In earlier films there is always an explanation, a "what's happening" moment. In these films explanations are either not forthcoming, cursory and ignored, or cannot be acted on. Although the rescue mission in *Aliens* discovers a lab with living and dead examples of one stage of the alien life form, and the android crew member Bishop works in it throughout the film, we know little more at the end of this sequel than we did at the end of the first film. Although Seth would seem to have several sources of information and help: the team members who designed the components of his machine for him and Veronica or her editor, both of whom would logically know of other scientists, none is forthcoming. Little time is given to speculation about causes or solutions in either film. Logic, even science fiction logic, seems useless. Perhaps this traditional moment in science fiction, fantasy, and horror films is dispensed with here because the force represented by both themes cannot be unmasked.

Vivian Sobchack states that "the fear in SF films springs from the future possibility that we may—in a sense—lose contact with our bodies" (39). In these films it seems that the loss is not only probable, but may have already occurred. The victories we see are limited, and temporary. The open-ended nature of *Aliens*, already a sequel and likely to produce another, produces concerns that the alien is returning to earth in one of the survivors, or that some aliens remain alive on the planet to try to use us as hosts again. Veronica intends to abort Seth's (or Brundlefly's) child, destroying what may be the last vestige of his humanity. In both cases the bad faith and "inhuman" judgment of corporations must be feared. Despite two failures, "the Corporation," which seems to own space, may still believe it can profit from the Alien. Unlike the research in the original *Fly*, Seth's was financed by a corporation, and it may wish to pursue his invention despite his death. The absent presence of the corporation and the dominance of corporate interests over human needs runs through many of these films.

According to Fredric Jameson, mass culture performs "a transformation work on social and political anxieties and fantasies which must then have some effective presence in the mass cultural text in order subsequently to be 'managed' or 'repressed' " (141). It appears that the latter half of what Sobchack calls the second Golden Age of science fiction film is dominated by fears about the loss of fundamental humanity through the use of technology. This fear is so strong that the role of scientist has either disappeared completely from recent horror and science fiction film or become that of an impotent observer of nature gone wrong.

Works Cited

Cavell, Stanley. *The World Viewed.* Cambridge, Mass.: Harvard University Press, 1979.

Jameson, Fredric. "Reification and Utopia in Mass Culture." *Social Text* 1, no. 1 (Winter 1979): 130–48.

Modleski, Tania. "The Terror of Pleasure: Contemporary Horror Film and Postmodern Theory." *Studies in Entertainment: Critical Approaches to Mass Culture.* Ed. Tania Modleski. Bloomington: Indiana University Press, 1986.

Sobchack, Vivian. *Screening Space: The American Science Fiction Film.* 2nd. ed., enlarged. New York: Ungar, 1987.

Sontag, Susan. "The Imagination of Disaster." *Against Interpretation.* New York: Dell, 1966. 209–25.

Sharon A. *Russell*

The Problem of Novelization: *Dead and Buried* and *Nomads* by Chelsea Quinn Yarbro

Most examinations of the relationship of novel and film begin with the novel and discuss the problems of the translation of a written text into a visual medium. Those studies based in literature tend to defend the sanctity of the written word and attack its destruction in the film. Those studies that concentrate on film usually begin with the premise that the literature wasn't all that great to begin with and that the work has benefited from its translation. It is generally accepted by both sides of this controversy that poorer literature makes better films and that great works suffer most in the process of translation.

The subject of the relationship between the literary work and its cinematic adaptation has been treated in film criticism as far back as Sergei Eisenstein's article on Dickens and Griffith. While recent criticism tends to attempt to walk the middle ground, not favoring either side, there are certain standard features of each work that these critics examine. *Made into Movies: From Literature to Film* by Stuart Y. McDougal is fairly typical. Textbooks like this one certainly provide a beginning for an examination of the relationships between these two media. McDougal raises questions about the translation of literary devices into film when he analyzes plot/story relationship, character, point of view, "the world of inner experience," figurative discourse, symbol and allegory, and time. Seymour Chatman also deals with some of these devices in "What Novels Can Do that Films Can't (and Vice Versa)." He concentrates on the relationship between literary description and the presentation of visual details in a film and deals to some extent with point of view.

The novelization of a film has been largely ignored by the critics on both sides. It is generally considered a bastard art form, mainly useful as a potboiler for its author. Even Chelsea Quinn Yarbro's dedication of *Dead and Buried* reads: "*For Donald*: craft for art and a Toyota" (iii). Most of the time a novelization provides greater exposure for the film during its initial run by allowing people to relive the cinematic experience. Sometimes the publication of novelization precedes the release of the film. The actual source of the novelization is not the film, but the script of the film. But a film script is generally much closer to the final film than it is to any literary version of the work. The major alterations that occur during the filming relate to the order of events, the rewriting of dialogue, or the deletion or addition of incidents. The changes in the sequence of events will often take place during the editing of the film. Evidence resulting from a comparison of the three versions of Dead and Buried suggest that the finished film is the result of a script revision. The film and novelization share many changes from the original script. The novelization of script, however, requires the restructuring of the work. While original dialogue is often retained, and incidents may occur in the same order as the script, the changes that are made suggest a great deal about the differences between reading and seeing when the traditional movement from literature to film is reversed.

Chelsea Quinn Yarbro is a widely published author in the popular genres of horror, science fiction, fantasy, and mystery. Her interest in the occult has also resulted in records of contact with the supernatural world. Except for the two novelizations, a few short stories, and two mysteries, all of her horror and science fiction genre work is set either in the past or the future. The tracing of the connections between the novelizations and the films may have general implications for the novel/film relationship, but it also confirms the styles and themes of Yarbro's other fiction.

The tools for study of traditional literature as applied to film analysis do illuminate certain features of this type of literary venture. While the distinction between story and plot is important for an understanding of the structure of any narrative, Yarbro does not significantly alter the arrangement of events in either novelization. Both versions of Dead and Buried present the story in a fairly linear plot. Yarbro suggests a slight time shift when she begins with a prologue that contains the opening scene of the film. But the division of this opening into a prologue does not really alter its connection to subsequent events. Both film and novel take place over a few days in the town of Potter's Bluff, although they deal with events that have been set in motion over a period of time.

They open with similar versions of the death of a young photographer who is looking for interesting photographic opportunities as he wanders the beach. A young girl offers herself as a model, removes her blouse, and excites him. At first he doesn't notice the gathering crowd of strange people who surround him. In the novel he is sprayed with gasoline and set on fire. In the film he is beaten, caught in a fishing net, then burned. In the script, his face is placed in battery acid. All follow with a quick transition to a burning Volkswagen van and the introduction of the main characters. While the firemen put out the blaze, the sheriff, Dan Gillis, waits for the arrival of the town mortician and coroner G. William Dobbs. As Dobbs takes the victim out of the car, he screams, and all present are shocked to find out that the supposed dead man lives. (In the script, Dobbs finds the victim's pulse.) The sheriff's subsequent investigation into the burning and the discovery of the strangeness of most of the local citizens become both cause and effect of this incident and the other deaths that lead to the resolution of the plot. All of the events take place in a linear series even though reference is made to aspects of the story that have taken place before the actual plot begins.

All versions of *Nomads* follow the same structure. The plot alternates between two time periods: the present, experienced by all of the characters, and the immediate past, relived by Dr. Eileen Flax who, because of her contact with the dying Jean-Claude Pommier, is forced to experience his past. The structure of this plot is crucial to the effect of the works, but it is not presented in the same manner in all three. The different effects achieved by the alternation of the two times is less a result of the organization of the plot than it is an effect of such elements as interiority and the operation of the genre conventions.

Just as the plot/story distinction is important in the individual work but not really relevant to a comparison, so characterization is not an especially significant tool for this analysis. It is obvious that films and novels use different methods to create character. Films use casting, clothing, setting, and dialogue, while novels may use direct description as well as dialogue. Scripts also contain character description that may or may not be reproduced in the film. In her novelizations, Chelsea Quinn Yarbro did not have the advantage of knowing how the scripts would be cast. She does make some changes in the characters, but these changes seem to be related to her style. Often a novel will have more characters than the film, but Yarbro makes no effort to add or significantly alter characters, with one exception. She does invent a young male hustler who gives Pommier information lacking in the film.

Such narrative elements as point of view and its expression in internal discourse provide most of the traditional discussion of the adaptation of novel into film. In the cinema, the movement is always toward the externalization of the internal events of the novel and the shift from a localized point of view to that of the camera, often synonymous with that of the omniscient narrator. Even though the camera is always the narrator, films often take the point of view of specific characters. It is easy to limit much of the information to a single character's experience; what is difficult is the presentation of the narration through the point of view of a particular character. During most of *Dead and Buried*, we follow the sheriff as he investigates the strange series of events in Potter's Bluff. His limited perspective is especially evident in a scene toward the end of the film when he thinks that his car has hit a man. He gets out of the car, finds a detached arm stuck in the grill, sees the man grab the arm and run away. Dan looks for the man in the fog, and enters an empty building. A chicken flies, and he fires a shot. During this entire sequence we share Dan's viewpoint. At other moments, the difference between film and novel becomes more complex. Toward the beginning of the film, after the discovery of the burning person, Dan enters the diner in the town, the scene of many of the events in both versions. He talks to the townsfolk, his friends, and neighbors. In the novelization, the third person point of view favors him. All we know is what Dan knows. In the film, the audience recognized that the same people who just participated in the murder of the young photographer are now acting out their normal roles in the town's life. We still don't understand the connection between their actions and their motives, but we see things that Dan does not see until the end of the novel. Yarbro, the novelist, deliberately chooses to control the information in a way that is not possible in the film, because the camera must show all.

In film, novel, and script, *Nomads's* structure is based on a dual point of view. While there are moments in all when we experience an omniscient, objective perspective, most of the time the works alternate between Eileen's current life as an emergency room doctor who is suddenly taken over by visions of another person's life, and those experiences of Jean-Claude Pommier that she relives. In all cases, once we enter the world of Pommier, we lose track of the "narrator" of those events, Eileen, until some event forces us back to an awareness of her. Pommier's part of the story traces those days that immediately precede his death and the transference of his memories to Eileen. Pommier, an anthropologist who has spent most of his life in the field, comes to Los Angeles with his wife to teach. His research has been concerned with the tracking of nomads in various parts of the world. Pommier discovers that similar nomads actually exist in Los Angeles. He encounters a group of weirdly dressed people. They are attracted to his house because of the mass murder that occurred there. This violent group travels the streets in a black van, and they are only visible to other nomads or to those who live on the fringes of society. Pommier tracks the nomads and is, in turn, tracked and destroyed by them.

The alternation of points of view in all versions is also accompanied by an alternation in time. Of course, in both literature and film, these shifts are not unusual. Flashbacks and even flash forwards are standard cinematic devices. Certainly literature has long had devices for shifting time and point of view. In all versions, these transitions are indicated visually. In the film, the transition is rather abrupt, often only a simple cut from one story to the other. These cuts are confusing because John McTiernan, the scriptwriter, uses a different type face to indicate Pommier's story, but he uses no special devices to indicate these shifts in the film. It is often difficult for members of the audience to follow them, a fact that he even acknowledges in the script. "Meanwhile, Pommier—" (It's not really meanwhile, but to the audience it now *seems* it.)(74). The novelization seems to be able to indicate these shifts much more clearly. Yarbro leaves a space between paragraphs that the reader associates with the change in perspective. She also carefully includes clues about the shift in the opening paragraph of each change.

The conflict between the camera's omniscient perspective and the limited knowledge of the character is even more complex in *Dead and Buried*. The camera must show the viewer the black van and its inhabitants, but these evil spirits, "inuat," are only supposed to be visible to those who are in some way connected with their world. In the novel, we are always aware that we are experiencing the flashbacks from Pommier's point of view. In the film, we follow Pommier in the same way that he follows the inuat. Are we susceptible to their power because we, too, can see them? The film requires a suspension of disbelief difficult to maintain. If we think that they are visible, we can't understand why everyone can't see them. While there are certainly instances when cinematic conventions allow us to see things visible to only one of the characters, McTiernan never includes scenes that would allow us to fully understand the difference. There is a scene in the novelization where Pommier encounters a young male hustler who explains who can see the inuat and why. Yarbro, the experienced novelist, realizes the need for a clarification of the supernatural characteristics of this group. Because we can see these people, the film is confusing. The nomads just look like obnoxious punk rockers, not visitors from another reality.

Yarbro's mastery of the translation of cinematic transition in *Nomads* indicates a growth in her understanding of the process from her work with *Dead and Buried*. In the latter, she indicates cuts in the script by a three-dot ellipsis between paragraphs, a device that soon becomes tiresome. But this problem in the translation of a script to novel is an indication of the different narrative devices that must be considered when examining this kind of adaptation. The novelization must reintroduce literary devices absent from the script. While dialogue can often be taken directly from the script, all of the descriptive material surrounding this dialogue must be added. Not only must the author be concerned with the translation of cinematic transitions like fades and cuts, the description of characters and decor, additions of large blocks of information, but also on the very minute level, each line of dialogue has to be developed to indicate the tone and attitude of the character speaking the line. These additions have to indicate a tone only suggested by the script where there may be some indication of how the line may be spoken.

The increase in Yarbro's skill in the addition of the larger descriptive passages can also be seen in a comparison of *Dead and Buried* and *Nomads*. By the time she writes the latter, she no longer includes such passages as the one that opens chapter 9 of *Dead and Buried*. "Pallid narrow clouds like keloid scars seamed the pink belly of the sky as the light faded" (121). In *Nomads*, the descriptive passages provide information about the characters' past that make present events much clearer, information that may have been present in the script but that is absent from the film. These passages also make much clearer the role of the inuat and their relationship to the other nomads that Pommier has tracked. But at the same time that more information is conveyed, some scenes tend to get wordy because Yarbro must include descriptive material that is visually suggested or omitted entirely in the film. While McTiernan tends to let this part-for-the-whole characteristic of film get out of hand so that the film is too compressed, Yarbro often includes lengthy transitions that amplify a simple cut in the film.

When the different descriptive passages in a novelization and film are added to the varying amounts of information delivered by camera and narrator, the result is two rather different texts in the case of *Dead and Buried.* In the film, the recognition of characters in dual roles as ritual murderers and as working members of the community means that the viewer knows more than the central character, wants different questions answered, and has a different set of expectations. We know that there is something very wrong in Potter's Bluff from the beginning and that its citizens are a lot weirder than the sheriff imagines. In the novelization, the reader identifies with Dan's quest and shares his shock when he learns that everyone in the town is actually dead and kept in repair by Dobbs the coroner, a man who takes great pride in his work. We are as amazed as Dan to find out that Janet, Dan's wife, is Dobbs's best creation. We are further shocked by the final revelation that Dan, too, is one of the undead. In the film, the objective point of view leads us to this information earlier, although we are uncertain about Janet until we see movie lights associated with the ritual murders in her closet.

By the end of both works we are aware of Dobbs's real occupation, but the tension in the novel comes from the revelations of the extent of the town's involvement. In the film, increased information leads to a definite shift in tone. Because the film must show the town's involvement, director Gary Sherman, pushes that aspect by reveling in violence. In the novel, all of the deaths are by fire. In the film, each victim is killed in a different manner, sometimes more graphically than indicated by the script. The conclusion of the film is a kind of apocalypse of visuals. We finally see examples of the kinds of films that the zombies have been making during each death scene. In the novel, Dan discovers that Janet is one of the undead when he watches a film that she has asked him to develop. He projects the film at home and discovers that his wife is a murderer. In the film, this scene is followed by a film and slide show at the mortuary where another film reveals not only Janet as murderer but also Dan as her victim. The script presents a third ending. Dan receives another roll of film. When he watches it at home, he finds out that he strangled the hitchhiker killed earlier in the film.

It is difficult to separate the changes in these two films from the demands of the genre in different media and the stylistic choices of author versus director. But in both *Nomads* and *Dead and Buried,* there are clear examples of Yarbro's stylistic intervention. The process of novelization, the movement from script to novel, may present even clearer evidence of choices determined by style than can be revealed by a study of the adaptation of literature into film. Novelization is also the process of translation of a collaborative effort to one individual's perspective. Changes from novel to film may be the result of any one of a number of people involved with the film, but changes in the other direction can only be the result of the author's preference. One of the most obvious changes in *Dead and Buried* is the choice of music. In her other novels, Yarbro exhibits an interest in classical music. (She has even composed music in this mode.) All of the music that Dobbs plays while he works comes from the big-band era. In the novel, specific pieces of classical music are indicated.

In both novels, events are changed slightly in ways that suggest Yarbro's thematic concerns. A young couple in her version of *Dead and Buried* survives; they die in the film. Yarbro admires the kind of courage and resourcefulness that these characters display, and she rewards their efforts. In her novels, Yarbro consistently presents strong, independent female characters in central and supporting roles. Eileen Flax in the novel *Nomads* is much stronger than she is in the film, where she is often reduced to the role of screaming female. This shift is especially evident in scenes near the film's end. Eileen has found Pommier's house and his widow, Veronique. The inuat surround the house, and the two women hide in the attic. While the house is being destroyed, Eileen is forced to view Jean-Claude's death. In the film, she is incapable of coherent action and thought. In the novel, she engineers the survival of both women, and her increased strength balances the two points of view. In the film, Pommier is most important, and the film becomes a vehicle for Pierce Brosnan.

The increased importance of Eileen's point of view gives the novel a stronger and clearer ending than that of the film. In all versions, the two women escape from the house and drive away. As morning comes, they are out of the desert of Los Angeles and into an area of trees. (The relationship between deserts and nomads has been more clearly established in the novel.) They are suddenly followed by a man on a motorcycle. In the novel, Eileen takes over the driving; in the film, Veronique drives. Eileen states that no matter what happens, they must not stop. The driver passes them and pulls up on the side of the highway. As they pass him, they realize that it is Pommier, who has now become a nomad. Eileen looks back at him through the rear window, and the camera pans over to a sign stating: "Entering California." The novel amplifies this image by adding, "The cyclist . . . began the long ride back to the place he belonged, where he could feed" (232). Yarbro adds another brief scene. The two women arrive in Taos. Veronique discovers a photographic gallery. She notices a photo of a Hopi on a rock. "It appeared that the lone figure was—she studied the Hopi hunter intently—was 'trespassing' " (232). It has been clear throughout the novel that nomads are also trespassers. The escape in the film is absent from the novel; the women have also become nomads, a fact reenforced by their ability to see nomads.

The problems of novelization have largely been ignored by scholars of literature and film. This brief analysis has begun to suggest some of the relationships between the two media. Obviously there is still much work to be done. Genre studies might benefit from further exploration of both the development and effect of horror in novel and film. Further work could also be done with the structure of the two works. A well-written film script has a very definite structure that remains present in the finished film. It would be interesting to see if such a structure influences the chapter organization of the novelization. An analysis of several novelizations might establish the extent to which a book must remain true to the script to satisfy audience expectations. From this brief analysis, it is evident that traditional approaches to cinematic adaptations of novels have limited usefulness in such a study. The emphasis must shift from an examination of how literary devices translate into film to an exploration of the literary equivalents of cinematic techniques.

Works Cited

Chatman, Seymour. "What Novels Can Do that Films Can't (and Vice Versa)." *On Narrative*. Ed. W. J. T. Mitchell. Chicago: University of Chicago Press, 1981. 117–36.

Eisenstein, Sergei. "Dickens, Griffith, and the Film Today." *Film Form* and *The Film Sense*. Ed. and trans. Jay Leyda. Cleveland: Meridian Books, 1965. 195–255.

McDougal, Stuart Y. *Made into Movies: From Literature to Film*. New York: Holt, Rinehart and Winston, 1985.

McTiernan, John, screenwriter. *Nomads*. Dir. John McTiernan. Prod. Elliot Kastner in association with Cinema 7. Kinesis Productions, 1980. Hollywood: Script City.

Shusett, Ronald, and Dan O'Bannon, screenwriters. *Dead and Buried*. Dir. Gary A. Sherman. Based on an original story by Jeff Millar and Alex Stern, 1981. Hollywood: Script City.

Yarbro, Chelsea Quinn. *Dead and Buried*. New York: Warner, 1980.

———. *Nomads*. New York: Bantam, 1984.

V

Fusion, Transfusion, and
Transgression in the Fantastic

Joe Sanders

"My God, No!": The Varieties of Christian Horror Fiction

Both religion and horror fiction deal with ultimate concerns such as the purpose of human life, the survival of the soul, and the existence of absolute values. Thus, horror literature written in a culture that still is at least nominally Christian refers rather frequently to Christianity. But it is difficult to imagine a genuine combination of the two. Christianity offers worshipers safety through certainty of a personal savior; on the other hand, horror literature objectifies its readers' uncertainty, but suggests that an unthinkable doom probably is waiting for everyone. Although best-sellers such as *The Exorcist* and *The Omen* show that Christianity and horror make a commercially potent mixture, examining samples of the several types of such fiction also confirms that the compound is usually unstable and prone to decompose. Nevertheless, some successful fiction *does* pay equally serious attention to the impulses behind Christianity and horror.

One variety of Christian horror fiction, based directly on a Christian outlook, borrows threatening elements from horror literature in order to show how desperately people need to be saved from fear. Therefore, such work cannot depict horrible objects as overwhelming. For example, in Charles Williams's *Descent into Hell*, Pauline Anstruther at first feels menaced by a terrifying vision, but later learns to see it as an opportunity to share love. Not all characters in Christian fiction find salvation, but they can be defeated only by their own choices. God never sends mortals more anguish than they can bear. If they look around, they will discover that someone has been sent to help them shoulder their crosses. Pauline has Peter Stanhope. Marina, in Russell Kirk's *Lord of the Hollow Dark*, has the redoubtable Manfred Arcane. In the same way, in Frank E. Peretti's *This Present Darkness*, though the angelic warriors sent to defend a small college town against demons and their New Age allies find only one just man at first, they are confident that "there are others. There are always others" (13). In such fiction, no one is forced to face the unimaginable alone, and, in fact, if they are pursued, it is by the hound of Heaven. But such fiction thus avoids profoundly disturbing horror.

A subdivision of this variety of Christian horror fiction assumes that the powers of evil are especially active now because we are approaching or are *in* the period of tribulation before the millennium. Thus, Frank De Felitta's *Galgotha Falls* shows a millennium-obsessed pope personally confronting the Devil to win the soul of a tormented Jesuit; the struggle is awful, but the saved priest later reassures a woman scientist who has found religious faith by witnessing the conflict that on the Last Day "science and religion, matter and spirit, will reveal their unfolding purpose to mankind simultaneously" (341). Likewise, the apparent victories of evil in the first books of the *Omen* series ultimately occur in the context of Christ's eventual victory over the Antichrist.

Other stories attempt to achieve horror while referring to religion—but actually ignore the substance of Christianity. Though they contain supernatural forces with some Christian resonance, such works announce that those religious concepts or images have been mistakenly applied to older, pre-Christian forces. Characters must ignore the meaningless Christian labels in order to attune themselves to living, healthy powers. For example, in F. Paul Wilson's *The Keep*, what at first seems to be the familiar image of the cross used to imprison a vampire turns out actually to be the hilt of the sword that will be used to kill him. Also, Stephen King's *Salem's Lot* shows vampires apparently driven back by a crucifix; later, though, when a priest's faith falters, the master vampire seizes his cross and breaks it apart. As he tells the doomed priest, "Without faith, the cross is only wood" (355). On the other hand, when King's hero is chopping through a barrier in order to attack the master vampire, he finds a truer source of power:

> He was a man taken over, possessed, . . . the possession was not in the least Christian; the good was more elemental, less refined. It was ore, like something coughed up out of the ground in naked chunks. There was nothing finished about it. It was Force; it was Power; it was whatever moved the greatest wheels of the universe. (408)

William Peter Blatty's *The Exorcist* also belongs in this category since, despite the story's religious trappings, the possessed child is not freed by exorcism but by a doubting priest's personal rage, which leads him to challenge the demon to come out and fight him man-to-fiend.

Another variety of fiction that mixes horror and Christianity appears to take religion more seriously; at least it does not call it a mistake to apply traditional religious labels to the powers that disturb human lives. However, the bizarre changes the writers ring on the traditional concepts, exaggerating and inventing for the sake of shock effect, separate such fiction from genuine Christianity. In Jeffrey Knovitz's *The Sentinel*, for example, the church coerces grief-stricken sinners to do penance by guarding the gate of Hell, which currently opens off the second floor hallway of a New York apartment house. If this sentinel is distracted or if a new penitent does not undergo a supernatural transformation to become the aged and infirm watcher, the hosts of the damned will swarm out and seize the Earth. William H. Hallahan's *The Monk*, on the other hand, describes Satan, in the form of a hawk, patrolling the world to kill all babies who have the purple aura of perfect goodness, lest one survive to adulthood and forgive the angel Timothy (who once was Satan's ally during his rebellion but has since repented); meanwhile, an adept order of priests has managed to disguise one child's aura. Overall, such stories are action-packed, exciting, and meaningless in Christian terms. In fact, since they intensify horror by depicting either a less-than-beneficent God or an actively divided universe in which good and evil battle on more or less equal terms, such stories frequently end with evil triumphant; such is the case in *The Guardian*, Knovitz's sequel to *The Sentinel*, and in Mark Manley's violently nihilistic *Blood Sisters*.

Still another branch of horror fiction shows more familiar forms of good and evil—except that one of these powers has disguised itself as the other. Only a few people recognize this deception, and the established church does not help people make the distinction. For example, in James Herbert's *Shrine*, an evil force from the past masquerades as a divine visitation in order to prey on humans; it enjoys huge success because it can appeal to all eager self-deception in humans (436). Herbert's less-than-pure hero survives largely because of his unwillingness to surrender his self-aware alienation in order to worship, though he does wind up gingerly attending services at the Church of Our Lady of the Assumption (458).

In the same vein, good takes the guise of evil in Ramsey Campbell's *Obsession*. Campbell's characters feel that their adult lives have been poisoned by a Faustian bargain they made as adolescents, so they retreat into solitary torment. As the action develops, however, they realize that if they can be honest and open, their problems can be solved, and they do so. At the very end, the one character who feels too saturated with guilt to be redeemed prepares to commit suicide. As he stands on a cliff in a gathering storm, though, he becomes aware of a light inside the darkness, and he reevaluates his experience: "What kind of evil was it that had shown him that giving in to temptation led to greater and greater suffering? Perhaps it was precisely the opposite of what he had assumed" (308). Believing this, he feels that even in death he is moving toward the light— toward safety and peace. Such a story, in which horrible experiences are used to teach people a lesson, resembles the outlook of the overtly Christian works listed earlier. However, the hopeful interpretation is dragged in at the last moment, Campbell never identifies that disguised light, and the suicide is the only character to have any kind of transcendent revelation. Moreover, he has no opportunity to share his insight; the other characters must simply muddle along in their agnostic ways. Overall, any vague spiritual illumination the characters receive seems a poor reward for the insanity and pain they have suffered. The anxiety rings true; the hopeful resolution false. Campbell's failure is especially disappointing because he is touching a real nerve; in fact, Campbell's novel may get out of control because he has been seized by his concern, unlike writers who more carefully pick images and themes—but who also tend to evade the depths of their avowed subjects.

Another of Campbell's novels, *The Nameless*, shows the same pattern: unrelenting tension in a situation collapsing into defeat and despair, reversed by an unexpected, unlabeled force that appears too abruptly to be reconciled with the earlier action. Barbara Waugh, Campbell's heroine, becomes obsessed with tracking down a Mansonesque cult that kidnapped her young daughter, Angela, years before. Although Campbell does not say so directly, the cultists are Satanists, whose goal is to commit such atrocious acts of torture that they destroy their victims' sense of identity; this negation of significance creates an opening for a formless darkness (Satan) to enter existence. In particular, the cultists have depraved Angela until she takes the lead in planning the unnatural act of trapping her mother and torturing her to death. But though Barbara almost despairs after her capture, she is saved by the providential appearance of her husband's ghost, which awakens Angela's good nature, so that she turns on the cult and destroys them before taking her own life. After Angela's self-immolation, Barbara's lover (who also has been enthralled by the cult) tries to make sense of what has happened, while

> gripping her [Barbara's] arm so painfully that it wasn't clear if he meant to reassure her or himself. He sounded as if he was trying to understand or to believe. "They couldn't kill her [Angela], they could only corrupt her. And they didn't manage that, not completely. She's given herself another chance." (312)

To put it bluntly, this scene is an ideological mess. The triumph of good is not only unexpected, but unconvincing. After the perpetual anguish that the reader has witnessed and shared, it seems arbitrary for a good power (once again left unnamed, a choice that unfortunately resembles the cultists' technique of destroying personal significance) to intervene to save one character. Barbara responds to her lover's attempt at consolation not so much with awakened faith as with desperate yearning: "She had to believe that was true. . . . She watched the undying flames and tried to believe while she waited through the chill gray time until dawn" (312). Once again, light appears in the midst of darkness. But once again, the novel's final impression is of desperate contrivance.

Overall, thus, not only do Christianity and horror seem incompatible in theory, but a look at several of the different ways Christianity is treated in horror fiction confirms that the two often do not mix well.

Nevertheless, artistically successful Christian horror fiction can and does exist, doing with conviction what Campbell does out of desperation. To understand its effect, consider again the question readers find unresolved at the end of Campbell's novels: Can faith justify such suffering? This is the issue debated during the terrestrial action of the Old Testament book of Job, after the opening that rationalizes God's decision to let Satan torment Job and before God's final bullying appearance to tell Job to be silent and accept His will. If Job were certain that God existed, but God either withheld His presence or expressed Himself in a way that Job or the reader was unable to accept, the biblical debate would be unresolved, and the pain would remain. Some works of literature do achieve this level of spiritual horror. One might argue that Christ is the means by which God demonstrated His presence in human existence and that, there-fore, works ignoring this are by definition *non*-Christian. However, since these works deal with religious questions in a determinedly Christian context, and since at least some of the characters consider themselves to be Christians and argue for their beliefs, the fact may be that this full awareness of Christianity's claims is necessary for the most profound horror. It may be that the deepest possible horror is the inability to fully realize—or communicate—Christ's loving presence.

Take, for example, Joseph Sheridan Le Fanu's "The Mysterious Lodger." Le Fanu sets up the religious context early. The narrator is an atheist, scoffing at his wife's piety until he rents a room to a lodger who at first encourages the husband's "paganism" by witty, sneering oration but then begins demonic per-secution of the man and his family. As he terrifies everyone in the household and brings about the children's deaths, the lodger scoffs at the idea that a merciful God would permit such suffering. Fortunately, though even the devout wife is shaken by the lodger's blasphemous taunts, the narrator meets a new companion, "beautiful and kinglike" (360) in manner, who calms him and encourages him to submit to God's will, however dreadful it may appear to limited human understanding. The narrator accepts that advice, even when he is about to bury his daughter, whose death the demon lodger has caused:

> Sore and desolate was my heart; but with infinite gratitude to the great controller of all events, I recognized in it a change which nothing but the spirit of all good can effect. The love and fear of God had grown strong within me—in humbleness I bowed to his awful will—with a sincere trust I relied upon the goodness, the wisdom, and the mercy of him who had sent this great affliction. (368–69)

This faith is maintained even when the demon informs the man that the child actually has been buried alive. Consequently, the man's angelic companion is able to advise him how to expel the demon from his home. Though the house itself is tainted and must be destroyed, the narrator and his wife have other children and enjoy a long, loving married life afterward.

"The Mysterious Lodger" certainly is an odd story, quite unsatisfactory if taken at face value, since the final assurance is clearly insufficient payment for the characters' anguish. In particular, the little girl's agonized suffocation in her coffin is a gratuitous atrocity, explainable only as one more especially bitter pill the narrator must swallow. E. F. Bleiler is uneasy at including the story in a collection of Le Fanu's work, since "it is very unlike anything else that Le Fanu wrote in subject matter, presentation, values, and style" (vi). Jack Sullivan, however, relates "The Mysterious Lodger" to Le Fanu's other work with his description of how, in another of Le Fanu's stories, "the tension between the artificially injected faith in Christian redemption and the more dramatically realized terror of the void reflects a painfully divided consciousness" (39). Of "The Mysterious Lodger" itself, Sullivan says that "it is as if Le Fanu wants to affirm the Christ figure, but finds the demon more compelling and authentic. What begins as a religious allegory becomes a grotesque parody of one" (40). Readers cannot be sure which interpretation is correct, whether Le Fanu intended one thing and produced another or whether his story is a deliberate, poker-faced mockery of Christian assurance. Rather than being an uncertain, juvenile botch, Le Fanu's story may be a deliberate success at disconcerting and disturbing readers. Despite the narrator's conquest of his disbelief, we are left in unresolved doubt, hanging somewhere between the certainty of Christianity and the uncertainty of horror. We can appreciate the attraction of each, but we cannot free ourselves from the other.

Letting go of doubt is so difficult that it may require letting go of the self that doubts. Christianity speaks of the necessity for rebirth, and Peretti's evangelical novel mentioned earlier associates this with "inner brokenness" (339), a condition to be welcomed because it prepares one to be reconstructed by God. Nevertheless, accepting a reworking of the existing self is difficult. In "Holy Sonnet XIV," John Donne prays,

> Batter my heart, three person'd God; for you
> As yet but knocke, breathe, shine, and seeke to mend;
> That I may rise, and stand o'erthrow mee, 'and bend
> Your force, to break, blowe, burn and make me new.
>
> . . . .
> . . . for I
> Except you'enthrall mee, never shall be free,
> Nor ever chast, except you ravish me. (Bennett)

To someone less fervent in belief, this prospect of being ravished and remade can be more frightening than desirable. Humans naturally cling to their identities, and perception of a supernatural transformer's approach may suggest Howard Phillips Lovecraft's description of how horror fiction excites "in the reader a profound sense of dread, and of contact with unknown spheres and powers; a subtle attitude of awed listening, as if for the beating of black wings or the scratching of outside shapes and entities on the known universe's utmost rim" (16). What Campbell suggests but Le Fanu shows is that acceptance of Christianity is the outcome of a shattering of beliefs, a transformation of personal consciousness. An individual experiencing the approach of such conversion may have difficulty remembering that the ultimate result will be for the better, since the ultimate result will not be *him*; what matters is the fact that the precious, familiar self is about to be seized and reshaped.

If this perception is difficult to hold in mind, maintaining the drives of Christianity and horror in the same piece of fiction is still more difficult. But it can be done. Brian Moore's *Cold Heaven* is an example of successful Christian horror fiction. Although Marie Davenport was educated by nuns, she identifies religion with her parents' neglect, in particular her father's virtual abandonment after her mother's death. She has had to grow up without her parents; now she hates religion. Marie's coldly unlikable husband, Alex, is a doctor, but she has fallen in love with another doctor, Daniel, and during a stolen weekend with Daniel, Marie has a vision of the Virgin Mary demanding that she inform priests that the headland where She is standing is holy and must become a place of pilgrimage. Marie refuses, angry at the intrusion and afraid that if she gives in she will never be free to be her ordinary self (58). Exactly one year later, Alex is killed in an accident but vanishes from the morgue; Marie fears that he has been resurrected to force her to speak out. When she traces Alex to a motel near the site of the vision, Marie finds him in a strange condition between death and life, becoming more or less "normal" according to whether she does what is expected of her or not. In the following scene, Marie discovers that Alex has slipped into death again, and she responds simultaneously with rage at God for His part in killing Alex and with mortification for what *she* has done.

He was lying in the bed under the lit bedlamp, his eyes open. "Alex?" she said. He did not answer. She went toward the bed and . . . saw that he was dead. His mouth was open. His eyes were open. He was not breathing. . . . She lay down on the bed beside her dead husband and in fear and guilt and desperate affection laid her cheek against the dead flesh of his cheek, put her arms around his dead body and held him. . . . She left the corpse and walked across the room to the window. . . . Alex is dead. He is dead because of me. Daniel will come tomorrow but it will make no difference. Nothing will be the same. They have done this to Alex to punish me. They did not kill me in that accident because they still plan to use me. They killed Alex. They killed him to warn me.

She looked out of the window at the dark shape of the headland. I thought I had free will. I thought I had the right to ignore what happened to me. But what use is it to talk about rights when they have shown that there is no right or wrong, when everything I thought was superstitious and false might be true, but not true in the way those nuns believe it to be true. Oh, I have news for you Mother St. Jude. God is something you could never understand, something we call God but it may not be God at all. Something evil. And yet I am to blame. I blame my pride, my selfishness, for even after the accident, if I had done what was asked of me, Alex would have been spared. (90–91)

Marie is wrong: Alex is returned to life again so that she is able to save him by—painfully and bitterly—doing what is demanded of her. But though she modifies her behavior just enough to satisfy the letter of the supernatural command, she evades its spirit. She refuses to worship the power that is compelling her to act. This is a disturbing choice, especially in *Cold Heaven's* conclusion. When the vision reappears before nuns whom Marie has led to the site, she decides that she has obeyed the command and can refuse to do any more. She denies seeing the second apparition, and a kindly, superficial priest reassures her that her testimony about its first appearance will not be revealed. And so Marie is free to experience the griefs and responsibilities of ordinary life. She is also, from a Christian perspective, self-damned, having rejected the love of her heavenly Mother and the commands of her heavenly Father. Still, considering the torture resulting from that love and brutality of those commands, a reader can understand Marie's reluctance to embrace the power that ravishes her.

Is that power the Christian God? The story sets up a Christian context, and readers interpret events in that framework, as does Marie. Certainly there is a consciousness at work that is superior to the laws of the natural world. It can control weather to send down lightning bolts at appropriate moments, and it even can raise the dead. However, it shows no personal interest in Marie in a form to which she can respond; it speaks through the command: Do my will! If she hesitates, it is as willing to kill as to resurrect (194). Speaking of humanity as wayward children, the New Testament book of Hebrews advises us that "for the moment all discipline seems painful rather than pleasant; later it yields the peaceful fruit of righteousness to those who have been trained by it" (Heb. 12:11). But the "discipline" Marie receives is in exactly the wrong form, administered in exactly the wrong way, to "train" her.

Most of the novel's action is seen through Marie's eyes, but we get enough glimpses of other people's interactions with her to realize that she frequently is misinterpreting them, convinced they are agents of the conspiracy against her integrity. Marie herself sometimes realizes that she is acting in a paranoid manner and questions her own sanity. Yet, often enough, the characters *are* lying to her; moreover, she *is* being persecuted, driven by a Something that lets itself be seen only through a glass darkly. Marie grudgingly does what she must, but she clings to her resentment, her "right not to believe" (261). In any event, without Marie's worship or love, force still prevails. "Free will" may exist, but a power also exists that can coerce humans into choosing to act because it can threaten them with unbearable consequences. And it will do so. "Thy will" *will* be done, whatever humans pray.

Such is the mood of Christian horror fiction. For any less-than-totally-devout humans, horror is the other side of awe at the approach to the more-than-human. Even believers pray, in honest distress, "I believe, O Lord; help thou mine unbelief." Christian horror recognizes the reality of this attitude and depicts a person stranded by a God who is not so much invisible as inscrutable, superior both to doubt and worship.

Works Cited

Bennet, Joan, ed. *Four Metaphysical Poets: Donne, Herbert, Vaughn and Crenshaw.* New York: Vintage Books, 1960.

Blatty, William Peter. *The Exorcist.* 1971. Reprint. New York: Bantam, 1972.

Campbell, Ramsey. *The Nameless.* 1981. Reprint. New York: Tor, 1985.

———. *Obsession.* 1985. Reprint. New York: Tor, 1986.

De Felitta, Frank. *Galgotha Falls.* 1984. Reprint. New York: Pocket Books, 1985.

Hallahan, William H. *The Monk.* New York: Morrow, 1983.

Herbert, James. *Shrine.* 1983. Reprint. New York: Signet, 1984.

King, Stephen. *'Salem's Lot.* 1975. Reprint. New York: Signet, 1976.

Kirk, Russell. *Lord of the Hollow Dark.* New York: St. Martin's, 1979.

Konvitz, Jeffrey. *The Guardian.* 1978. Reprint. New York: Bantam. 1979.

———. *The Sentinel.* 1974. New York: Ballantine, 1976.

Le Fanu, Joseph Sheridan. "The Mysterious Lodger." *Dublin University Magazine.* (1850). Reprinted in *Ghost Stories and Mysteries.* Ed. E. F. Bleiler. New York: Dover, 1975, 332–372.

Lovecraft, Howard Phillips. *Supernatural Horror in Literature.* 1927. Reprint. New York: Ben Abramson, 1945.

Manley, Mark. *Blood Sisters.* New York: Charter, 1985.

Moore, Brian. *Cold Heaven.* New York: Holt, Rinehart and Winston, 1983.

Peretti, Frank E. *This Present Darkness.* Westchester: Crossway Books, 1986.

Seltzer, David. *The Omen.* New York: Signet, 1976.

Sullivan, Jack. *Elegant Nightmares: The English Ghost Story from Le Fanu to Blackwood.* Athens: Ohio University Press, 1978.

Williams, Charles. *Descent into Hell.* London: Faber and Faber, 1937.

Wilson, F. Paul. *The Keep.* New York: Morrow, 1981.

Cynthia L. Walker

"They're Fusing Just the Way They Should": Fusion, Transfusion, and Their Negative Correlates in *The Second Chronicles of Thomas Covenant*

While *The First Chronicles of Thomas Covenant* explore the concept of imminence in a dualistic world and posit the necessity for standing in the eye of the dualistic paradox, *The Second Chronicles of Thomas Covenant* demonstrate the next logical step, the need to fuse that duality into a new creation, an alloy not born of the land. Although Covenant's white-gold ring is the alloy par excellence of the trilogy and although power is as much an issue in this trilogy as it was in the last, Donaldson is using the concept of the alloy in order to examine the duality of power itself. Only an alloy, one who has accepted and fused the contradictory parts of himself, has the power to make real choices; otherwise he is vulnerable to possession by the parts of himself he is denying, and any so-called choices he makes are going to be controlled by that denial.

In order to make this point, Donaldson provides a number of examples of fusion, the uniting or blending of elements or entities into a whole, as well as a number of examples of its negative correlate, possession, one entity's domination of another from within. He also examines that which approaches but does not substitute for fusion—transfusion, the transfer of some vital quality from one entity to another—and its negative correlate, vampirism, the appropriation of some vital quality from another entity. While the acts of transfusion and vampirism are temporal in nature, fusion and possession are continuing states, though they can be halted, as when Lord Foul abandons his possession of Joan in exchange for Covenant's agreement to sacrifice himself. The major events in the trilogy involve at least one of these concepts and through them Covenant, Linden, and the reader discover their own power and learn how to wield it.

The prologue, through its emphasis on possession, vampirism, and transfusion, prepares the reader for the changes that have occurred in the Land since Covenant's last visit. The prologue begins with the negative correlates of possession and vampirism. Lord Foul has possessed Joan and is using her as a tool to induce Covenant to return to the Land. Yet Joan is responsible for her vulnerability to possession, for she has adhered to a self-image believing that she is perfectly all right, that denies parts of who she is. Abandoning a diseased husband and being perfectly all right are not easily reconcilable, and rather than attempting to fuse these opposing aspects, Joan looks for cures outside herself, eventually coming to believe she is a prophet and projecting the sins she cannot accept in herself onto those she regards as more deserving of punishment.

While Joan appears only in the prologue of *The Wounded Land,* her situation sets the tone for the rest of the trilogy both by foreshadowing the behavior of the main characters and by demonstrating what the other characters must work beyond if they wish to be more than Lord Foul's tools themselves. Her alternation between uncontrollable violence and catatonia is a response pattern later to be echoed by Covenant and Linden. And as she looks elsewhere, first to psychology, then to religion, and finally to Covenant, for healing and power and resolution, so will Covenant look for the One Tree, so will Linden covet the white gold, both hoping to acquire some tool that will mend the bifurcation in their souls. Donaldson carefully maps Covenant's and Linden's slow progress toward the recognition that they alone can fuse their internal selves into an alloy, a recognition that Joan never achieves.

Once Covenant and Linden arrive in the Land, Donaldson fleshes out and cumulatively builds on the concepts he presented in the prologue. *The Wounded Land* focuses on vampirism and transfusion; *The One Tree* focuses on possession; *White Gold Wielder* has fusion as its central focus. Covenant's and Linden's initial experiences in the Land expose them to varying degrees of vampirism. As Sunder combines his blood with his sunstone to raise water, so the Clave combines blood and banefire to control the sun bane, so Hollian uses her blood and her *lianar* to foretell the sun. In each case, for one object to be powerful, it must be fed by the other. Such depletions are decimating whole peoples, such as the *Haruchai,* and will eventually destroy all the inhabitants of the earth, as Lord Foul intends.

The vampirism represents, in most cases, a basic distortion of nature, a distortion ostensibly made possible by the destruction of the Staff of Law, rather than by a conscious allegiance to evil. One of the first and most distressing examples of such vampirism involves the Land's use of its natural elements: "The wood lay on a pile of ash burning warmly. The people he had known here would never have voluntarily consumed wood for any purpose. They had always striven to use the life of wood, the Earthpower in it, without destroying the thing they used" (WL, 73–74). Yet now no manifestation of life is cherished, and a people that can burn wood can burn themselves or shed each other's blood.

Such vampirism is initially presented in the prologue when the Fantastics cast their hands into the fire to evoke their Master: "Blankly she put her right hand into the flames. The fire seemed to mount as if it fed on the woman's pain" (*WL*, 47). These believers do not question the nature of a God that would feed on such pain. Similarly, Sunder, the Graveler, does not question his use of human blood and his sunstone, *orcrest*, to support his people, nor does Hollian question her shedding of her own blood to read the sunbane and to perform minor acts of healing.

The ultimate form of vampirism in the novel is, of course, the Sunbane itself, perpetuated by the Clave: "The shedding of blood to invoke the Sunbane only made the Sunbane stronger. Thus Lord Foul caused the increase of the Sunbane without cost to himself" (*WL*, 333). And that, of course, is the salient characteristic of vampirism and possession—they are without cost to the one who feeds and controls the other.

Opposed to vampirism is transfusion, in which a willing donor gives of himself in order to aid another. One primary example of transfusion is the Waynhims' gift of blood to Covenant so that he may speed to Revelstone. However, the ultimate example of a transfusion, of a giving of one's own powers or nature to assuage another's need, is the magnificent finale to *The Wounded Land*, in which Covenant uses the flames of the *caamora* and his white gold to fashion a fire that will bring peace to the dead giants of The Grieve (484–85).

While *The Wounded Land* focuses primarily on vampirism and transfusion, it also prepares the reader for Donaldson's treatment of the more complex issues of possession and fusion, issues which are the primary focus of the remainder of the trilogy. Possession is the necessary alternative to fusion, and both alternatives exist within the psyche, within the Land, and within the mind of the Creator. Possession is predicated on denial; fusion, on acceptance. Both in the Land and in the psyches of Linden and Covenant, the denial prevails. The creation story that Covenant relates to Linden and is overheard by Sunder reveals the pervasiveness of this denial:

> For while he had labored over his creation, he had closed his eyes, and had not seen the Despiser, the bitter son or brother of his heart, laboring beside him—casting dross into the forge, adding malignancy to his intent. (*WL*, 113–14)

As Pitchwife later explains to Linden, all power is an articulation of its wielder (*The One Tree [OT]*, 169). Pitchwife's pitch, Covenant's ring, the Creator's "love and vision" control what may be expressed, but not the essence of the expression itself. The Creator's blindness to the brother of his heart, to his true nature, is what empowered the Despiser in the first place and enabled him to plant banes within the earth. The Creator's subsequent attempt to banish the Despiser by imprisoning him within the Arch of Time was hardly a step toward psychic or cosmic integration. Linden Avery is the trilogy's closest mortal parallel to the Creator. Having dedicated her life to healing some of the banes of the earth, she has, at the same time, denied the presence of evil, both within the world and within herself. That is why Linden is so shocked at the sight of Joan and why Gibbon-Raver's touch and his question "Are you not evil?" (*WL*, 268) have such an insidious effect on her self-confidence. The self she has so carefully created has been constructed as a bastion against the evil that she knows she contains within her and that she is determined to refuse. But her very refusal gives it autonomy and the power to possess and corrupt the parts of her that are truly good.

For Linden, as well as for the other characters, it is not merely a matter of accepting duality, of accepting the fact that she is good and bad, but of accepting that good and bad are synonymous, since they are simply articulations of power. For example, her health-sense may be destroying her, but it also saved her life, since it gave her the percipience to know that she and Cail needed Voure when they were infected during the Sun of Pestilence. However, like the Creator, Linden has chosen to banish evil, and her periodic bouts of psychic and moral paralysis mirror the Creator's impotence with regard to the Despiser.

What Linden recognizes about Covenant, that from the same source "arose both his power and his defenselessness" (*OT*, 178), is true of her as well. The sensitivity that enables her to have health-sense, to perceive that presence of Ravers and hurricanes, is the same sensitivity that would permit her to possess Covenant and wrest his power from him. Thus, she refuses to enter Covenant's mind unless circumstances are so critical that she is absolutely forced to. Only the First's threat to amputate Covenant's arm can compel her to enter him after his venom relapse precipitated by the Raver-possessed rat. When Infelice suggests that Linden retrieve from Covenant's mind the location of the One Tree, Linden refuses, despite her anxiety about the intention of the *Elohim*. As a result of her refusal, Covenant is subjected to the catatonia imposed on him by the *Elohim*, and it is only the Kemper's possession of Covenant that eventually compels her to risk possessing him herself.

It is no surprise that she is both angered and terrified at the *Elohim's* contention that she is the Sun-Sage and that Sun-Sage and Ring-Wielder were foreseen to be one. As the quest proceeds and it becomes more and more apparent to her that she may well have to take Covenant's place, her terror mounts. Only in the final pages of the trilogy does she learn that fusion is the answer to possession; this knowledge enables her to fuse within herself the attributes of Sun-Sage and White-Gold Wielder.

Donaldson's treatment of fusion is considerably more subtle, since he is examining two different kinds of fusion—a combining of two aspects or individuals, which might more appropriately be called union than fusion, and, more important, a combining of three or more characteristics or entities. While a union of two can create a new entity, such as the union between the Kemper and the croyel, it is fusion that, in Donaldson's cosmogony, creates the true alloy, since something must serve as the medium by which the other elements are combined.

Thus, genuine fusion or wiving, as Pitchwife would call it, requires at least three elements or entities, whether they be physical or psychological, and all the real accompishments in the trilogy are achieved through fusion. Donaldson is far more concerned with the psychological/spiritual ramifications of fusion, but he uses a number of physical examples to drive his point home. Fusion is a medium for healing on the physical plane and integration on the psychological/ spiritual plane, and all of the significant examples of fusion occur in the final book of the *Chronicles*, building cumulatively to the stunning climax of *White Gold Wielder*. The first two examples occur in Revelstone in the Hall of Gifts. In a parody of Pitchwife's craft, as well as of the death of the First's father, "by some cunning of Gibbon-Raver's power, Honninscrave had been fused into the floor. Kneeling, he had sunk into it to the middle of his thighs and forearms as though it were quicksand. Then it had solidified around him, imprisoning him absolutely" (245). After Honninscrave is freed by Nom and possessed by Gibbon-Raver, Nom embraces him, and the Raver contained within him, thus fore-shadowing the embrace scenes between Caer Caveral, Sunder, and Hollian, as well as Linden, Findail, and Vain. In doing so, Nom kills Honninscrave, who chooses to make his death meaningful, and rends the Raver, thereby gaining the capacity for speech. As Pitchwife's pitch is the medium by which the stone is fused, and Gibbon-Raver's power is the medium by which Honninscrave is fused to the floor, so Honninscrave is the medium by which the Raver's intel-ligence is fused with the sandgorgon. In each case, something is required to bring the disparate elements together to make possible the alloy.

Immediately following these two rather minor examples of fusion occurs one of the most significant ones—Covenant's use of the banefire to make an alloy of himself: " 'I guess you could say it's been fused. I don't know how else to describe it. It's been burned into me so deeply that there's no distinction. I'm like an alloy—venom and wild magic and ordinary skin and bones melted together until they're all one. All the same. I'll never be free of it' " (271). At any rate, Covenant will not be free of it while he lives, and it is just such an alloy that Linden needs to make of herself, by using her own will, her freedom of choice to fuse her desire for power and her fear of power, to fuse the raver and the healer within her.

The novel concludes with a double example of fusion, but first Donaldson gives Linden parallel opportunities to choose against possession and, in addition, provides the reader with a pictorial demonstration of the effects of resistance.

En route to Kiril Threndor, Linden is possessed by the *moksha* Jehannum, thereby forcing her to experience herself as truly evil and providing her with a final opportunity to choose a response other than paralysis to her awareness of evil within herself (432–33).

Linden's refusal yet again to succumb to moral paralysis enables her to rec-ognize the extent to which the contradictions in her mind have controlled her behavior, her sense of herself. Through accepting the contradiction, as Cove-nant accepted the venom in his blood, she is ultimately able to make an alloy of herself: "She was evil. And yet her instinct for healing falsified *moksha*. That contradiction no longer paralyzed her. She accepted it. It gave her the power to choose" (443).

Having escaped possession and paralysis, Linden is immediately beset with the opposite temptation, possessing Covenant in order to prevent him from giving his ring to Lord Foul. This too she refuses: "Deliberately, she let him go—let love and hope and power go as if they were all one, too pure to be possessed or desecrated" (445–46). Power, in its various manifestations, has been an obsession of many of the characters in this trilogy. Like Covenant, Linden has both feared and coveted power. Once she accepts her contradictory impulses, Linden, like Covenant, learns that real power comes only when one gives up the power one has, as Linden does when she walks out of Covenant's consciousness; as Covenant learned after his experience in the banefire, when he declared that he would never use his power again; as the reader learns when Covenant gives Lord Foul the white gold.

The price of resisting a part of oneself is paralysis or self-destruction, as Covenant and Linden have finally discovered. Lord Foul, however, is unwilling to accept that he is just one aspect of humanity (440). Donaldson uses Foul's maniacal resistance visually to represent the ultimate consequences of attempting to resist a part of oneself. All Foul accomplishes by resisting Covenant's specter is to make Covenant that much stronger, since Covenant merely absorbs the power Foul blisters him with. Although Covenant does not use power, Foul empowers him with every blow and diminishes himself accordingly.

Foul may be out of the picture, but the Sunbane isn't, and Linden, like Covenant before her, needs the opportunity to learn to use *herself* rather than her power. And Findail and Vain need to fulfill their mysterious purposes. Through Linden's embrace, Findail's earthpower, Vain's structure, and her own passion for health and healing fuse into a new Staff of Law.

Yet the healing of the Land still remains to be accomplished, and for this Linden must make of herself a tool as she makes a tool of the ring and the staff: "But she had learned from Covenant—and from the Raver's possession. She did not attempt to attack the Sunbane. Instead, she called it to herself, accepted it into her personal flesh." In accepting the Sunbane, Linden goes Covenant one better. Covenant absorbed the power that Foul blasted him with, but Linden does more than absorb the Sunbane; she heals it and returns the energy to the Land (463–464). Linden has learned true healing and has discovered the only true tool is herself.

From Lord Foul possessing Joan to force Covenant's return to the Land to Linden Avery, White Gold Wielder, using her own life to alter the sunbane, Donaldson has given us example after example of the misuses and uses of power, of self. Vampirism, possession, transfusion, union, and fusion are all aspects of the paradox of power, and all but the last are accessible to anyone, be he giant or Stonedowner, Raver or *elohim*. And even fusion is ostensibly available to all, at least on the physical plane. But the ability to make of oneself an alloy and, hence, to be a tool for whatever purposes one chooses, has to be earned through a rigorous process of self-awareness and self-acceptance. As Pitchwife points out, "unearned knowledge rules its wielder, to the cost of both" (*White Gold*

Wielder, 360). Earned knowledge, particularly earned self-knowledge, allows one to rule oneself, to choose one's own meaning, which, as Donaldson has so carefully pointed out, is the only true form of power. If power is an articulation of its wielder, then the only real tool is one's own life. Donaldson, through *The Second Chronicles of Thomas Covenant*, has given his readers the knowledge that we, like Covenant, like Linden, can choose to make our lives a tool as powerful as white gold.

Works Cited

Donaldson, Stephen R. *The One Tree*. New York: Ballantine, 1982.
———. *White Gold Wielder*. New York: Ballantine, 1983.
———. *The Wounded Land*. New York: Ballantine, 1980.

Mickey Pearlman

The Element of the Fantastic and the Artist Figure in the Novels of Muriel Spark

Kierkegaard said that "his task was 'to create difficulties everywhere' " (Bretall, 194) and as Tom Hubbard and other critics have noted, "Muriel Spark does likewise" (179). The seventeen novels of Muriel Spark are suffused with the surrealistic and foreshadowed by the fantastic. Hers is a world where shadows fall the wrong way (in *The Hothouse by the East River*), typewriters type out their own stories (in *The Comforters*) a woman writes the script for her own murder (in *The Driver's Seat*) and there are strange, symbolic phone calls from unidentified voices (in *Memento Mori*). Fortunately, in addition to the blackmailers, betrayers, grotesques (of both genders and many nations), the committed or odious Catholics, the parade of eccentric sexual misfits, egocentrics, malingerers, and fetishists, Spark provides the reader with an artist figure who attempts to cope with the fantastic, to reinvent reality, and who represents the power of creativity in an ephemeral, confused and complicated society.

Caroline Rose in *The Comforters* is a critic and a writer. She is writing a book, *Form in the Modern Novel*, and is struggling to break through the inertia that many writers experience when confronted by the blank page. Ms. Rose is having trouble with "form," a typical Sparkian concern, because in Spark's often absurd world, it is difficult, if not impossible, to superimpose form on experience. (In fact, Spark's latest novel, *The Only Problem*, deals obliquely with the book of Job, but, more profoundly, with understanding the experience of Job—giving it a "form" that humanity can accept. Understanding why God punishes Job so harshly is, for Harvey Gotham, the "only problem" worth solving.) Caroline Rose is unable to analyze the form of the modern novel, and thus she becomes a character in her own story. She is both Spark's main character in *The Comforters* and a character in her own work, *Form in the Modern Novel*. This is a device that Spark develops more fully, but with more intricate machinations, in *Loitering with Intent*.

The concept is clear: there is a tenuous demarcation here between what is real and what seems to be real, between the fantastic and the commonplace, which is established in her first novel. At the end of *The Comforters*, Caroline Rose's typewriter begins without her assistance to type out a novel whose story line is the life of Caroline Rose. The typewriter becomes, in effect, a novelist, and is able to record both the spoken and unspoken thoughts of Rose and of her former lover, Lawrence Manders, and his mother, Helena. Caroline refers to the typewriter as the "typing ghost." (176)

> "I suppose Caroline wants to get her book off her hands. But I don't know their business at all really. I wish they would do something definite, but there it is."
> "Caroline's 'book,' " he said; "*do you mean the book she is writing or the one in which she lives?*" [emphasis added]
> "Now, Willi! Caroline is not a silly girl. She did have a little upset and imagines things, I know. And then there was the accident. But since that time she's recovered wonderfully. My dear Helena. I do assure you that Caroline has been receiving communications from her Typing Spooks continuously since that time." (211)

In *The Comforters* the typewriter is referred to as a "ghost" and Caroline's lover is named "Manders." In Ibsen's play *Ghosts*, the pivotal character is named Pastor Manders and the central issue of the play is a discussion of the masks that human beings prepare and present to the public. The play is also about the elusiveness of reality (if it exists) beneath those masks. In my view Spark includes this allusion to Ibsen, this submerged "joke" and many others like it in order to accentuate her questions about reality, surrealism, and fantasy and to underscore the importance of the objects and the names in her novels.

Caroline Rose's enemy in *The Comforters* is an unappealing, malicious former servant named Georgina Hogg. There are several interesting components to her character. First of all, "Georgina" (like Caroline and Louisa, both in this novel) is a feminized version of what is, essentially, a masculine name. The use of these names is important. They imply that there are diffused or ambivalent identity problems at play. ("Edwina" in *Loitering with Intent* is the most masterful of these creations.) Georgina is described as being "like a lump of food on the chest which will move neither up nor down" (42). Her last name, "Hogg," is not only supposed to remind us of her piglike nature, but, as Carl Jung said, "in the minds of many people, the pig is closely associated with dirty sexuality. (Circe, for example, changed the men who desired her into swine)" (Jung 343). In Allan Massie's opinion "the name Hogg is not arbitrarily chosen. It refers us to James Hogg and *The Confessions of a Justified Sinner*, that most remarkable analysis of the consequences of erecting false gods and following their teaching. For, from the beginning, Muriel Spark recognizes that it is not just a choice between indifference and true religion. There is also false religion, seductive and destroying. The name Hogg is a warning; it takes us into that world which so many of her characters will inhabit" (98). Georgina, therefore, is the focus of several patterns that Spark creates in order to reinvent reality. She has a suggestive name, she is a mastering servant, her sexuality is confused, and so on.

The subplot in *The Comforters* revolves around a "phony Baron" and two characters named "Hogarth." Clearly, using the name of the eighteenth-century British portraitist here was not unintentional, particularly since the first name of one of Spark's "Hogarth" characters is Mervyn, reminiscent of "Merlin," the magician/seer who is always associated with the fantastic. The magical qualities suggested by Merlin are associated here with the Hogarth characters. And in this book Spark's sexually confused character is a cross-dressing homosexual named Ernest who is self-indulgent and effete. He is the antithesis of the seriousness that his name suggests.

> [Helena Manders] thought how Caroline with her aptitude for 'placing' people in their correct historical setting had once placed Ernest in the French court of the seventeenth century. "He's born out of his time," Caroline had explained, "that's part of his value in the present age." Lawrence had said placidly, and not long ago, "Ernest never buys a tie, he has them made. Five-eighths of an inch wider than anyone else's." (133)

The point here is that confused sexuality is aligned with suggestive names and interesting questions about time. Creativity and identity are problematic in a world that is always invaded by the fantastic and both suggest the disorder and chaos that invade the world of Spark's characters in New York, London, Italy, and elsewhere. The creative characters, the writers and artists, attempt to impose order, to make sense of flux and pattern from randomness. Caroline Rose is the first of Spark's female characters to suffer the pain of confusion and, as Nancy A. J. Potter has noted, she is

> engaged in finding a spiritual peace by recourse to various "comforters"— a lover, his family, St. Philumena's retreat house, her artistic friends, and, finally, her will. Her progress is impeded by concentrations of improbable and melodramatic obstacles: mysterious voices, talk of Black Masses, diamond smuggling gangs, and [the] disgusting . . . Mrs. Hogg. (115)

Caroline, like many of the females who follow her in later novels, is surrounded by the supernatural and the suspicious—the water that engulfs Georgina Hogg, the blackmailers who surface repeatedly in Spark's work to suggest the elusiveness of the dependable. As with January Marlowe, the writer character in *Robinson*, there is also turmoil within; it is not only the external circumstances that pose the problem. Spark suggests that Caroline's conversion to Catholicism mirrors her other profane attempts to locate the stable and unfluctuating. But she is surrounded; she hears voices, her typewriter is a plagiarizing novelist, the other characters are cripples (emotional and physical), Satanists, phony unctious Catholics—all contained by a world that is populated by false or useless comforters.

A completely different twist on the artist character emerges in Spark's 1968 novel, *The Public Image*, written two years after her much-debated and longest work, *The Mandelbaum Gate*. Spark researched her 1966 novel about Barbara Vaughn, a half-Jewish, half-Protestant convert to Catholicism, while she was covering the Eichmann trial in Israel for the British press in 1961. The novel won the James Tail Black Memorial Prize in 1966, but as Spark herself, and many other critics (with the glaring exception of Patricia Stubbs) have noted, "It's out of proportion: the beginning is slow; the end is very rapid" (*Dictionary of Literary Biography*, 599). Fortunately, she realized that the spareness and economy that define her genius, the liveliness of style and fast pace, were buried by an overflow of words. "I got bored," she said, "because it was too long, so I decided never again to write a long book. Keep them very short" (*Dictionary of Literary Biography*, 599).

Spark took her own advice in *The Public Image*, a spare and brittle novel with the hollow spaces and reverberating echoes suggested by a symbol that appears often in the novel—a shell. Annabel Christopher, "a puny . . . English girl from Wakefield, with a peaky face and mousey hair," (7) has been transformed through the manipulation of the movie director, Luigi Leopardi, into the "English Lady-Tiger" of the film world in "Italy, the Motherland of Sensation" (24). Annabel is an actress of sorts, and in this role she is another artist figure in Spark's canon. But unlike Caroline Rose and Fleur Talbot, who attempt to create reality through the act of writing books and giving birth to fictional characters, Annabel is the personification of someone else's "fantasy"; she is created by Leopardi and Frederick Christopher, her husband.

Annabel, the former waitress in a coffee bar, "a little chit of a thing," (7) is an unusual female character for Spark. She is, in fact, "stupid, [with] . . . the deep core of stupidity that . . . thrives on the absence of looking glass," (9) who has somehow "fallen on her feet" (6). She has none of the plodding dullness of other witless women in Spark's work and she has none of the emasculating energy of Spark's vipers. What she understands is that "she did not need to be clever, she only had to exist" (11); "she did not need to perform" (11). "She thought of appearances in this way, they were 'roles' " (21) and she understood that the public image would inevitably replace the private truth. "Annabel has become so identified with her movie star image as the 'English Lady-Tiger' that reality no longer exists. She has become a well-produced, self-created artifact, falsifying her memoirs in the manner of her own popular films" (Pullin 72).

The mastermind behind Annabel's image, a precursor of Lister in *Not To Disturb*, is her husband, Frederick, who is angry, envious, and manipulative. Frederick becomes so incensed by Annabel's success that he carefully orchestrates both his own suicide and a fake orgy at Annabel's apartment in order to discredit her and to destroy the "public image" he has worked so hard to create. He jumps from a scaffold at the Church of St. John and St. Paul, scene of Paul's martyrdom, while Annabel is bearing the intrusion of an assortment of film world gadflys, fashionable drug users and assorted hangers-on into her apartment in Rome. The apartment is large and empty of furniture but full of sounds—in many ways it too is a shell. Frederick hopes to deny Annabel the role of grieving widow/adoring wife so popular in Italy by implicating her in his morbid death. (Suicide is also illegal in Italy.) It was, said Annabel, " 'worse than a nightmare because it has been a reality, with a worse and heavier reality to follow and finish off the night with a thud on the floor of her mind' " (47). But Annabel, schooled by the two men in replacing reality with fantasy, finds that she can become the orchestrator of a new public image. She proves, as Faith Pullin has noted, "the greater 'artist' of the two" (72) by galvanizing the neighbors "in attitudes of grief and sympathy for the press just as successfully as if the scene had been studied and rehearsed for weeks" (68). She creates a fiction for the now-dead Frederick that makes him the accidental victim of a band of adoring fictitious women from whom he was supposedly trying to escape. The manipulated becomes the manipulator, and Annabel emerges again the untainted and bereaved wife.

Frederick's alter ego here is a nasty betrayer type named Billy O'Brien who attempts to blackmail Annabel through five maudlin and incriminating letters left behind by Frederick. The publication of these letters would force Annabel to discard the role that has now become reality and to adopt a new image. Annabel says, " 'It's the widowed Lady-Tiger or nothing,' " (101) and at the novel's end, she climbs back into her handy shell, foregoes the coroner's inquest, takes her baby, Carl ("the only reality of her life"), and leaves for the airport and "freedom."

> She was pale as a shell. She did not wear her dark glasses. Nobody recognized her as she stood, having moved the baby in a sense weightlessly and perpetually within her, as an empty shell contains, by its very structure, the echo and harking image of former and former seas. (125)

Annabel Christopher has often been compared with Lise, the antiheroine of Spark's next novel, *The Driver's Seat*. The difference is, however, marked. Lise is an identityless wanderer, a chaotic and sick package in a plain wrapper. Annabel, perceived by the public as an enticing, sexual vamp, is, underneath her image, the epitome of evenness and order. She is a contradiction even in sexual terms.

> "In fact, I don't like tiger-sex. I like to have my sexual life under the bedclothes, in the dark, on a Saturday night. With my night dress on. I

> know it's kinky, but that's how I like it. . . . And I don't like it upside down," she said. (101)

Muriel Spark, whose novels are a showcase for "kinky" sex, here transforms utterly "normal" sex into kinkiness. In a world where the unusual is the norm, the usual is abnormal.

Spark makes an additional statement about the function of the artist figure in the character of Frederick, a man who is personally offended by his wife's supposed "shallowness." He has two problems here: one is the recognition of Annabel's adaptability and the other is the acknowledgment of his own short-comings. As a serious filmmaker, Frederick wants to play God, and in this pose he is closer to Jean Brodie (in *The Prime of Miss Jean Brodie*), Lister (in *Not to Disturb*), and the Abbess Alexandra (in *The Abbess of Crewe*) than he is to Miles Mary Robinson or Harvey Gotham, two other male artist figures in Spark's novels. What strikes the reader in the three male portraits of Robinson, Gotham, and Christopher is the presence of a cold and detached intellect without the redeeming qualities of empathy and tenderness. Spark's masculine artist figures are detached, alienated, unsympathetic. When Frederick says of Annabel that she is " 'a beautiful shell, like something washed up on the sea-shore, a collector's item, perfectly formed, a pearly shell—but empty, devoid of the life it once held' " (12), he suggests his own persona.

Spark's view is that Annabel must divest herself of the carefully crafted "public image" in order to experience the "pregnant" possibilities of reality; she must escape the confines of the carefully crafted shell of her public identity. This idea of an internal, suffocating structure is supported by a reiterated number pattern that Spark uses in *Robinson* (the number three) and in *The Girls of Slender Means* (the number five), which subtly underscores, again, the element of the fantastic and the surreal. In this novel the emphasis is again on the number three. Before Annabel's face-saving press conference, there are three neighbors in the apartment (65); there were three guests left after the party (a journalist, a forgotten girl asleep on the bathroom floor, and a "small, sober, wiry Italian girl") (53); Gerda, an obnoxious daughter of the doctor who certifies Frederick's death, "stump[s] three steps closer to her mother as if to protect herself from Annabel" (64); the Christophers have moved back to Italy "at least for three years" (32); Annabel calls to check on her baby every three hours (35); Frederick waits "three weeks for the release of [Annabel's] film" to argue with her (20); and, finally, Frederick's funeral is at three o'clock (108).

The number pattern intensifies the sense of entrapment, of the glaring arti-ficiality of the "public image" in a hollow world with the fragile yet hard-baked surface of a shell.

Spark's first novel of the eighties, *Loitering with Intent* (1981), is a multilayered, cantilevered puzzle box, a kind of mirrored skyscraper demarcated by multiple levels of reality. Muriel Spark, the novelist, once again creates a novelist (here Fleur Talbot) who has written a book called *Warrender Chase*. So far, the pattern is familiar, a writer creating a writer. "Fleur takes a job helping the snobbish and, it transpires, spiritually predatory Sir Quentin Oliver to edit—indeed, to write—the memoirs of people who belong to his Autobiographical Association" (Treglown 36). Obviously, no writer can write another person's autobiography, but we now have a fictional writer (Fleur) writing fictionalized or improved accounts of the supposedly "real" lives of the Autobiographical Association members. Muriel Spark then explains that the association members have rejected the "lives" with which Spark has endowed them and, with Sir Quentin's encouragement, appropriated the lives of the characters in Fleur's book. In fact, "Sir Quentin uses a stolen proof of the novel as a blueprint" (Treglown 36) since he is dissatisfied with the prosaic "real" lives of his members. " 'Life' plagiarizes art in *Loitering with Intent*," and the members of Sir Quentin's circle, "a galare of the infirm and eccentric" (Treglown 36; see also *Memento Mori*) begin, one by one, to resemble the characters in Fleur's book, who are also sickly and zany. Sir Quentin, an evil impressario (Fleur calls him " 'a psychological Jack the Ripper' "), eventually dies in an automobile crash as has the Warrender Chase of Fleur's novel.

The reader accepts the idea that we have a writer (Spark) who creates a writer (Fleur), who then creates a set of characters (in *Warrender Chase*) who exchange personalities with a set of characters in Spark's novel *Loitering with Intent*. As a secondary theme there are two writers (Spark and Fleur), looking back on their experience as writers, and in this sense the novel is a double memoir. Fleur Talbot is by now a successful novelist who is recalling the events surrounding the completion of her first novel, *Warrender Chase*, in 1950. Spark is loitering with the intent of understanding her own career. *Loitering with Intent* "clearly stands in (as it were) a multiple solipsistic relation to Muriel Spark's *The Comforters*, published in 1957, which was about a character in a novel who has finished writing a study of the Novel and goes away to write a novel" (Treglown 36). Fleur claims that the entire account is true, and it is symptomatic of Spark's genius that her fictional characters are believable as interpreters of reality. As Fleur says,

> "While I recount what happened to me and what I did in 1949, it strikes me how much easier it is with characters in a novel than in real life. In a novel the author invents characters and arranges them in convenient order. Now that I come to write biographically I have to tell of whatever actually happened and whoever naturally turns up. The story of a life is a very informal party; there are no rules of precedence and hospitality, no invitations." (43)

It is important to note that the reader accepts Fleur as "real" and also believes her assertions that her fictional *Warrender Chase* characters are easier to deal with than the fictional people of Spark's *Loitering with Intent*.

Both sets of characters (in *Warrender Chase* and in *Loitering*) have an irritating, jarring quality about them, even those who are more innocuous than Sir Quentin. Velma Richmond says that "the novel presents an unmistakably Sparkian combination of peculiar characters, grotesques whose human frailties are exposed but also tolerated . . . until they become . . . menacing and dangerous" (156). Fleur says that Warrender Chase is " 'privately a sado-puritan who for a kind of hobby gathered together a group of people specially selected for their weakness and folly, and in whom he carefully planted and nourished a sense of terrible and unreal quiet' " (59). Sir Quentin, of course, a lunatic manipulator, does the same thing with the association members since he is Chase's mirror image. He plays Providence with the lives of others and in this is reminiscent of Jean Brodie (Little 177). But his members, unlike Brodie's students, are all mildly deranged, depressed, dyspeptic, or dotty. (Naturally, Fleur's friend, who is married to Fleur's bisexual lover, is named "Dottie." Dottie's husband's lover is a colorless, anxious poet by the name of Gray Mauser.) Again, the names are suggestive and they reinforce Spark's message. There is, too, a self-serving and vicious female housekeeper, Beryl Tims, descended from Georgina Hogg (*The Comforter*) and Mabel Pettigrew (*Memento Mori*). They are all mastering servants, although they are less Machiavellian and sinister than Lister in *Not to Disturb*. Mastering servants are a Sparkian reminder that reality becomes increasingly tenuous as the social order and the concomitant role definitions break down and that fantasy starts to look normal. The only entrancing and lovable character is Sir Quentin's mother, Lady Edwina, who is sure of nothing, including her bladder control, which is undependable at best. Edwina serves as Spark's symbol of reversal or contrariety in this novel. She is incontinent and apparently senile but Fleur recognizes that Edwina is the only clear-sighted character in the group. She is also the oldest character, but with the courtesy of a shrewd justice she outlives her vile and vindictive son.

Loitering with Intent is a central novel in the study of Spark's work. What is happening in the evolution of Muriel Spark is that all the patterns, that is, suggestive names, sexual deviates, mastering servants, litanies, writer and artist characters, emerge in this work. They are interwoven by Spark with her thematic concerns, that is, identity, reality, fantasy, sexuality. The patterns speak to the issue of technique, of how Spark does what she does. The themes exemplify Spark's concerns throughout her career from *The Comforters* to the present.

Spark's novel, *The Only Problem* (1984), uses for its central character another writer, this time a Canadian male, Harvey Gotham. Harvey has money so he can afford to spend his days ruminating about the plight of Job, the archetypal sufferer, and his false and unfeeling comforters. (As noted, Spark's first novel also alluded to this story.) Gotham is writing a monograph on the Book of Job since for him "the only problem" worth addressing is the dichotomy between a supposedly benevolent God and the "unspeakable sufferings of the world" (22).

Harvey, of course, identifies with Job; he too has problems: he has an amateur terrorist for a wife (she is also an adulteress), a lover (his wife's sister) who goes off with the father of his wife's illegitimate child, and so on. He is a man with no answers, but with plenty of questions, holed up in a little cottage in St. Die, France. What he wants now is solitude, privacy, and access to George de La Tour's sublime painting *Job Visited by his Wife*, which is housed in a museum at Epinal, a nearby town.

Harvey Gotham is one of Spark's most committed writers, but he differs from her other artist characters in a significant way. He is an observer, not part of the problem or the solution. He is "in fact, . . . a scholar, a fundamentalist; he is a man who questions and who is at the same time resigned—perhaps stoically, at any rate impassively, resigned—to receiving nothing in the way of affirmation, however serious the inquiry" (Brookner 1).

He does not expect answers because he knows there is no explanation for the suffering of Job—only acceptance of the fact. "As Emerson said of the fall of man, 'It is very unhappy, but too late to be helped' " (Dillard 75). And so he spends his days speculating about God's actions regarding Job and Job's submission to his suffering.

> What was the answer to Job's question: Job's question was, why does God cause me to suffer when I've done nothing to deserve it? Now, Job was in no doubt whatsoever that his sufferings came from God and from no other source. The very rapidity with which one calamity followed upon another, shattering Job's world, leaving him destitute, bereft and sick all in a short space of time, gave dramatic evidence that the cause was not natural but supernatural. The supernatural, with power to act so strongly and disastrously, could only, in Job's mind, be God. And we know he was right in the context of the book, because in the Prologue, you read specifically that it was God who brought up the subject of Job to Satan; it was God, in fact, who tempted Satan to torment Job, not Satan who tempted God. (107)

Like the biblical man, Harvey is visited by a succession of comforters, all of whom interrupt his peace and invade the emotional space that he has constructed as a silent wall between him and the world. (Muriel Spark has said in an interview that she lives on the continent because she has too many friends in England.)

The first visitor is another artist figure, Harvey's brother-in-law, Edward Jansen, the ex-cleric, now an actor who needs money. Edward is a role player who says that he "knows when [he's] playing a part and when [he's] not. It isn't every actor who knows the difference. The majority act better off stage than on" (17). Once again fantasy is thin; Edward reinvents himself every few years and he has now realized that he acted the part of a curate as a curate.

> In . . . days [past] Edward had been a curate, doing so well with church theatricals that he was in demand from other parishes up and down the country. It wasn't so very long before he realized he was an actor, not a curate, not a vicar in bud. (26)

He currently sees himself in the role of advocate for Harvey's wife, Effie, the sometime terrorist who is pregnant by an electronic salesman named Ernie Howe. (The electronics industry is responsible for the current profusion of duplicating devices so prevalent in Spark's work, which underscore the difference between reality and the fantastic, the real and the surreal.) Effie wants a divorce and as large a settlement as she can get; she thinks she deserves it since Harvey left her on the Autostrada when she stole two large chocolate bars from a snack bar as social protest. Effie is pure Muriel Spark, because she is a reversal of our expectations. No one expects a studious, serious scholar like Harvey to be married to an impulsive, counterculture type. Harvey is a man locked in the past of the Old Testament; Effie is a woman committed to destroying the past. Her underground name is Marion (a derivative of Mary!), she belongs to the Front de la Liberation de l'Europe which plans to free Europe from capitalism by bombing supermarkets. She is Spark's nomination for one of the beautiful people of the current scene whose moral sense is ugly, if topical. In a telephone interview with Herbert Mitgang, Spark admitted that Effie is an Italian Red Brigade type. She said that " 'terrorism sometimes begins with a generosity of spirit, but some people have built-in violence—almost as though there were a terrorist chromosome. Nobody can sympathize with the real terrorists' " (quoted in Brookner 1). In other words, Spark understands that violence is sometimes unrelated to causes, it is arbitrary, and in some people, innate.

Effie is a political dilitante—she plays at liberation, scurrying around the continent causing trouble and protesting the artificiality of life, of which she is a distinct part. For her life as a terrorist is a game and a role to play; she is similar in that sense to Edward. They are activists; Harvey is reclusive and passive. But Spark suggests that even passive people "have an effect on the natural greenery around them regardless of whether they lay hands on it or not; some people . . . induce fertility in their environment and some the desert, simply by psychic force" (14). Harvey is the type of postmodernist hero who creates a desert.

Ruth, sister of Effie, is the next visitor. She brings with her Effie's baby girl, Clara. (Velma Richmond points out that "Clara . . . means light") (173). She replaces her sister as Harvey's "wife." (This is ironic in view of the 'levirate law' of Deuteronomy 25:5–6) which says that "if a man died childless, his nearest kinsman was obligated to marry the widow and to consider the first born son as the dead man's heir" [Trawick 298].) Instead of Harvey being replaced by a brother, Effie is replaced by a sister. In Jewish tradition, the story of Ruth is the tale of the faithful follower, and this Ruth follows Effie.

Ruth is a religion lover; it is "her bread and butter" (The Only Problem 51), and, like many of Spark's female characters, she seems attracted to detached, ascetic, religious types who are not noticeably interested in sex. But she is not all generosity of spirit. She reminds Harvey that the wife of Job suffered, "but whoever wrote the book made nothing of her. Job deserved all he got" (51).

Ruth wants to be rid of Edmund now that he is an actor, and she seems curiously satisfied to live for awhile in a chateau that Harvey buys while he works in a simple cottage near the gate. Ruth is a comforter; she stays out of Harvey's way, is his sometime mistress, and takes care of Clara. "You feel safer when you're living with someone who's in the God-business" Harvey tells her (49). She soon leaves for an escapade with the same Ernie Howe who has impregnated her sister. So Harvey, in a sense, becomes Edward, Ruth replaces Effie with both Harvey and Ernie, and Edmund, her husband, has previously slept with Effie. In other Spark novels, her artist characters (see *The Comforters, Loitering*) become characters in the fictional world that they create. To some degree in *The Only Problem*, the characters are distorted reflections or doubles of each other.

The element of the fantastic reoccurs since Ruth and Effie look alike, and they both look like Job's wife as depicted in de La Tour's painting. Job's wife wears a turban; in the painting she leans over her troubled husband. When Effie lies dead in a Paris morgue, her turbaned head is bent at the same inquiring angle as that of Job's wife in the de La Tour picture in Epinal (177). This kind of doubling is a consistent pattern in the novels of Muriel Spark.

Harvey has other visitors—Nathan Fox, an androgynous type who likes house-work and babysitting, who is in love with Effie, and was a student of Ruth's. He has a degree in English literature which has apparently prepared him to do nothing. Nathan, too, has an interesting biblical name since in Hebrew, Nathan is "Nahum," a name that means "a comforter" (Andersen 40). In the Old Testament he is the prophet sent by God to rebuke David for his behavior with Bathsheba. Nathan Fox arrives during the Harvey-Edward-Ruth episode, but he is less a minister against sin than an audience for it. Perhaps Spark is saying that we are too immured in absurdity for effective rebuke.

There are visits from Harvey's English lawyer, Stewart Cooper, after Effie is arrested for killing a Parisian gendarme and the police arrive to question Harvey about his possible involvement. Even Aunt Pet, resident of Toronto, who is interested in family honor, not the suffering of Job, arrives. The point here is that Harvey Gotham, like Job, is besieged, and that the threads of his closely woven existence are unraveling. He seems powerless to stop the onslaught and becomes a character in an unfinished morality play about innocence and guilt, and good and evil. Gotham is experiencing firsthand the nature of suffering. He is, in fact, losing his sense of self, partly through his identification with Job, a man beset and bereaved, and through his spectacular neglect of material things, which is making the role of isolated thinker more familiar. He is "endlessly speculative and obsessed" (Philpott 80), like Job, who, Harvey says, " 'not only argued the problem of suffering, he suffered the problem of argument. And that is incurable' " (32). Harvey is insistent that Edward visit the crocodiles at the London zoo to confirm that the eyes of these "leviathans of Job" open vertically. (Harvey says that " 'it is written of Leviathan "his eyes are like the eyelids of the morning",' " (69) and the problem of "seeing," of understanding, becomes pervasive.)

Unfortunately, Harvey is not as intrinsically interesting a character as those previously created by Spark. "There is something attenuated about her rendition of Harvey's story. Her reluctance to probe her characters' psyches and motives is carried to an extreme here, as is her penchant for obliqueness" (Kakutani 34). Like many postmodernist characters, Harvey is offended by an intrusive society, he suffers from a self-imposed loneliness and a total identification with the role of victim, of man in contemporary society beset by the indignities of potential chaos. For instance, he thinks the police will not raid a house if they believe a baby is inside, so he hangs baby clothes on a clothesline outside his cottage. And, as fantastic as this idea seems, it works. An additional advantage is that it will deter "well-meaning women" from approaching him. Spark's characters like to find ways to be protected from the attractions of the opposite sex. (Caroline Rose in *The Comforters* can't sleep with her boyfriend anymore because she is now a Catholic; January Marlowe in *Robinson* picks one man to talk to on an airplane so the others will lose interest, and so on.)

However, if Harvey Gotham is not the colorful, quirky, maladjusted male we are used to in Spark, he is persistent, honest, and thoughtful—all qualities highly valued in characterizations by Spark. His friends and his comforters add to his burden; they have no answers to the agonizing and insolvable questions that consume him. "It is the very nature of friendship to prove inadequate to the demands of prolonged catastrophe" (Brookner 1). The more intrusive they become, the more immersed Harvey Gotham becomes in the inexplicable puzzle of Job. Finally, after three years of work on his monograph, the return of the pregnant Ruth with the child, Clara, and the death of Effie, Harvey emerges from his emotional retreat as Job emerged from his pain to live "one hundred forty years in the Lord's blessing (42:12–17)" (Richmond 171). Harvey's epiphany is that "the *Book of Job* will never come clear. It doesn't matter; it's a poem" (127); it is inscrutable. This seems to be a comment by Spark on much of contemporary life—the terrorists without and the terror within, the fragmenting sense of self, the inability to connect the individual with the universal experience. Velma Richmond says that "Spark balances Harvey's precise, studious analysis of the pivotal text of the Bible with the bizarre and disturbing details of modern life in which instability of personal relations and acts of terrorism are commonplace. . . . The only problem, human suffering, has not and will not change" (Richmond 175–176).

The Only Problem is a reflection of the mature vision of Muriel Spark. It was published twenty years after *The Comforters*, a novel in which Spark originally contemplated the nature of suffering and the failure of the sufferer to be comforted. This is a sad and somber novel; it leaves the religious reader to depend on faith, without evidence that the suffering represented by Job will dissipate in the foreseeable future. For the reader without a committed and positive religious outlook, it is Muriel Spark's subtle reminder that faith and devotion saved both Harvey Gotham and Job. Without these virtues the twentieth-century individual becomes, inevitably, one of the worthless and unknowing comforters, and part of the fantasy in Muriel Spark's world.

Works Cited

Andersen, Christopher P. *The Name Game*. New York: Simon and Schuster, 1977.

Bretall, Robert, ed. *A Kierkegaard Anthology*. 1946. Reprint. Princeton: Princeton University Press, 1973.

Brookner, Anita. "How Effie Made Him Suffer." *New York Times Book Review* 15 (July 1984): 1.

Dillard, Annie. *Living by Fiction*. New York: Harper Colophon, 1982.

Hubbard, Tom. "The Liberated Instant: Muriel Spark and the Short Story." *Muriel Spark: An Odd Capacity for Vision*. Ed. Alan Bold. Totowa: Barnes and Noble Books, 1984.

Jung, Carl. *Man and His Symbols*. New York: Dell Books, 1976.

Kakutani, Michiko. "Review of the *Only Problem* by Muriel Spark." *New York Times* 26 (June 1984): 34.

Little, Judy. *Comedy and the Woman Writer: Woolf, Spark and Feminism*. Lincoln: University of Nebraska Press, 1983.

Massie, Allan. "Calvinism and Catholicism in Muriel Spark." *Muriel Spark: An Odd Capacity for Vision*. Ed. Alan Bold. Totowa: Barnes and Noble Books, 1984.

Philpott, Joan. "Gift of Age." *Ms.* 14 (1984): 28.

Potter, Nancy A. J. "Muriel Spark: Transformer of the Commonplace." *Renascence* 17 (1965): 115.

Pullin, Faith. "Autonomy and Fabulation in the Fiction of Muriel Spark." *Muriel Spark: An Odd Capacity for Vision*. Ed. Alan Bold. Totowa: Barnes and Noble Books, 1984.

Richmond, Velma. "The Darkening Vision of Muriel Spark." *Critique* 15 (1973).

Rowe, Margaret Moan. *"Muriel Spark" Dictionary of Literary Biography* 15. Detroit: Gale Research Co., 1983.

Spark, Muriel. *The Comforters*. Philadelphia: J. B. Lippincott Co., 1957.

———. *Loitering with Intent*. England: Triad/Granda, 1982.

———. *The Only Problem*. New York: Putnam's, 1984.

———. *The Public Image*. New York: Knopf, 1968.

Trawick, Buckner B. *The Bible as Literature: The Old Testament and the Apocrypha*. New York: Harper and Row, 1970.

Treglown, Jeremy. "A Literary Life." *Times Literary Supplement* 22 (May 1981).

VI

The Fantastic and Science

Joel N. *Feimer*

Bram Stoker's *Dracula*: The Challenge of the Occult to Science, Reason, and Psychiatry

"There are more things in heaven and earth, Horatio, Than are dreamt of in your philosophy."

(Shakespeare, *Hamlet* 1.5.166–67)

Je pense donc je suis.

(Descartes, *Discours de la méthode* IV)

Bram Stoker's *Dracula*, which was written in 1897, summoned ancient histories of horror and age-old beliefs in occult phenomena to mount a challenge to the rising arrogance of reason, science, and psychiatry. What Stoker's novel objects to most is the insistence of the mainstream of modern thought on the reality of a quantifiable universe that excludes all possibility of the objective existence of the occult. The legend of Dracula can be traced to the early Renaissance figure of Vlad the Impaler, whose documented cruelties spawned Stoker's tale of preternatural horror (McNally and Florescu 34–81). The vampire itself has haunted humankind from its earliest consciousness of evil (Cavendish 9–10). Vampires originated with the ancient Mesopotamian *lilitû* and the classical lamia who sought the souls and life forces of ancient man, haunting his waking visions and nightmares.

In fact, the earliest extant references to vampire figures may be found in *The Epic of Gilgamesh*, parts of which date from the second millennium B.C. In a terrifying dream of the underworld to which he will soon travel in death, Enkidu is transported by a vampirelike man-bird to preview the horrors of the house of Erishkigal (Sandars 92; Heidel 60). In one of the related legends of Gilgamesh's youthful exploits, the hero exorcises the demoness Lilith from the goddess Inanna's sacred willow (Heidel 94). Thus, even in the most ancient literary records, vampires were forces to be reckoned with and were perceived as stealers of souls.

Such powerful occult phenomena and demonic enemies still had the power to capture the imaginations, if not the actual spirits, of the people of the Renaissance and the seventeenth century, as the evidence and punishments of the witch trials of that era attest (Trevor-Roper 90–192; Hughes 163–95). Hamlet's fear that his father's apparition might be some demon playing on his grief in order to tempt him to damnation (Shakespeare 625–34) was extremely plausible to Shakespeare's audience. Even the imperturbable Horatio has his skepticism silenced by the armed ghost of Hamlet's father. However, with the publication of his *Discourse on the Method* (1637), René Descartes assures the ultimate victory of the voice of reason and heralds a new age of enlightened empiricism that the modern field of psychiatry inherited.

Once Descartes observed that the only thing of which he could be certain was the fact that he was thinking (63), the existence of all entities that could not be verified, quantified, or otherwise measured by scientific instruments was cast into doubt. Among these discredited essences were God, the Devil and his legions, and a corresponding host of occult activities and principles. By degrees, as the centuries progressed, it become foolish and then certifiably pathological to believe in such things as gods, demons, witches, and vampires. Anyone who professed to do so was considered to be either a charlatan or delusional; in some cases, he or she could be both (Jung 26–46). Gestures and events that were once believed to be ominous have been reduced to the proverbial Freudian slip (Freud *A General Introduction to Psychoanalysis*, 59–65). More important, experiencing visions, hearing voices, and seeing apparitions have become signs of neuroses, or even full-blown psychotic episodes (Jung 9–20; Freud *A General Introduction*, 255–83, *Totem and Taboo*, 86–87). In modern psychiatric theory, all occult phenomena are denied any reality beyond that of a symptom or, at most, an idea that possesses substance either in the conscious or the unconscious of the human psyche (Jung 3–5).

The stance that the fledgling field of psychiatry had assumed, which was based upon its rejection of the phenomenological validity of occult experiences, was challenged immediately by Bram Stoker's *Dracula*. It is a significant coincidence that Stoker's novel was published only five years before Jung defended his medical dissertation before the Faculty of Medicine of the University of Zurich in 1902 (Jung 7, n.1). The principle subject of Jung's dissertation is a youthful Miss S. W., whose visionary experiences the good doctor diagnoses as delusional compensations for inadequacies in her life and hysterical responses to pressures and stresses of her adolescence (Jung 22–35). Later, as the force of her visions wanes, the unfortunate young woman attempts to restore it with chicanery and is eventually unmasked as a fraud (Jung 46). Significantly, Jung's ministrations to Miss S. W. seem to be as ineffectual as were those of John Seward to Renfield in Stoker's narrative. While the cause of Jung's ineffectuality cannot be determined from his presentation, that of Seward's inadequacy to help Renfield is blatantly manifest. Renfield is not delusional; there really is a demonic vampire who possesses him, an ancient evil presence against which theories of modern psychiatry are about as effective as a pistol against a *Tyrannosaurus rex*. As one critic has observed, the power of the novel to capture its audience "seems to depend on its very inexplicableness, its nonsensibleness to generate a kind of tension that is unrelieved and ultimately unexplained" (Twitchell *The Living Dead*, 133). It is precisely this quality of the inexplicable reality of Dracula that frustrates Seward's attempts to deal with the "illnesses" of Renfield and Lucy Westenra and makes the vampire so formidable.

Curiously, most of the recent criticism of *Dracula* has been directed at exploring psychoanalytic approaches to the book. The work of McNally and Florescu combines "biography" of Vlad Tepes, the historical inspiration of Stoker's vampire count, with rudimentary psychoanalysis (123). Twitchell (*The Living Dead* and *Dreadful Pleasures*) and Johnson (20–36) psychoanalyze the sexual orientation of Stoker's characters. Their work is important and contains its truths, but it ignores one significant, if not crucial, aspect of the novel. Psychiatry and psychoanalytic theory fail miserably when called upon to answer the challenge that Dracula delivers to modern consciousness. Stoker's *Dracula* combines history, legend, and occult lore (as well as, ironically, contemporary theories of the psyche) to create an arch-villain who, like the ghost of Hamlet's father, disrupts the rational certitudes and securities of the quantifiable universe upon which the rational bias of modern man insists (Twitchell *Dreadful Pleasures*, 137–42, *The Living Dead*, 48–54).

Count Dracula's story is in itself unbelievable, a *nosferatu* (undead) who was a participant in the atrocities of the violent ages of the early Renaissance, quiescent for centuries, but brooding and planning an invasion of the modern world from his forgotten corner of Eastern Europe. When his plans are laid, he rises like a fate to conquer an unwary world that has forgotten, to its peril, that such enormities as Dracula exist. The luminous reason of the Enlightenment had cast a shadow over such things as vampires, rendering them invisible but still potent.

The fact that modern Europe has become skeptical of ancient beliefs concerning the existence of such monsters is Dracula's greatest advantage. How can a world that does not acknowledge his possibility ever combat his reality? That the threat is a real one is demonstrated by the fact that Dracula is able to seduce his first victim, Lucy Westenra, into what he hopes will become an ever-growing legion of the undead in spite of the efforts and techniques of modern medicine to save her. Lucy, whose name means "light" or "bright one" ("light" in the West [Twitchell *Dreadful Pleasures*, 129]), changes form and nature as she is methodically, relentlessly possessed by this demon from a forgotten time and place (Twitchell *Dreadful Pleasures*, 134–35, *The Living Dead*, 136–37). From pure and lovable, a desirable young woman who inspires love and self-sacrifice in every man she meets (she receives three proposals of marriage in one day [Stoker 67], and four transfusions of life-sustaining human blood from the men who adore her [Stoker 169]), Lucy is metamorphosed into a wanton whose bestial desires and lust for blood drive her into the night to prey on helpless children. The change is first manifested in an unguarded moment as Lucy lay sleeping after one of her ordeals, "Whilst asleep she looked stronger, although more haggard, and her breathing was softer; her open mouth showed the pale gums drawn back from the teeth, which thus looked positively longer and sharper than usual; when she awoke, the softness of her eyes evidently changed the expression, for she looked her own self, though a dying one" (Stoker 172). In her completed form of one of the *nosferatu*, Lucy's pale purity has disappeared. Her hair is dark, her lips full and voluptuous, engorged with the substance of her unhallowed feasts. As one of her former suitors, the psychiatrist, John Seward, observes, "The sweetness was turned to adamantine, heartless cruelty, and the purity to voluptuous wantonness," and her eyes were "Lucy's eyes in form and colour; but Lucy's eyes unclean and full of hell-fire, instead of the pure and gentle orbs we knew" (Stoker 235). Thus, aspects of Lucy's form and spirit have been altered by the evil that has captured her.

Lucy's transformation is effected in spite of the vigilant presence of her physician, her fiancé, her mother and Dr. Abraham Van Helsing, the old scholar and man of universal knowledge who finally recognizes and accepts the reality of Lucy's bane. After Lucy's mother has unwittingly allowed the vampire access to her daughter, Van Helsing exclaims:

> "God! God! God! What have we done, what has this poor thing done, that we are so sore beset? Is there a fate amongst us still, set down from the pagan world of old, that such things must be and in such way? The poor mother, all unknowing and all for the best as she think, does such thing as lose her daughter body and soul. . . . Oh how we are beset! How are all the powers of the devils against us!" (Stoker 152)

The helplessness of Lucy's would-be protectors results from their experience with the ancient obscenity who stalks the present cloaked in the obscurity of modern ignorance.

Fortunately for Lucy's soul and for the rest of humankind, Van Helsing, the humanist with the far-ranging mind, discovers and accepts Dracula's presence. Van Helsing gathers the necessary information from ancient lore with which the vampire can be opposed, forms a league of six believers who turn the tables on Dracula and hound him from England, and finally directs the pursuit that hunts the vampire toward his lair in the wilds of Eastern Europe and exorcises him. With a combination of selfless dedication to the cause, knowledge of ancient lore, determination, and raw courage, Van Helsing's league of six purge Dracula's homeland of its evil and dispatch the count and his minions to a long-delayed confrontation with the Eternal Judge.

That is, in part, the bare outline of the story. Woven into Stoker's tale is an allegory of the dangers of rational skepticism and of too heavy a reliance on science and the quantifiable to explain the universe.

Apropos of this theme is the fact that one of the main characters and narrators of the story is Dr. John Seward, a psychiatrist who studies insanity as if it were only the result of some treatable disease. One of his most notable patients is a man named R. M. Renfield, who in medical terms is zoophagus; that is, he eats live things in the expectation that he will absorb his victims' life force directly and thus live forever (Stoker 72–73, 80–83). He begins with flies, progresses to spiders and birds, and plans on moving on to cats when he is finally balked by his physician, who has been carefully observing and monitoring Renfield's behavior. I should add at this point that Renfield's theory works only if he ingests his victims while they are still alive. One can only guess at what species Renfield will stop if he is left to continue. His insanity is an obscene parody of the promise of Christ to bestow eternal life on those of His faithful who partake in the communion of His body (for a discussion on the connection between vampire beliefs and Christian dogma, see Twitchell *The Living Dead*, 13–16). What Dr. Seward does not discover until almost too late (too late, indeed, for Renfield) is that his patient is not merely insane. Unlike Jung's Miss S. W., Renfield is neither delusional nor deceptive. He is possessed by the evil influence of Dracula, to whom he has sworn allegiance in return for the promise of a never-ending supply of ingestible life-forms (Stoker 122–24, 131–33).

This aspect of Stoker's novel is a direct challenge to the nascent study of the soul, psychology/psychiatry, which assumes a scientific stance in its approach. Science cannot assert that the soul is divine spark with celestial origins, or it moves from psychology to theology, from the presumed quantifiable-knowable to the mystical, where knowledge is predicated on a leap of faith. This inability of medical science to deal with the mystical and to acknowledge the actuality of the preternatural Dracula is the most real and present danger of the modern age that the novel *Dracula* exposes.

As Stoker attempts to demonstrate through his characterization of Van Helsing, it takes profound insight and great elasticity of mind to accept the presence of the demonic preternatural in the scientific modern world. As Van Helsing explains to his reluctant young colleague:

"You are a clever man, friend John; you reason well, and your wit is bold; but you are too prejudiced. You do not let your eyes see nor your ears hear, and that which is outside your daily life is not of account to you. Do you not think that there are things which you cannot understand; and yet which are; that some people see things that others cannot? But there are things old and new which must be contemplated by men's eyes, because they know—or think they know—some things which other men have told them. Ah, it's the fault of our silence that it wants to explain all; and if it explain not, then it says there is nothing to explain." (Stoker 213)

The arrogance of science cum psychiatry assumes the preternatural exists only as hysterical delusions of deranged psyches. There is always the threat that the acknowledgment of the objective presence of forces such as Dracula will bring charges of insanity to the proposer. The skeptical Seward comments on Van Helsing's diagnosis of Lucy's undead state and the prescribed treatment, " 'I wonder if his mind can have become in any way unhinged. Surely there must be *some* rational explanation of all these mysterious things' " (Stoker 227). With the courage of conviction that is supported by his acceptance of experience, Van Helsing leads his band of modern men and women of the scientific age first to accept the horrifying reality of Dracula, and then to proceed to gather the requisite data on the preternatural, ironically employing the techniques of scientific observation and painstaking research to formulate a plan of defense against this ancient demon from Transylvania.

Van Helsing and his five companions, Dr. Seward, Arthur Holmwood (Lucy's betrothed), Quincy Morris (the moral viking from the New World, another of Lucy's suitors), and Jonathan and Mina Harker (the last one of Dracula's intended brides), take up this impossible quest as if it were a fated mission. They dedicate themselves to the final annihilation of Dracula and his vampiric extended family. As the companions prepare their assault on evil, Van Helsing defines the dangers and describes the forces that have brought Dracula into the lives of these six people and, in a larger context, into a struggle for supremacy with the modern world:

> "I have told them how the measure of leaving his own barren land— barren of peoples—and coming to a new land where life of man teems till they are like the multitude of standing corn, was the work of centuries. Were another of the Un-dead, like him, to try to do what he has done, perhaps not all the centuries of the world that have been, or that will be, could aid him. With this one, all the forces of nature that are occult and deep and strong must have worked together in some wondrous way. The very place, where he has been alive, Un-dead for all these centuries, is full of strangeness of the geological and chemical world. There are deep caverns and fissures that reach none know whither. There have been volcanoes, some of whose openings still send out waters of strange properties, and gases to kill or make to vivify. Doubtless there is something magnetic or electric in some of these combinations of occult forces which work for the physical life in a strange way; and in himself were from the first some great qualities. In a hard and warlike time he was celebrate that he have more iron nerve, more subtle brain, more braver heart, than any man. In him some vital principle have in strange way found their utmost; and as his body keep strong and grow and thrive, so his brain grow too. All this without that diabolic aid which is surely to him; for it have to yield to powers that come from, and are, symbolic of good." (Stoker 354)

This is the novel's only concession to "naturalism," but what a strange naturalism it is. Occult forces recumbent in "caverns measureless to man" combine with the diabolical to produce this formidable enemy to man. However, Dracula is vulnerable to the symbols of redemption that God has made available to man through the sacrifice of Christ, and furthermore it is "God's own wish" that the six companions "have redeem one soul already, and we go out as the old knights of the Cross to redeem more" (Stoker 354, 355).

As one reads these words and ponders their implications, he realizes one of the primary purposes of Stoker's narrative. At the dawn of the age of psychiatry and the certitude of "normalcy," Bram Stoker was cautioning his contemporaries and their posterity against too rigorous insistence on the rational against the tyranny and arrogance of the normal. Such attitudes render the human perception of reality handicapped, fettered with presumption, with the assumption that it can be certain concerning the parameters of possibility. These limitations render humanity vulnerable to the palpable realities that they exclude from normal consciousness. In the light of Stoker's tale, the human soul is reduced to the psyche, to the grave peril of humankind.

Works Cited

Cavendish, Richard. *The Black Arts*. New York: Putnam, 1967.

Descartes, René. *Discourse on the Method*. *The Rationalists*. Trans. John Veitch. Garden City: Doubleday, 1962, 39–96.

Freud, Sigmund. *A General Introduction to Psychoanalysis*. 1924. Trans. Joan Riviere. Reprint. New York: Washington Square, 1960.

———. *Totem and Taboo*. Trans. James Strachey. New York: Norton, 1950.

Heidel, Alexander. *The Epic of Gilgamesh and Old Testament Parallels*. 1946. Reprint. Chicago: University of Chicago–Phoenix, 1963.

Hughes, Pennethorne. *Witchcraft*. 1952. Reprint. Baltimore: Penguin, 1970.

Johnson, Alan P. " 'Dual Life': The Status of Women in Stoker's *Dracula*." *Sexuality and Victorian Literature*. Ed. Don Richard Cox. Knoxville: University of Tennessee, 1984. 20–39.

Jung, Carl Gustav. *Psychiatry and the Occult*. Trans. R.F.C. Hull. Bollingen 20. Princeton: Princeton University Press, 1977.

McNally, Raymond T., and Radu Florescu. *In Search of Dracula: A True History of Dracula and Vampire Legends*. New York: Galahad Books, 1972.

Sandars, Nancy K., trans. *The Epic of Gilgamesh*. 1960. Reprint. New York: Penguin, 1972.

Shakespeare, William. *Hamlet*. *Shakespeare: The Complete Works*. Ed. G. B. Harrison. New York: Harcourt, 1948.

Stoker, Bram. *Dracula*. 1897. New York: Dell Laurel, 1965.

Trevor-Roper, H. R. "*The European Witch-Craze of the Sixteenth and Seventeenth Centuries*" and Other Essays. 1956. New York: Harper Torchbooks, 1969.

Twitchell, James B. *Dreadful Pleasures: An Anatomy of Modern Horror*. New York: Oxford, 1985.

———. *The Living Dead: A Study of the Vampire in American Romantic Literature*. Durham, N.C.: Duke University Press, 1981.

Gregory L. Zentz

Physics, Metaphysics, and Science Fiction: Shifting Paradigms for Science Fiction

One of the most common questions being asked about the field of science fiction today is, Why are there so few original new stories? One of the more common answers is that science has caught up with science fiction. That response would seem to be shortsighted. It is perhaps more accurate to say that science has caught up with the ability of language to talk about it. Scientists, especially physicists, are increasingly using metaphor, simile, analogy, and, sometimes, educated handwaving to describe new theories and discoveries.

In *The Tao of Physics*, Fritjof Capra elucidates the parallels between these new concepts and Eastern philosophical thought. In it, he suggests that one method of breaking through the logical, deterministic paradigms that our languages are based on is through adoption of a Zen Buddhist device called a koan. Koans accentuate the paradoxical nature of language. They employ metaphor, simile, and analogy, and often integrate nonsense, paradox, and contradiction, which encourages the mind to jump beyond the limitations of language itself.

Transcending these limits is valuable to physicists and, by extension, to science fiction writers. A study of Eastern philosophical thought would be an excellent way for a science fiction writer to gather insight into new ideas and ways of presenting the difficult and confusing new sciences.

Jules Verne wrote exciting, adventure-oriented fiction which tended to appeal to the nineteenth-century preoccupation with the marvels and possibilities of science. In *Hector Servadac, or Off on a Comet* (1877), he used the device of a convenient astronomer to give a description of the planets to a group of people riding a piece of comet-sundered earth, in effect educating them. In his *Underground City* (1877), he presents all that was known about the properties of coal, in effect educating an audience made receptive by the appeal of the adventure involved (Gunn 73).

We see science fiction being used effectively, if not intentionally, to educate people about classical mechanics. But what of the new physics? Albert Einstein, in 1905, introduced the special theory of relativity. In it he melds Newtonian mechanics and electrodynamics. In 1915 he introduced his general theory of relativity, working gravity into the special theory. He gained insights into how to do this through thought experiments which, without the benefit of mathematical interpretations, is difficult for the educated layperson of today to grasp—in the terms of conventional language.

The ramifications of Einstein's theory of relativity are innumerable, but perhaps one can get a feel for the subtle change in thinking that he brought about. All that was thought to be known as directly evident, self-presenting, true, or a priori, was altered and the concepts involved stepped out of the range of our normal, three-dimensional thinking. Alan Nourse, considering the concept of four dimensions as indicated in space-time, writes:

> We are reaching a point at which language cannot describe what is actually happening; the "language" of modern physics has become the language of mathematical analysis and nonverbal symbols. The physicists working on the frontiers of research literally cannot describe, explain, or even discuss their work in any language of words. Books . . . can only describe this work in terms of coarse generalities and inaccurate, inadequate, or sometimes misleading analogies. And it seems probable that the more the physicists' work impinges on our lives, the more difficult it will become for us even to grasp in terms of generalities what that work is all about. (Nourse 672)

Edward Harrison elucidates the historical perspective on this by writing in his book *Masks of the Universe* (1985):

> Throughout history devout people have felt convinced that their universe was the Universe, their mask the true face. . . . Then, within an ace of explaining everything worth explaining, the old and outworn universe dissolves in the ferment of social upheaval and transforms into a new and youthful universe full of challenge and expectation. (2)

The attempt at understanding the new physics concept of multiple dimensions, for example, is filled with difficult conceptual barriers that make the undertaking frustrating at best. This difficulty was anticipated by nineteenth-century mathematicians, who were already dealing theoretically with such concepts. In a humorous attempt at communicating descriptions of dimensions other than three, mathematician Edwin A. Abbott wrote the book *Flatland* (1884). In it, he describes a two-dimensional world with inhabitants struggling to conceive the "natural" three-dimensional world of common experience. The central character in Abbott's book tries to explain what we had discovered to be the third dimension:

> "[It is not] at all silly," said I, losing my temper; "here for example, I take this Square," and, at the word, I grasped a moveable Square, which was

lying at hand—"and I move it, you see, not Northward but—yes, I move it Upward—that is to say, Northward but I move it somewhere—not exactly like this, but somehow—" Here I brought my sentence to an inane conclusion (Abbott 114)

Isaac Asimov writes about *Flatland*, "Since we can easily imagine a Universe transcending Flatland, might there conceivably be some Universe transcending ours in which . . . " (Abbott xii).

Such logic, of course, breaks down in that argument, but such is the nature of the concepts. We have seen how someone in a two-dimensional world might attempt to speak of a three-dimensional world. How then might someone in a three-dimensional world speak of a fourth dimension? Let us consider time as the fourth dimension. The concept itself predates Einstein, and indeed he never felt that time was exactly like the other three dimensions we are familiar with, just that it functioned as a fourth dimension. In any event, there are a great many stories that utilize the concept of time travel previous to Einstein. Examples of this can be found in such works as *A Christmas Carol* (1843), by Charles Dickens; *A Tale of the Ragged Mountains* (1843), by Edgar Allen Poe; *The Clock that Went Backward* (1881), by Edward Page Mitchell; and *A Connecticut Yankee in King Arthur's Court* (1889), by Mark Twain. However, the first story to try to envision a device and scientific rationale for time travel is H. G. Wells's *The Time Machine* (1895).

Wells's attempt to explain time travel as a fourth dimension can be illustrated by the following passage from *The Time Machine*:

> "The geometry, for instance, they taught you at school is founded on a misconception. . . . Clearly," the Time Traveler proceeded, "any real body must have extension in *four* directions: it must have length, breadth, thickness, and—duration. . . . *There is no difference between time and any of the three dimensions of space except that our consciousness moves along it.* . . . Here is a popular scientific diagram, a weather record. This line I trace with my finger shows the movement of the barometer. Yesterday it was so high, yesterday night it fell, then this morning it rose again, and so gently upward to here. Surely the mercury did not trace this line in any of the dimensions of space generally recognized? But certainly it traced such a line, and that line, therefore, we must conclude was along the time dimension." (Wells 2–5)

Clearly, addressing some scientific concepts in an intelligible manner has been difficult since before the discovery of the new physics. Einstein's work on the photoelectric effect in 1905 built on Max Planck's earlier concept of radiant energy being composed of quanta. Einstein showed that light was indeed quantized into photons, thus bringing out the first great paradox of the new physics, the particle-wave nature of light. We later find that quantizing of things on the submicroscopic level becomes vital to many different concepts within the new physics.

Quantum mechanics was officially delineated in 1927 in what became known as the Copenhagen Interpretation of Quantum Mechanics, which claims, basically, to be an effective model that reflects what one will observe under given conditions. It works for all the experimental situations that we can devise, so it is useful. One begins to see a willingness to consider science as a modeling tool that doesn't necessarily reflect reality; this is much as Ptolemy, claiming that his epicycle universe did not need to reflect reality as long as it worked.

Regarding this, Zukav writes in *The Dancing Wu Li Masters* that "the rational part of our psyche, typified by science, began to merge again with that other part of us which we had ignored since the 1700s, our irrational side" (37).

The major players in the new physics emerged at that time and consisted of such names as Niels Bohr, Louis de Broglie, Erwin Schrodinger, Wolfgang Pauli, Werner Heisenberg, and Paul Dirac. They experienced many paradoxes with the new theory, not the most perplexing of which was the duality of light, being both a particle and a wave. They found the atom to be mostly empty space, with an electron's location relative to the nucleus a matter of mathematical probability rather than mechanistic certainty. Contradictions, paradoxes, probabilities, and duality of existence became common.

In combining all the new concepts of the atom, for example, Zukav finds that "atoms are hypothetical entities constructed to make experimental observations intelligible" (107).

Still, even before Einstein, one finds examples of the science fiction writer's intuition regarding the complexities of science that lay on the horizon. A good example of science fiction's prescience and descriptive abilities can be found before the formal formulation of quantum mechanics in Garrett P. Serviss's *A Columbus of Space* (1894):

> "[Just] a single grain of radium contains in its padlocked atoms energy enough to lift a million tons three hundred yards high. . . .
>
> [I tell you that] I've solved the mystery of the atoms. I'm sure you'll excuse me from explaining my method" (there was a little raillery in his manner), "but at least you can understand the plain statement that I've got unlimited power at my command." (5–9)

Despite the typical formula of the adventure variety of science fiction prevalent in the twenties, there were, nonetheless, attempts to deal with the new physics concepts by means other than merely asking the reader to suspend disbelief as Serviss does above. Maintaining the example of understanding time as a fourth dimension we see in *The Man Who Mastered Time*, by Ray Cummings, such descriptions as

You must think along entirely different lines, in terms of, I shall say, the new science. I mean that the actual reality underlying all the manifestations we experience is not temporal or spatial or material, but a blend of all three. It is we who, in our minds, have split up the original unity into three such supposedly different things as time, space and matter. . . . The mathematics language of science would bore you. Let me give you a popular illustration—an illustration, by the way, that I saw in print long before Einstein's theory was made public. For instance, think about this: A house has length, breadth and thickness. The house is matter, and it has three dimensions of space. . . . Could a house have any real existence if it did not exist for any time at all? (2–3)

Joseph Wood Crutch wrote about the way man viewed reality as follows:

Consistency with known facts and fruitful workability are . . . the only characteristics by which we would ever be able to recognize Truth if we found it. . . . Ptolemaic astronomy was "true" as long as it explained all known facts and proved fruitful so far as the regulation of the calendar and all the other uses to which it was put were concerned. . . . [Such a pragmatic point of view in] the hands of William James . . . became a defense of the rights of a will to believe—not, as seems sometimes to be assumed, whatever you would like to believe but whatever would be useful and *not inconsistent with the known facts.* [Italics added.] (145)

An excellent example of the "science as a useful model" philosophy is found when Isaac Asimov addressed the Cartesian division between the *I* and the world of experience, as elucidated by Krutch above, in his story "Reason" (1941). In it, he introduces a robot who was created to run a sophisticated solar energy collection station along with a human complement. The robot takes a crewman by surprise when he says:

"I began at one sure assumption I felt permitted to make. I, myself, exist, because I think—" Powell groaned, "Oh, Jupiter, a robot Descartes!" (Pohl 32)

Asimov continues with the robot proving that it couldn't have been made by men. It further rationalizes the existence of a Master who had to have made them instead and decides that in any event some facts should not be questioned too closely. When approached by the humans with the facts of the existence of the earth, planets, stars, and so forth, the robot responds:

"That He [the Master] supplied you with these laughable ideas and far-off worlds and people is, no doubt, for the best."

[Powell eventually responds.] "You can prove anything you want by coldly logical reason—if you pick the proper postulates." (Pohl 40–41)

In the end, the robots run the station flawlessly, let the *deluded* humans come and go at will, and harmlessly pursue their mechanical metaphysics. The argument for tolerating this is given by a pragmatic crewman in the following dialogue:

"How are we going to trust him [the robot] with the station if he doesn't believe in Earth?"
"Can he *handle* the station?"
"Yes, but—"
"Then what's the difference *what* he believes?" (Pohl 43)

One is reminded of Krutch's statement above that Ptolemaic astronomy was "true" as long as it explained all known facts and proved all the other uses to which it was put.

In the story "My Name is Legion" (1942), Lester del Rey addressed the new physics concept of four dimensions and its time-travel elements by inventing a machine made of "a few tubes, coils, condensers, two little things of my own, and perhaps five watts of power feeding in—no more" (Pohl 97).

However, rather than just asking the reader to suspend disbelief because it sounds scientific, he goes into an excellent justification, not for how the machine works but rather for why he can't explain it. This too is designed to make the reader feel more comfortable with his inability to comprehend the concept. In the story, Myers invents a machine which will bring thousands of duplicates of Hitler, younger and older versions, to the same temporal and spacial location. Hitler asks the scientist how the machine works and Meyers answers,

"Unless you can think in a plenum, my Leader, I can't explain. . . . Oh, mathematicians believe they can—but they think in symbols and terms, not in the reality. Only by thinking in the plenum itself can this be understood. . . ."
"What," the Leader wanted to know, "is a plenum?"
"A complete universe, stretching up and forward and sidewise—and durationally; the last being the difficulty. The plenum is—well, the composite whole of all that is and was and will be—it is everything and everywhen, all existing together as a unit, in which time does not move, but simply is, like length or thickness."
The Leader nodded doubtfully, vaguely aware that he seemed to understand, but did not. If the machine worked, though, what matter the reason? (Pohl 97)

In science fiction, analogy has often been resorted to in order to give the reader insight into a concept. A good example of analogy in talking about multiple dimensions, in this case where time is the fifth dimension and the fourth is a dimension existing at a right angle to the three spatial dimensions we are aware of, can be found in Arthur C. Clarke's story "Technical Error" (1946). In it he educates the reader through the device of having one of his characters putting two equal right triangles of paper on the surface of a table. He arranges them so they are mirror image to each other. He then flips one of them over, effectively moving the triangle through the third dimension, to make them identical and, "similarly, to change a solid, three-dimensional body, such as a man, into its analogue or mirror image, it must be rotated in a fourth dimension" (Pohl 249).

There are many other examples of science fiction writers grappling with difficult concepts in the new physics. What has sprung up, however, is general acceptance of certain terms and ideas used to talk about what is essentially impossible to discuss with conventional language. Such terms as hyperspace and time warps are almost permanent residents in the lexicon of the science fiction writer. They are often used in lieu of an explanation under the reasoning, perhaps, that a term has been explained so often that it's automatically accepted. It is more likely resorted to as means of avoiding having to invent, describe, or postulate new ways of circumventing the known limitations of science in order to make a story flow, especially since most ideas would seem to be fantasy due to the semantic limitations of the new physics. Technically oriented, or *hard*, science fiction readers often don't want to be exposed to pure fantasy.

In the words of Lester del Rey:

> A number of devices and conventions were adopted because they were necessary to avoid holding up everything in a story while time passed or an explanation could be found. Thus, special relativity makes flight at the speed of light or greater impossible. . . . That meant that a writer must either allow for decades or centuries of travel to reach another star—or he must find some way around the limitation of velocity.
>
> In early stories, considerable space was devoted to explain how rapid travel between stars was possible. Most of the methods boiled down to one, however: if faster-than-light travel through space was impossible, men had to find some kind of space where that rule didn't apply. Eventually, this was simply called hyperspace and became a conventional device used by most writers. The readers quickly accepted it, because the explanation for it all had been flanged up in previous stories. (del Rey 84–85)

We have looked at some of the aspects of the new physics and the types of language difficulties brought about in talking about such things as space-time and curved space. Yet space-time and curved space are just words that attempt to describe and can't really. It wasn't only dimensions and speed of light relativism that developed in the new physics; it was also the concepts of interconnectedness and wholeness.

The interconnectedness and holism of the new physics is illustrated by the Einstein-Podolsky-Rosen thought experiment. Two electrons with opposite spin values are separated. The spin value of either one is determined by the very act of measuring that spin value, thus the other's spin is determined the instant the first one is measured. We seemingly have instantaneous communication faster than the speed of light.

Einstein thought there were factors involved that we just were not aware of and that the limitation of the speed of light was real. Niels Bohr, quoted by Fritjof Capra in *The Tao of Physics* (1776), said, " 'The two-particle system is an indivisible whole, even if the particles are separated by a great distance; the system cannot be analyzed in terms of independent parts' " (Capra 303).

The readers of technical science fiction are unique to the masses in that many are effectively using hard science fiction as a method of lubricating their journey through the highly technical and often incomprehensible world of modern physics. A list of the areas of science that the hard science fiction writer has to work with now includes supersymmetry, supergravity, superstring theory, dimensional compactification, multidimensional theory, a fifth fundamental force, antimatter, quantum-relativistic atomic models, infinity, anthropic theory, a plethora of subatomic particles, singularities, and more. This list doesn't even include all the other sciences and opportunities therein.

Considering the new physics taxes the conventional Western way of evaluating and intellectualizing observations and theories. Eastern philosophical thought offers an entirely different way of evaluating the world about us. It is important to look at the outline of Eastern thought.

There are several formalized types of Eastern thought, with many shared concepts. They are Hinduism, Buddhism, and Chinese thought, consisting of Taoism and Confuscianism, with Zen, which utilizes elements of all.

Let us look at Zen carefully. Zen is a Japanese construct of Buddhist/Hinduist mysticism, Taoist naturalism, and Confucian practicality. Zen is only interested in the attainment of enlightenment, which is largely Buddhist in intent. Strong parallels to the new physics, however, are seen in its attitude to language. Capra says that, "More than any other school of Eastern mysticism, Zen is convinced that words can never express the ultimate truth." (108).

One of the Zen techniques of enlightenment is the use of koans. According to Capra,

> *Koans* are carefully devised non-sensical riddles which are meant to make the student of Zen realize the limitations of logic and reasoning in the most dramatic way. The irrational wording and paradoxical content of these riddles makes it impossible to solve them by thinking. They are designed precisely to stop the thought process and thus to make the student ready for the nonverbal experience of reality. (35)

There is no set formula for a koan, for by its very nature it must transcend conventional thought both in its own definition and in what it points to.

Philosopher D. T. Suzuki, writing in *An Introduction to Zen Buddhism* (1954), said that the Zen master Hakuin knew that

> ordinarily a sound is heard only when two hands are clapped, and in that sense no possible sound can come from one hand alone. Hakuin wants, however, to strike at the root of our everyday experience, which is constructed on a so-called scientific or logical basis. This fundamental over-throwing is necessary in order to build up a new order of things on the basis of Zen experience. . . . [The seeming nonsense of it is] meant to open up the secret chamber of the mind, where the devotees can find numberless treasures stored. . . . It is only intended to synthesize or transcend—which-ever expression you may choose—the dualism of the senses. So long as the mind is not free to perceive a sound product by one hand, it is limited and is divided against itself. (105–06)

Roderick Chisholm writes in *The Theory of Knowledge* about the importance of self-consistency to the theory of knowledge. Epistemology, of course, addresses the question of how we know what we know and to what degree we can know that we know. He indicates that the traditional Western philosophical sources are external perception, memory, self-awareness (reflection, or inner conscious-ness), and reason (Chisholm 122).

Zukav talks about what we know, or rather, what we think we know in the following passage:

> "Reality" is what we take to be true. What we take to be true is what we believe. What we believe is based upon our perceptions. What we perceive depends upon what we look for. What we look for depends upon what we think. What we think depends upon what we perceive. What we perceive determines what we believe. What we believe determines what we take to be true. What we take to be true is our reality. (310)

Upon more intensive study, what can be known eventually about the new physics may transcend traditional epistemic paradigms without being episte-mically inconsistent. If one realizes that to the Eastern philosopher reality has a very fluid structure, based upon a transcendent kind of experience as opposed to a purely analytical evaluation, then the interest in Eastern thought becomes clear. This interest affects both the physicist, who must evaluate what he or she sees, and the writer, who wishes to communicate the incommunicable.

The value of using koans as a descriptive tool in science fiction has been evaluated and used, as in physicist Gregory Benford's *In the Ocean of Night* (1977). Evaluating Benford's use of "nonsense as catalyst" requires reading the entire book. How might a quick, if somewhat simplistic, attempt at creating a koanlike explanation of a new physics concept appear, then?

A koan might be developed to introduce the contradictory wave and particle nature of light. For example, after giving a student, or reader, a good understanding of the wave nature of electromagnetic radiation and detailing the concepts of photons and quantized packets of energy, and after the student concentrates over time on both concepts, the student might then ask the question, Is light really an electromagnetic wave or is it actually a packet of quantized energy? The master (science fiction writer) might then answer with a powerful Yes!

The student, grounded in the comprehensible basics and not expecting a seemingly nonsensical answer, is challenged intellectually to transcend his logical, mechanistic thought patterns and could well come to a state of enlightenment regarding the reality of the particle-wave nature of light.

In a rush, the Joyceian stream of consciousness might progress in the reader's mind like this: The particle is a wave though it cannot be both, and the wave is a particle and impossible, and the particle has no mass and the wave is electromagnetic, and electromagnetics are waves having no mass, and the particle has no mass though energy is mass, so the paradox continues as electromagnetics are mass since mass is energy and a particle that cannot have mass, and they thus are united with the wave defining time so that time becomes mass at speed through vacuum that is empty, though vacuum is full of particles not existing, and where energy is not such that vacuum is where mass is not, but mass and energy are defined, then, by vacuum and vacuum exists not in reality, giving variations on a theme, being a phantom scar that drifts across the eye but will not keep still, unfocused, fleeting, leading finally to appreciation, not understanding, but empathy in transcendence defying language inexactly alluding to appreciation by others' insight Brahman *Dharmakaya* Tao, the Absolute!

Eastern thought has as its highest goal the attainment of the essential nature of the universe, Brahman, *Dharmakaya*, and Tao. The new physics seems to be striving for a similar essential. It is looking for the grand unification theory that many think will answer all the questions of physics. Physicists think they can find it by studying the first instant of the big bang, the great singularity. Paul Davies writes in *God and the New Physics* (1983) that this absolute knowledge "[will] follow from a magnificent mathematical theory that will encompass all of physics (in the reductionist sense) in one superlaw" (Davies 216).

Nourse quotes Dr. George Gamow, who said that while "there was still plenty of interesting and exciting work to be done in the physical sciences, there would probably be no great undiscovered areas of physics suddenly appearing for investigation" (Nourse 670).

That statement, however, is hotly disputed and may be dated due to recent developments in physics. Even so, there are many more parallels that can be derived between the new physics and Eastern thought. If physics is about to be unified, then it would seem that all aspects of existence would be unified and made intelligible. Davies acknowledges the difficulty of doing this through his use of the qualifier "reductionist" above. The unification of space-time, to the reductionist physicist, consists of a mathematical model. In the words of D. T. Suzuki,

> [To Eastern mystics, appreciation of space-time consists of] a state of complete dissolution where there is no more distinction between mind and body, subject and object. . . . We look around and perceive that . . . every object is related to every other object . . . not only spacially, but temporally. . . . As a fact of pure experience, there is no space without time, no time without space; they are interpenetrating. (158)

What is it that the Eastern mystic is seeing? Understanding the mystical perspective, accompanied by one's own knowledge of physics, could indeed give insight into how to get others to understand the seeming incomprehensibility of the new physics. The argument that since the new physics is seemingly mystical in its descriptive elements, and since Eastern philosophical thought is inherently mystical in its intent, then the two must have something in common, is of course invalid. What is valid is that people whose goal is to communicate in a language of words couched in the realm of practical experience that which seems to defy ready description might garner some insight into how best to communicate such concepts from thought systems that are based in paradox, enigma, contradiction, and nonsense.

No one knows for sure the direction that science or society will take in the upcoming years. If one accepts that the future will bring major revolutions in what we know and indeed in how we think (and there is no reason to think that we have reached any Hegelian apex of development in our societal, much less scientific, evolution) then the science fiction writer of today finds himself in the delightful position of being able to write during a time when science may soon lag far behind science fiction once again, much as the fanciful mythological fiction was replaced by Verne, Wells, and Serviss. Even so, if science fiction can address the mainstream of the new sciences without sacrificing what essentially defines it, then it can continue to act as a bodhisattva for a technically bewildered society, suffering the nausea of complexity, so close on the heels of the death of God. One asks if certain textbooks might not be better read and understood, even in teaching classical physics, if they were put in the vein of a science fiction story.

Still, so-called hard science fiction should incorporate speculation based on theories that are supported, or at least generally perceived, as reasonable possibilities based on current theory at the time it is written. Stumbling while walking the razor's edge separating science fiction and fantasy is easy, so it's best to keep in mind the constraining words of physicist Richard Morris:

> New ideas and new conceptions have been produced at such a prodigious rate that it is sometimes difficult to distinguish between scientific fact,

scientific speculation, and philosophical inquiry. As a result, the contemporary reader of books on the new physics is often either left bewildered or given the impression that certain speculative ideas have become more generally accepted than they really have (xii).

Nevertheless, Eastern thought appears to have much more in common with the new physics, in terms of its ability to describe and categorize, than our conventional Western semantics and logic systems by themselves. Just as physics is now seen to be a model of reality rather than a representation of it, so too, can Eastern thinking be conceived as a model, a kind of Rosetta stone, for the new physics.

It would seem, then, that an understanding and appreciation of Eastern philosophical thinking would be a good starting place for the enlightened science fiction writer to look for inspiration and guidance in formulating new descriptive tools, styles, and stories.

Works Cited

Abbott, Edwin A. *Flatland*. 1884. Reprint. New York: Harper & Row, 1983.

Benford, Gregory. *In The Ocean of Night*. 1972. Reprint. New York: Bantam, 1987.

Capra, Fritjof. *The Tao of Physics*. 1976. Revised. Boulder, Colo.: Bantam, 1984.

Chisolm, Roderick M. *Theory of Knowledge*. 1966. Englewood Cliffs, N.J.: Prentice-Hall, 1977.

Cummings, Ray. *The Man Who Mastered Time*. 1924. Reprint. New York: Arno, 1975.

Davies, Paul. *God and the New Physics*. New York: Simon and Schuster, 1983.

Del Rey, Lester. *The World of Science Fiction, 1926–1976*. New York: Garland, 1980.

Gunn, James. *Alternate Worlds*. Englewood Cliffs, N.J.: Prentice-Hall, 1975.

Harrison, Edward. *Masks of the Universe*. New York: Macmillan, 1985.

Krutch, Joseph Wood. *The Modern Temper*. 1929. New York: Harcourt Brace Jovanovich, 1957.

Morris, Richard. *The Nature of Reality*. New York: McGraw-Hill, 1987.

Nourse, Alan E. *Universe, Earth, and Atom: The Story of Physics*. New York: Harper & Row, 1969.

Pohl, Frederik, Martin Harry Greenberg, and Joseph Olander, eds. *Science Fiction of the 40's*. New York: Avon, 1978.

Serviss, Garrett P. *A Columbus of Space*. 1894. Reprint. Westport, Conn.: Hyperion, 1974.

Suzuki, D. T. *An Introduction to Zen Buddhism*. 1954. Reprint. New York: Grove Press, 1964.

Wells, H. G. *The Time Machine*. 1895. Reprint. New York: Ventura, 1980.

Zukav, Gary. *The Dancing Wu Li Masters*. 1979. Reprint. New York: Bantam, 1984.

VII

The Fantastic World—Space and Time

Ingeborg M. Kohn

The United States in Contemporary French Fiction: A Geography of the Fantastic

Europe's fascination with the Americas constitutes an important literary/artistic theme, especially in France, where, beginning with the Renaissance—from Montaigne to l'Abbé Prévost to Chateaubriand to Sartre to Robbe-Grillet, the geography of a continent has often become part of an *imaginaire du fantastique*.[1]

Two novels by important contemporary writers, Hervé Guibert's *Les Lubies d'Arthur* (1983) and Monique Wittig's *Virgile, Non* (1985) both published by the avant-garde *Les Editions de Minuit*, are proof that the tradition continues. They are two of the most recent examples of a telescoped, transcontinental metamorphosis; each text shows how, once again, the geography of the United States has been transformed into landscapes of the fantastic.

Ideally suited as their theoretical framework is Jean Baudrillard's *Amérique* (1986), a sociological study that elucidates concepts of comparative culture and sets out to prove that the United States is already a "utopie réalisée," a utopian realm unaware of having reached that status. This vision is based on a special valorization of geography; in his proposed "reading," or mapping of U.S. territories and its peoples, the concepts of surface and superficiality tend to blend into an etymological entity, a new reality of *hyperréalité*: "L'Amérique n'est ni un rêve, ni une réalité, c'est une hyperréalité" (neither dream nor reality, but a hyperreality).[2] Baudrillard's interpretation relies on a semiotic approach: he reads America's geography and demography as a system of signs constituting this hyperreality, and concludes that they spell impending doom:

> I have searched the future and already accomplished social catastrophe in geology, in the outward turning of depth witnessed by the striated spaces, in the formations of salt and stone, in the canyons into which tumble fossilized rivers, in those immense chasms of slowness, erosion and geology, and in the verticality of the megalopolis. This nuclear form, this future catastrophe, I knew of it in Paris. But in order to understand it, one must

make the journey, which realizes what Virilio calls the aesthetics of disappearance.[3]

Baudrillard also argues that Americans have become insensitive to the signs around them. Since we are constantly involved in shaping them (as well as being shaped by them), we are too close to distinctly perceive them; we are part of an ever-changing, constantly evolving sign system. He suggests that America's "truth" only becomes apparent to Europeans, since they can recognize here "le simulacre parfait, celui de l'immanence et de la transcription matérielle de toutes les valeurs" (the perfect simulacrum, that of the immanence and the material transcription of all values).[4]

That is why the protagonists of Guibert's and Wittig's texts are perfect examples with which to test Baudrillard's theories on hyperreality and simulation.[5] They are strangers in a strange land, travelers with no past and only a hypothesized future, free of intellectual ballast or any other baggage that could tie them to specific points of reference or origin. Both Arthur and the narrator of *Virgile, Non* (also called Wittig) are explorers for the sake of exploration.

The narrations of their encounters with American hyperreality also confirm Todorov's definitions concerning literature of the fantastic: it is the principle of indetermination, and a skillfully maintained hesitation between the real and the possible, that underlie and inform each novel. Guibert's hero Arthur and his lover-companion Bichon, Wittig's first-person narrator and her guide Manastabal have embarked on a journey into limited, identifiable geographical/national regions; it is their enterprise of revalorizing local particularities that creates new utopias of the grotesque and the sublime.

Their motive is the exploration of the mind; the literary vehicle is that old convention of the traveler in a strange land. Both texts attempt a mapping of the psyche, but their setting is fictional space defined by geographical boundaries. The tone is strictly apolitical, and there is no message or value judgment. The adventures of the narrators/protagonists, though bizarre, often seem rather insignificant; if their tales are impressive it is not so much because of *what* they experience, but because of a persistent foregrounding of visual elements, or rather because of *how* their settings/surroundings are perceived by them, and by the reactions they provoke.

Arthur and Bichon, the traveling companions in *Les Lubies d'Arthur* (Arthur's whims, or follies), have sailed from Canada around the world before reaching San Diego. But since a first encounter there proved its natives too inhospitable, they decide to make their entry to the United States from the Gulf of Mexico. After a failed attempt to Corpus Christi, that "vilain" (ugly, nasty) port, they continue their journey to Annapolis, where, unfortunately, not a single slip is available for mooring. They finally land in Halifax, Nova Scotia, and sell their boat to "une jeune fille fataliste." The fact that they travel all over the world before landing again in Canada is significant: the United States is saved for last, meaning that the most incredible of adventures takes place in its territory.

Their point of entry is along the Canadian border, which they cross in a bus headed for Montgomery, because "Arthur had heard that there one could buy a beautiful car cheaply" (71). Both the name of their destination, Montgomery, and the object of desire, a car, belong to the domain of the real; but ambiguity begins to cloud the picture as soon as the reader consults the atlas and realizes that geographical references are often very vague or misleading (there are six towns and more than two dozen counties in various states all called Montgomery).

Thus, a first element of the fantastic is the semantic aspect of America's geography—the naming and the renaming of places that evoke a feeling of recognition and déjà vu combined with a sense of confusion or even shock when one encounters the name (and even more so when one sees) places like Paris, Texas, or Moscow, Idaho.

Arthur and Bichon's effort to experience the vastness of the United States is rendered in terms unmeasurable by time; after having sailed around it, from San Diego to Halifax, their inland peregrinations also take place without clocks or calendars. Unorganized, yes; but not entirely at random. It seems that they are sufficiently intrigued by the phonetic and semantic qualities of America's geographic nomenclature to seek out and travel to certain places on the sole promise of a name, intrigued by the evocatory powers and random associations of ideas provoked by towns named Ogalalla, Kokomo, Crève-Coeur.

Montgomery is a disappointment; they arrive during the flood season (the only clue given that this might be Montgomery, Alabama, flooded by the Alabama River), not a good time to buy a car because the entire city is submerged by a tide of "carcasses d'automobiles" (71). It is for Arthur and Bichon a fantastic sight with mountains of abandoned cars, wrecks, or flattened chassis formerly stockpiled in salvage yards, now liberated by the surging flood waves, floating in the streets and parks of a city besieged by high water.

From Montgomery they travel to Devil's Lake, North Dakota, where they find the car of their dreams, an "old black tuf-tuf, generously banged-up, which sweated like a snail going downhill, but ran like a zebra going uphill" (71). Delighted with their purchase, they drive first to Kalamazoo, where they buy a magician's belongings (and his business license) at public auction, and then to Oklahoma City.

Now begins a most fascinating period. Arthur and Bichon find a manager, are initiated into the tricks of the magic trade, and then embark on a tour of triumphal performances, "from Halifax to Kokomo, from Moscow to Cobalt, from Eureka to Hannibal, from Racine to Seattle," leaving each city "the moment when their bluff was about to be called" (87).

They perform mostly at the desperate, sordid kind of places found in some rural areas, or big-city slums, the moth-eaten, crumbling theaters of small provincial towns, carny shows, circus barracks, sleazy seaside casinos. In this succession of scenes from America's low life, one sees Arthur and Bichon become adept at the worst type of hocus-pocus and hucksterism. They dream of riches because "Arthur wanted to become a true professional of magic, that is to say earn the most money possible" (87).

The other dream, or other American myth portrayed in the novel, is that of the car, which ultimately shatters Arthur's hopes, ends his career, and changes his life. It happens on July 13th: Bichon is killed in an automobile accident for which Arthur feels responsible. They had been driving along Blind River, between Indianapolis and "la Rivière du Loup" (Wolf River), when he lost control of the car, which plunged into a ravine. Again, it would be impossible to pinpoint the scene of the accident, since the geographic details are blurred. There is no Wolf River in the Indianapolis region, and Blind River is in Ontario, Canada.

Arthur escapes from the wreck, abandoning the car and its contents, including a small suitcase full of money, an indication that he has begun to lose his mind. The car explodes while he searches for Bichon, who has been thrown from the vehicle and dies impaled on the stripped trunk of a small fir tree. On his head has landed a glass disk (either a piece of windshield or a headlight) that gives him the appearance of wearing a halo. Arthur takes the glass, crushes it with a rock, and from then on carries the pieces in his hand—he never again opens his fist.

Grief-stricken, he begins a life of aimless wanderings, walking miles and miles barefoot, bearded, fist clenched. Hobo, transient, crazy man, and, soon, saint, or considered so. Subsisting on earth and leaves, he becomes sufficiently intrigued by the papers strewn along the roads to start a new hobby—or is it a crusade against highway littering? He begins to pick up papers, but he is selective, choosing only specimens that are still "a little strong and still a little virginal ("un peu forts et encore un peu vierges") (92), which he straps with strings around his chest. He carries them on his body like a medieval shield, or like an awful cataplasm; he is arming himself with a "coat" of totally useless "possessions," he becomes a visual metaphor of the bag man, or bag woman.

He also collects all the little pocket knives he can find in gutters and garbage cans. His plan is to eventually unroll or unfold that slowly accumulating crust of papers, to scrape it clean, and to inscribe something there with his "one good hand." But the message is never written—meaning either that there is none, or that it is impossible to express it in words. What he does leave behind is a self-portrait, painted shortly before his death.

During this period, he has slowly worked his way northward again, to the region around Halifax, having become both murderer and saint. A voice orders him to kill a village priest and to assume his functions. At first, he succeeds in fooling everyone; later he is found out and forced to flee after the parishioners discover that he has sucked the toes of the village idiot in the newly opened children's pedicure shop. He is caught, defrocked, undressed. But when the irate villagers tear his armor of dirty papers from his body, his left side starts to bleed as in examples of the stigmata; they recognize him as a Christ figure and fall to their knees.

He becomes their saint, and prisoner; his life changes for a brief time. As

cult figure and object of veneration, he is interviewed, photographed, interro-
gated, watched over jealously; he becomes a curiosity, a money-maker for the
community. But finally he escapes and wanders until he reaches a region where
he finds the strangest ground covering ever—rocklike, ocher-colored, shining—
which he scratches loose with his fingernail. He has struck gold.

Arthur, by now emaciated, nearly bald, and close to death, mixes this substance with the powdered residue of his blood in a glass tube the villagers had
used to collect his blood and sell it. Then he cuts his last remaining hairs, ties
them together with the frayed string that holds up his pants, and glues them
to the handle of a pocket knife whose blade he has broken off. After tearing
from his body what is left of the crust of papers, he washes them in a brook,
scrapes them, smooths them with his saliva, and flattens them into a canvas
with his fist. He takes the brush, the canvas, and the "paint" (the colored
powder made of the gold dust and dried blood particles, liquified with semen
from his testicles) and starts to paint his self-portrait. But he barely gets started;
death overtakes him after he has traced lines that "could have been part of an
eyelid" (117).

The author concludes that his body was never found, only this "painting."

Arthur, in following his "whims," covers thousands of miles, through rural
communities and urban centers, before he finally returns North and disappears;
Wittig's geography is much more restricted. Her traveler in *Virgile, Non* (also
called Wittig) explores only the city of San Francisco and surrounding beaches,
accompanied by the mysterious guide Manastabal. The first chapter announces
"un voyage tout ensemble classique et profane," advising the reader to expect
a confrontation of the classical and the profane. Manastabal's assignment is to
guide Wittig through a modern version of Dante's circles (a reenaction, or re-
creation, of the symbolic descent in the *Inferno*), from hell to paradise, to meet
the one who awaits her client in heaven, "celle qui t'attend au paradis" (10).

Their point of departure is not Dante's forest, but the wind-beaten, sandy
dunes of a deserted beach; a site located "in the middle of the earth" (8), causing
Wittig to wonder whether eventually she also will be carried across to some
point of entry by *her* Virgil—Manastabal, the ferocious looking, gun-toting,
tough woman who wears jeans.

Like Guibert's, Wittig's world is mostly a visual universe. The backdrop is
provided by the city of San Francisco, its referential framework a grid of street
and place names like Castro, Valencia, Dolores, the Mission District, Golden
Gate Park; but the sights of quaint row houses sloping up and down the hills
and other familiar vistas are distorted by the systematic projection and juxtaposition of a nowhere which could be hell, purgatory, or paradise. The anach-
ronisms of time and space set the tone for the outlandish scenes the two women
witness and at times participate in, a panorama of visions and events rendered
even more fantastic by the breakup of the *Divine Comedy*'s hierarchy. The
chronological order established by Dante (Hell, Purgatory, Paradise) has been
discarded; the two travelers find themselves going through regions that corre-

spond to alternate circles (from hell to limbo to paradise and back again)—until they finally reach the end, or summit, the kitchen of the angels ("la cuisine des anges") (136–38).

Nor are the various circles immediately identified as such. It is in a bar and pool hall (representing limbo), while drinking tequila, that Wittig inquires whether or not the harrowing experience just suffered in a laundromat corresponds to the first circle in hell—a question deemed unanswerable by Manastabal. Wittig, identifying herself as a lesbian, had provoked the rage of a crowd of women who were ready to attack and perhaps even kill her; but she was saved by the guide.

As in Guibert's novel, in which Arthur and Bichon are lovers, the theme of homosexuality in *Virgile, Non* is ever present but understated; in either text, the pairing of two men and two women could be interpreted to mean that "normal," heterosexual couples no longer "fit" into the fantastic surroundings or to emphasize the anachronistic aspect, that is, show that certain mentalities remain unaffected by change. In Wittig's novel, the analysis of gender becomes further complicated by the fact that the most interesting, most nightmarish scenes take place in various settings or "circles" which are populated by characters referred to simply as "âmes" (souls), a female gender noun in French. But there is no doubt that the souls in hell are all women, and the tormentors men; such as in the scene (or circle) of the leashes, set in a park where "souls" are caught like dogs, and then apparently disciplined, or "trained," or in the circle of the shooting galleries, where "souls," naked to the waist, their thoraxes cut open, serve as targets for the amateur sharpshooters trying to hit the bull's eye—the exposed heart (26–29, 89–92).

Another nightmarish vision is the scene taking place in and around "le palais de la bouffe," place of the great banquet hall (129–32). To reach it, one must pass through a square planted with avocado, orange, lemon, and baobab trees, but this complex is surrounded by a zone where bushes, trees, and all other vegetation has been completely defoliated, burned, or otherwise destroyed: this is the environment where "souls" live, in the "cabanes" (huts or shacks). Again, gender is indicated by the use of pronouns. "Elles" are the souls who are led by "ils" (the guards) to the great banquet hall in order to look at and smell the variety and abundance of food set out on tables. Guards, armed with whips and rifles, keep the starving souls at a distance; if one of them, desperate or crazed by the spectacle, dares to make a dash for one of the tables, she is whipped or shot. After this "ceremony," the souls are led out of the building and back to their dwellings. The land surrounding them has been deliberately made into a scorched earth zone so that the guards (in their towers) can closely monitor the souls and make sure that no one sneaks into the palace or finds anything edible outdoors.

At sundown, the "show" continues. Now they ("ils"—the men) arrive in their trucks, enter the palace, and begin to eat and drink noisily. The scraping of plates, the sounds of bottles being opened and glasses being filled, lips smacking and all the other noises of a joyous meal are amplified, broadcast by loud-speakers, and piped into the souls' dwellings. At the end of the meal, they are once more led into the palace and allowed to devour what is left: bones, car-tilages, skins, gristles, peelings, cold blobs of grease—sometimes on plates filled with vomit, cigarette ashes, or food chewed and spat out.

This scene, set in a no-man's-land resembling a battle zone with its miserable dwellings and its close proximity to buildings that symbolize great wealth, are a reminder of the anonymous ghetto areas that exist in most big cities, trans-formed into an allegorized remembrance; whereas in other passages, such as the description of a great annual parade (53–57), the background and the event itself are immediately recognizable as being particular to San Francisco.

To contrast and thereby emphasize the fantastic element of this event (which very much resembles the annual Halloween parade), there are precise references to geographic landmarks such as City Hall, the Castro district, San Francisco Bay, as well as a description of gaily decorated streets bordered by rows of houses, their facades painted mostly blue, white, and dark red. The paraders, all "souls" again (the female "âmes"), are grotesquely costumed; some are wearing tall feathers attached to their heads and/or buttocks, or rabbits' ears and tails (Playboy bunnies?). Those who belong to "various pornographic institutions, either public or private," wear chains around their ankles and wrists; some are tattooed; many of them are dressed in evening gowns which are publicity devices, advertising brands of beer, refrigerators, cars. In this circle of hell, those who have come to watch are all "ils" again, called the "enemy," a defiant, hostile, armed crowd of men ready to attack the paraders.

In some circles, the population is entirely made up of "elles." Such is the scene in the park at the end of Dolores Avenue, an elevated site from which one can see, at a distance, the outline of the old Mission's adobe buildings. This is where the "foire aux richesses" takes place, the wealth fair (60–64). Everything is available there, and it's all free—all the goods obtained by women through "plunder, theft, looting, pirating." They are displayed in a gigantic open market, everything from livestock to motor vehicles to postal sacks full of bank notes (dollars, of course), jewelry, food, clothing, tools, machinery and appliances, musical and other instruments, and even large containers of a white, extremely fine powdery substance (never named—but identified as being as good as gold or dollars, obviously cocaine). All these "recuperated" goods are available to "those who need them." Wittig wants an Appaloosa horse, but is rebuked by Manastabal who reminds her that they are not in a "western"—she does not need a horse in hell. So she settles for "a fistful of dollars."

Another circle where women are found exclusively is the region around "le lac du chagrin" (the lake of grief and sorrow), meeting place of the suicides (72–82). As in every circle of hell, there is a strong, biting wind sweeping the sand dunes, lashing out at Wittig, at her guide, and at the weeping "souls" walking about. They all wear long, purple, braided cotton cords around their necks; when two of them meet, they deeply bow to each other (in a kind of salute as exchanged by the opponents before a karate match), and then proceed to pull on the partner's cord until they have strangled each other.

Most of the circles represent regions in Hell; only four of them, called "les limbes" (limbo), represent purgatory. They are recognizable as the interiors of bars, cafes, pool halls, where Wittig (always drinking tequila) and Manastabal stop to reflect on what they have just seen. Six of the circles exemplify fragmentary visions of paradise—the most obtuse, the most cryptic of scenes that combine into a land of gentle breezes, aromatic odors, delightful music (what is heard is "l'opéra des gueuses," or opera of the harridans), territories where Wittig catches glimpses of the "angel" who waits for her in paradise. Their reunion takes place in the last chapter, entitled "la cuisine des anges" (the kitchen of angels). Again, the location could be narrowed down geographically, since the site commands a view of the bay and Golden Gate bridge. It depicts a joyous scene, in which angels arriving on their motorcycles (allusion to Hell's Angels?) are greeted by choristers chanting "Soupe, belle soupe du soir" (Soup, beautiful evening soup); perhaps an allusion to soup kitchens, or a wink at Lewis Carroll's equally fantastic Wonderland. In a distance, there is a small band of angels playing under a stand of pine trees—no lutes, harps, or cymbals, but clarinets, saxophones and drums. Other angels are busily preparing a feast in the vast open-air kitchen. The vision ends with the description of a procession, angels carrying in and then arranging baskets and crates of fresh fruit, vegetables, berries, and nuts in a courtyard, while an angel sounds the trumpet, announcing that everything is ready for "la cuisine des anges."

Both Guibert and Wittig have already created landscapes of the fantastic in some of their previous works; the reason why these novels are specifically set in the United States could be to emphasize, or problematize, the notion of space in literature, that is, the idea of space as cult and culture. Again, Baudrillard's Amérique points out that we live in a country dominated by a democratic culture of space ("une culture démocratique de l'espace"), where our concept of space (psychological or inner space, as well as the environment, including outer space) has created tolerance but also a growing indifference.

What Arthur and Wittig see in their American surroundings, and their interpretations of how they are perceived, are not just textual variations of the classical French genre of the traveler's tales (le récit d'aventures), that disjointed narrative type made famous by Lesage's Gil Blas or Voltaire's Candide, a mode still going strong in the recent past with New Novelist Robert Pinget's Graal Flibuste.

Arthur's "whims" (the yearning for self-gratification) remain unfulfilled. His dream of a beautiful car, of becoming an American-style magician (that is, making lots of money), and of living happily with Bichon, literally becomes lost in space—a prelude to the hero's own pathetic end and mysterious disappearance. His allusions to our national blights, obsessions, and idiosyncrasies are not presented from an ideological point of view, but rather as functions of geography that become landscapes of the fantastic, a fitting background to frame Arthur's experiences in America's "hyperreality." Wittig's account of her journey up and down the hills of San Francisco uses the lesbian theme as a leitmotiv (though less pronounced than in her two previous novels, *Les Guérillères* and *Le Corps lesbien*); her adaptation of Dante's allegorical journey also includes a random sampling of events and circumstances typically American. Her choice of San Francisco as the geographical site might have been influenced by its vertical dimensions; she creates a fantastic atmosphere by using (mostly nocturnal) views of the city and of the surrounding beaches as settings for the heroine's adventures.

To pose the question once again, why the United States?

Voyage of self-discovery, says Baudrillard. Europe can no longer learn from itself nor understand itself. Today, it looks toward America with the same mythical and analytical exaltation that once made its scholars study ancient civilizations—and with the same passion and prejudices. It is here, he insists, that one must look for "l'idéaltype de la fin de notre culture"; because from the American life-style (determined by and determining, our notion of space) will be abstracted "le tableau analytique complet" (the complete analytical picture) of "la fin de nos valeurs" (Baudrillard 21). This life-style, which Baudrillard interprets as utopian and sees as a revolution already accomplished, must be experienced in situ in order to appreciate the *envergure* (breadth, or spread) created by its geographical and mental dimensions. Only then can outsiders realize how, and to what extent, its shock waves (or fallout) have already reached and contaminated Europe.

Guibert's novel ends tragically; Arthur dies, poor, alone, and exhausted. Wittig's has a happy ending, she finds paradise, a land of plenty, where her personal "angel" awaits her.

America: Heaven or Hell?

In my reading, that which makes it "either/or" are neither Kierkegaardian notions of dread nor any other metaphysical or ideological considerations, but the authors' interpretations, their visions of a continent's geographical particularities. They have succeeded in showing us the mystery, the fantasy, and the "unreal" of American reality. Viewing us from abroad, through the prisms of their mental structures, they metamorphose real space, mythologize identifiable sites, and transform them into a dazzling panorama, into landscapes of the fantastic.

Notes

1. For example, Montaigne's essay "Des Cannibales," in *Essays*; l'Abbé Prévost's novel *Manon Lescaut*; Chateaubriand's *René*; Sartre's play *La P. . . respectueuse*; New Novelist Robbe-Grillet's *Pour une Revolution à New York*.

2. My translation. Baudrillard 57–58.

3. My translation.

J'ai cherché la catastrophe future et révolue du social dans la géologie, dans ce retournement de la profondeur dont témoignent les espaces striés, les reliefs de sel et de pierre, les canyons où descend la rivière fossile, l'abîme immémorial de lenteur que sont l'érosion et la géologie, jusque dans la verticalité des mégalopoles.

Cette forme nucléaire, cette catastrophe future, je savais tout cela à Paris. Mais pour la comprendre, il faut prendre la forme du voyage, qui réalise ce que Virilio dit être l'esthétique de la disparition. (Baudrillard 16–18)

4. My translation. Baudrillard 57–58.

5. Baudrillard's theory of le *simulacre*, or simulation: the substitution of signs of the real for the real. See also Jean Baudrillard, *Simulations*, trans. Paul Foss, Paul Patton, and Philip Beitchman (New York: Semiotext[e], 1983).

Works Cited

Baudrillard, Jean. *Amérique*. Paris: Grasset, 1986.

Guibert, Hervé. *Les Aventures singulières*. Paris: Gallimard, 1982.

———. *Les Lubies d'Arthur*. Paris: Seuil, 1983.

———. *Voyage avec deux enfants*. Paris: Gallimard, 1982.

Pinget, Robert. *Great Flibuste*. Paris: Editions de Minuit, 1964.

Wittig, Monique. *Le Corps lesbien*. Paris: Seuil, 1972.

———. *Les Guerillères*. Paris: Gallimard, 1969.

———. *Virgile, Non*. Paris: Seuil, 1985.

Jack G. Voller

Todorov among the Gothics: Structuring the Supernatural Moment

Tzvetan Todorov's well-known theory of the fantastic has some equally well-known and much-belabored limitations. Since its appearance, Todorov's schema has been questioned by scholars of the fantastic on the extreme narrowness of its central genre, the dualistic assumptions of its structuralism, and its inability (or refusal) to account for twentieth-century fantasy. Although I agree with many of these corrections, I do not seek to add to them. What I propose, rather, is to apply Todorov's basic model or structure to Gothic supernaturalism—an application that will permit important discriminations between the various modes of Gothic literature at the same time that it enables greater acknowledgment of Gothicism's social and historical value.

Todorov's study provides a useful point of departure because the Gothic supernatural experience is structurally cognate with the Todorovian moment of hesitation. Both involve a movement from mental equilibrium and epistemological security to a condition of profound uncertainty, to a moment of emotional and intellectual trauma that is followed by either validation of the original theory of knowledge or explosion of it. Todorov explains the process thus:

> In a world which is indeed our world, the one we know, a world without devils, sylphides, or vampires, there occurs an event which cannot be explained by the laws of this same familiar world. The person who experiences the event must opt for one of two possible solutions: either he is the victim of an illusion of the senses, of a product of the imagination—and laws of the world then remain what they are; or else the event has indeed taken place, it is an integral part of reality—but then this reality is controlled by laws unknown to us (25).

A correspondent structure informs the supernatural moment in Gothic text, but to appreciate the significance of this we need remind ourselves that this literary structure was first elaborated neither by Todorov nor by the Gothic novelists. The basic pattern of movement from certainty to trauma to subsequent recovery is the pattern of an aesthetic concept that dominated eighteenth- and early nineteenth-century literary thought and practice: I refer, of course, to the sublime.

Richard Payne Knight's formulation of the sublime experience may be taken, for the moment, as representative:

> All sublime feelings are . . . feelings of exultation and expansion of the mind, tending to rapture and enthusiasm; and whether they be excited by sympathy with external objects, or arise from the internal operations of the mind, they are still of the same nature. In grasping at infinity, the mind exercises the powers . . . of multiplying without end; and, in so doing, it expands and exalts itself, by which means its feelings and sentiments become sublime (367–68).

This experiential structure was elaborated by eighteenth-century thinkers as an intellectual and aesthetic stratagem enabling the pursuit of transcendence and recovery of the experience of God. Full discussion of this important aspect of sublimity is beyond the scope of this paper, but it has been ably demonstrated by Ernest Tuveson, Marjorie Hope Nicholson, David Morris, and Thomas Weiskel, among others.[1]

Although it occurs late in the sublime's greatest moment of popularity—in 1810 to be precise—Payne Knight's understanding of the experience is a traditional one. For John Dennis, Lord Shaftesbury, Thomas Reid, Knight and others, sublimity's expansion of the mind encounters or generates some feeling of spiritual consolation; this is followed by a return to the prior condition of being once the sublime experience is past. For this traditional sublimity, the correlation with Todorov's system is not dramatically evident, for there is no choice required of the mind either during or after the sublime experience: prior intellectual and emotional stability is simply and automatically recovered. There is no uncertainty; there are no options. There are, however, other interpretations of the sublime.

Knight's aesthetic is a polemic response to Edmond Burke's vastly influential theory of the sublime, a theory which shifted the experience of sublimity to a secular foundation. Traditionally, the sublime depended for its power upon the fact that it intimated the greatness and omnipotence of God, but this is not the case with the Burkean sublime, which understands sublimity to be a more purely physiological and aesthetic experience. On different grounds, Kant's sublime also shifts toward the secular, but because of its lack of influence on Gothic writers I must here pass over Kantian sublimity. Burke's interpretation of the concept, with its well-known insistence on terror as the basis of the sublime, became the dominant one in the popular mind of the late eighteenth century, largely because of its enthusiastic adoption by the writers of Gothic fiction.[2]

Burke found that the sublime generated a "state of the soul, in which all its motions are suspended, with some degree of horror. In this case the mind is so entirely filled with its object, that it cannot entertain any other, nor by consequence reason on that object which employs it. Hence arises the great power of the sublime, that far from being produced by them, it anticipates our reasonings, and hurries us on by an irresistible force" (57). Burke, uninterested in the supernatural in either its religious or Gothic sense, is always hurried back to the real world, that empiric domain where the "reasonings" always reassert control. He has abandoned the religious foundation of sublime terror that his predecessor John Dennis so vigorously advocated earlier in the century, yet Burke is no metaphysical daredevil. His empiricism and implicit Christianity never admit of epistemological doubt.

Gothic fiction, developing out of a number of eighteenth-century genres, incorporated into its emotional and narrative structures Burke's understanding of the sublime. This confluence of sublime theory and supernaturalism created what I call the supernatural sublime, a term that permits us to indicate its structural and emotional character at the same time that it marks a departure from earlier understandings of sublimity.

In an age that M. H. Abrams has identified as one of "progressive secularization,"[3] Gothic fiction did not always find that the sublime intimates the presence of God; at the same time, Gothic fiction often rejected a purely rational or empirical worldview.[4] Gothic literature, we know, is frequently populated by ghosts and devils, yet God is often absent. The supernatural sublime, then—at least in its more radical expressions, and this distinction is important—leads us beyond both traditional and Burkean sublimity. The expansion of the mind in the moment of supernatural horror does not lead one's thoughts to God, nor, given textual insistence on the supra-rational nature of the experience, is Burkean theory always an adequate intellectual refuge. Gothicism forges its own version of the sublime, one that, like Todorov's schema, foregrounds a moment of uncertainty or suspension. Raising its investigation of transcendent possibility to the highest register, the supernatural sublime becomes, like Todorov's fantastic-uncanny or fantastic-marvellous, a movement away from certainty, a movement that cannot be endured or sustained.

Both the Todorovian hesitation and the supernatural moment are dissipated in one of two trajectories of recovery. (I am excluding for the moment the Todorovian fantastic, that small genre for which the moment of hesitation continues beyond the text.) What we might call the conservative recovery in Todorov is that made by the uncanny, in which the hesitation is resolved by the disclosure that the "supernatural" was in fact only the result of misperception or error; prior theories of knowledge remain intact. The second category of recovery, which I term the radical, is Todorov's marvellous, which identifies the supernatural as such, thereby rendering previous epistemologies invalid.

Gothic supernaturalism may be structured in analogous fashion, its moment of supernatural encounter resolved by either strategy. Yet, unlike Todorov, I do not find that the final status of the supernatural is as important as the metaphysical consequence of that ontological determination. Supernatural or Gothic sublimity, after all, is a direct descendant of the conventional sublime, and we would do well not to ignore the metaphysical dimensions which carry over from one to the other.

One of Gothicism's modes of recovery from the supernatural endorses a conservative or traditional knowledge, and therefore corresponds (albeit on another level) to Todorov's fantastic-uncanny, in which the moment of hesitation is resolved in support of established laws of nature. The second Gothic mode is akin to the fantastic-marvellous, even though some of its works contain no supernaturalism, for it constitutes an insistence on the failure and inadequacy of received knowledge. (Todorov's fantastic, with its emphasis on the impossibility of certain knowledge, is aligned with this second category.)

This taxonomy is still slightly more complex, however, for in Gothic fiction, each mode of return may be expressed in either natural or supernatural texts. For example, in that conservative mode corresponding to Todorov's uncanny, we find Radcliffe's *Mysteries of Udolpho* keeping company with Walpole's *Castle of Otranto*. In the radical mode, akin to Todorov's marvellous, are texts such as Brockden Brown's *Wieland* and Lewis's *The Monk*. What matters is not the presence of ghosts (and, therefore, not ontology), but the use of supernatural or quasi-supernatural imagery to address questions with implications beyond those of a reader's or character's belief.

The first of these Gothic modes, cognate with Todorov's fantastic-uncanny, presents a conservative return, one in support of conventional moral or spiritual systems, as is true of the traditional sublime. Unlike Todorov's fantastic-uncanny, however, there are two strains of this conservatism, best represented by the novels of Ann Radcliffe and Clara Reeve. Radcliffe's productions may be located comfortably in Todorov's uncanny, for their supernaturalism is always finally excluded by rational explanation. Reeve employs genuine supernatural elements in *The Old English Baron* (1788), but this is a work in which a rigorous privileging of social, moral, and religious convention denies admission to Gothicism's anxious despair or revolutionary undercurrents. (To only a slightly lesser degree is this true of *Otranto*.) This validation of received wisdom allies the work with Radcliffe's novels, which are similarly conservative.[5] Both Reeve and Radcliffe vigorously insist on the ethical and metaphysical sufficiency of Christian thought.

The second mode of recovery from the supernatural encounter rejects these traditional consolations, for it finds either that the supernatural *does* exist (and without the familial benevolence of Reeve's ghosts or the heavenly connections of Walpole's), or that, as in the works of Hawthorne, Brown or Poe, heightened or unusual experience of "natural" phenomena—that is, the uncanny—demonstrates that received intellectual and spiritual wisdom are inadequate for assessing and responding to the complexities of the post-Enlightenment universe, if indeed response is possible at all.

In this second mode, the mind's recovery from its moment of encounter brings not consolation but terror. The sense of participation in a benevolent oneness that attends traditional sublimity is exchanged for a sense of despair, for an overpowering horror at the discovery that metaphysical consolation is problematic at best, if not utterly unobtainable. In *The Idea of the Holy* (1917), Rudolph Otto asserts that "representations of spirits and similar conceptions" are "early modes" of the desire to rationalize or account for religious mystery, and that they serve only to weaken or deaden the experience of that mystery (27). This, as regards the Gothic, is doubly inappropriate. Not only is the supernatural sublime a relatively late mode of what may be termed spiritual inquiry, the sense of lifelessness that for Otto characterizes investigation of this sort proceeds not from the incapacity of the signifiers, but from a perceived absence of anything positive or vital to be signified. The Gothic supernatural sublime reaches after a God who has become a *Deus absconditus*.

This is an appropriate point at which to illustrate the working of the supernatural sublime. It will be possible to move directly to the radical mode, for both strains of the conservative mode are, I believe, more readily understood, and what I have said of them already should sufficiently indicate their operation and nature.

The radical mode, however, is more complex, and in order to illustrate fully its operation I will concentrate on one well-known text, an example of the radical mode's supernatural strain, trusting that this discussion will cast light enough to suggest how the natural strain of the radical mode might work. My study-text is the Bleeding Nun episode from Lewis's *The Monk* (1795).

Readers of the novel will recall that the young cavalier Raymond is in love with Agnes; she, promised by her parents to the religious life, is under close guard in the castle of German relatives. To effect an elopement, Agnes plans to disguise herself as the spectral Bleeding Nun, a ghostly figure who every five years leaves her haunted chamber to spend an hour outside the castle walls.

Lewis carefully plans for this episode, for he seeks to elevate, by contrast with disbelief, the emotional register at the moment of the Nun's introduction. Agnes explicitly scorns belief in what she dismisses as "superstition," yet we will see that superstition suddenly becomes consonant with reality, that traditional formulations of knowledge (which declare ghosts to be impossible) become inoperative, the boundaries of possibility—even of nature itself—uncertain. By deploying superstition against a smug rationality, Lewis deliberately invites us to consider the larger implications of his supernaturalism.

Raymond's emotional state, heightened in anticipation of meeting the disguised Agnes, proves crucial to the episode's supernaturalism. " 'My bosom beat high with hope and expectation,' " he tells us, as it appears his desire to escape with Agnes will finally be realized. When "the lovely Ghost" emerges from the castle, Raymond rushes to it, uttering the following doggerel declaration of his love:

> "Agnes! Agnes! Thou art mine!
> Agnes! Agnes! I am thine!
> In my veins while blood shall roll,
> Thou art mine!
> I am thine!
> Thine my body! Thine my soul!" (155–56).

This drastic language of promise and possession binds Raymond to the ghostly Nun, although he does not discover the true ontological status of his "lovely Ghost" until the following night, due to a carriage accident and his subsequent unconsciousness.

When the Nun reappears to Raymond on the following night she first lifts her veil, disclosing the "haggard" and "bloodless" features of "an animated Corse" (160). This is the precise moment at which the supernatural encounter begins; the consequences of it reveal very clearly the operation of those principles I have identified as central to the supernatural sublime:

> I gazed upon the Spectre with horror too great to be described. My blood was frozen in my veins. I would have called for aid, but the sound expired, ere it could pass my lips. My nerves were bound up, in impotence, and I remained in the same attitude inanimate as a Statue. . . . Her eyes were fixed earnestly upon mine: They seemed endowed with the property of the Rattle-snake's, for I strove in vain to look off her. . . . In this attitude She remained for a whole long hour without speaking or moving; nor was I able to do either (160).

Her appointed hour having passed, the Nun departs after kissing Raymond and echoing his declaration of love. His response to her departure marks a very literal recovery from the suspension that characterizes the supernatural moment:

> Till that moment the faculties of my body had been all suspended; Those of my mind alone had been waking. The charm now ceased to operate: The blood which had been frozen in my veins rushed back to my heart with violence: I uttered a deep groan, and sank lifeless upon my pillow (161).

This is a near-perfect example of the supernatural sublime. The intensity of emotion with which the supernatural is confronted generates a moment of hesitation and uncertainty, a Burkean suspension of the motions of the soul. Raymond tells us his mind had remained "waking," but this means only that it avoided unconsciousness. No intellection occurs during the encounter; there is only rudimentary sensory awareness.

Lewis has rendered, literally and with precision, the Burkean moment of suspension, that sense of helplessness that must occur if sublimity is to intimate the presence of a transcendent object. But for the supernatural sublime there is no subsequent mental operation (conscious or otherwise) which constructs or intimates the divine. Raymond's only response to this and subsequent appearances of the Nun is to become further engulfed by the terror she inspires: "Far from growing accustomed to the Ghost, every succeeding visit inspired me with greater horror. Her idea pursued me continually, and I became the prey of habitual melancholy" (163).

As long as he is visited by the spectral Nun, Raymond is powerless to resume his life—that is, return to the woman for whom the Bleeding Nun is a demonic substitute—yet we need not see these visits as a series of supernatural moments. They are, rather, one prolonged moment, the duration of which emphasizes its effect. This points out what cannot be considered here, that the supernatural sublime may structure entire narratives as well as particular moments.[6] Since this is so, we may move to the last of Raymond's encounters with the Nun in order to assess fully the implications of this episode of the supernatural sublime.

At first it appears the recovery may be conservative, an endorsement of Christian metaphysics, for Raymond is aided by the Wandering Jew. Only he possesses the power to help Raymond, he claims, and he is, of course, a thoroughly Christian figure.

Or is he? The Wandering Jew is familiar from Christian myth, to be sure, and part of his narrative and thematic value involves his association with Christianity, for he exorcises the Bleeding Nun, whose nocturnal terrorizing has its origins in her transgression of Christian morality. Yet we must ask ourselves if this is sufficient to determine the episode's metaphysical tenor.

Our answer must be negative. While the Wandering Jew serves to end the supernatural moment—to close off the space of helplessness that threatens to swallow Raymond (and it is a narrative hiatus as well as one in Raymond's life)—he does not determine the direction of Raymond's recovery from that moment. Conventional Christianity supplies the novel's imagery as well as some of the moral reference points that enable us to say that Ambrosio's actions are "wrong," but in the final analysis it does not determine the novel's metaphysical implications. If it did, Christian theological precepts would inform the novel's supernatural moments, but this is not the case. In the recovery from this supernatural moment, there is no consequent movement toward divinity. The moment of helplessness does *not* prompt the mind to construe perceived absence or indifference as evidence of a transcendent presence; in *The Monk*, supernatural sublimity uncovers only horror—a horror that is never transformed by the mind, but only dissipated by the text.

The "terror and detestation" that the sight of the Wandering Jew and the cross on his forehead inspire in Raymond may be related to their status as signifiers of divine retribution, but the implications of this theological terror are never considered, its possibilities never invoked in the working out of the novel's moral, sexual, and metaphysical dramas. The means of laying the Bleeding Nun to rest are discovered by the Wandering Jew, but while he is eminently capable of inspiring fear and terror in those who observe him, he does not inspire that emotional or spiritual countermovement that is a necessary condition of the traditional sublime. Indeed, Lewis abruptly truncates the episode, as though he wishes to dismiss the Wandering Jew as promptly as possible once his narrative role has been played. After hearing the history of the Nun, Raymond (demonstrating remarkable obtuseness) inquires into that of the Wandering Jew himself. Told he will hear the story the following day, Raymond is content; the Wandering Jew takes the opportunity to vanish from both town and narrative without a trace.

Lorenzo, to whom Raymond has been telling this story, interrupts to marvel that his friend was unable to ascertain the identity of "the mysterious Stranger." Reporting that his uncle, the Cardinal-Duke, identified the man as the Wandering Jew, Raymond remarks, with an astonishing complacence, "For my own part I am inclined to adopt the only solution which offers itself to this riddle. I return to the narrative from which I have digressed" (177).

These are not the words of a man who has undergone a transcendent experience. The narrative to which he returns is that of his recuperation and of his return to the castle where Agnes was imprisoned. In one sentence, Raymond tells of burying the remains of the woman whose ghost had tormented him (this being the condition of the peace arranged by the Wandering Jew), and he turns then to the story of his continued pursuit of Agnes. The Bleeding Nun and any implications of her appearance or banishment are forgotten as quickly as her bones.

The mere fact that Christian supernaturals appear in this text—and in other radical Gothic novels—is not evidence that a transcendent deity informs the spiritual context of the work. It is in fact the *absence* of deity that such presence articulates, as we have just seen. In the Gothic world of the radical return, whether the sublimity is supernatural or not, it never occurs either to characters or authors to ask after God.

Todorov, concerned primarily with intergeneric relationships, and explicitly avoiding the question of "meaning," finds ontological determination a sufficient basis for his theory. If we shift Todorov's concern with ontology and epistemological hesitation to the metaphysical implications of these—a shift authorized by Gothicism's appropriation of the sublime—we find in Gothic fiction a coherent yet multivalent genre, and we may dispense with the generic fragmentation required by Todorov's schema. We also uncover further evidence that Gothic fiction is much more than the literature of emotional titillation, sexual frustration, or concern over the French Revolution: the concept of the supernatural sublime contributes to our growing appreciation of the Gothic as a literature of spiritual disquiet.

Notes

1. Marjorie Hope Nicholson, *Mountain Gloom and Mountain Glory: The Development of the Aesthetics of the Infinite*, Ithaca, N.Y.: Cornell University Press, 1959; Ernest Tuveson, "Space, Deity, and the 'Natural Sublime,' " *Modern Language Quarterly* 12 (1951): 20–38; David B. Morris, *The Religious Sublime: Christian Poetry and Critical Tradition in Eighteenth-Century England*, Lexington: University Press of Kentucky, 1972; Thomas Weiskel, *The Romantic Sublime: Studies in the Structure and Psychology of Transcendence*, Baltimore: Johns Hopkins University Press, 1976. The best general study of the sublime remains Samuel Holt Monk, *The Sublime: A Study of Critical Theories in Thirteenth-Century England*, New York: MLA, 1935; also useful is Walter J. Hipple's *The Beautiful, The Sublime, and the Picturesque in Eighteenth-Century British Aesthetic Theory*, Carbondale: Southern Illinois University Press, 1957.

2. For the influence of Burkean theory on Gothic authors, see David B. Morris, "Gothic Sublimity," *New Literary History* 16 (1985): 299–319; and Carrol Fry, "The Concept of the Sublime in Eighteenth-Century Gothic Fiction," *Mankato Studies in English* 1 (1966): 31–44. Radcliffe, perhaps the most popular Gothic novelist, was strongly influenced by Burke's *Enquiry*. See Malcolm Ware, *Sublimity in the Novels of Ann Radcliffe*, Copenhagen: Ejnar Munksgaard, 1963; Anne Radcliffe herself in a posthumous article (taken from the preface of her posthumous *Glaston de Blondville*) in the *New Monthly Magazine and Literary Journal* 16 (1826): 149–50; her *Journey through Holland and the Western Frontier of Germany*, (Dublin: Printed by W. Poter for P. Wogan, 1975); and Samuel H. Monk, op. cit., 218.

3. See M. H. Abrams, *Natural Supernaturalism: Tradition and Revolution in Romantic Literature*, New York: Norton, 1971. 13. On the nineteenth-century displacement of dogma, see also J. Hillis Miller, *The Disappearance of God: Five Nineteenth-Century Writers*, Cambridge: Belknap-Harvard, 1963.

4. See, for example, Peter Brooks, "Virtue and Terror: *The Monk*," *English Literary History* 40 (1973): 249–63.

5. A thorough examination of Radcliffe's conservatism is conducted by David Durrant, "Ann Radcliffe and the Conservative Gothic," *Studies in English Literature 1500–1900* 22 (1982): 519–30.

6. If we imagine certain Gothic texts as greatly expanded moments, we may readily see how the supernatural sublime has applications to larger narrative structures. A work such as *The Mysteries of Udolpho* features a young heroine whose idyllic childhood is disrupted by a series of traumatic events, chief among them her sojourns in two haunted houses, Udolpho and Chateau-le-Blanc. The supernaturalism of these episodes is of course eventually dispelled, and, recovering from all the tribulations which beset her, Emily returns to a new idyll in her childhood home. The pattern of the conservative supernatural sublime has here structured the entire three-volume text. Such a pattern is far from indigenous to Gothic or even fantastic works, to be sure, but we are justified in considering this an application of the supernatural sublime because the period of suspension is caused or signalled by the use of supernatural images and tropes.

Works Cited

Burke, Edmond. *A Philosophical Inquiry into the Origin of our Ideas of the Sublime and Beautiful*. 1759. Ed. J. T. Boulton, 2nd ed. New York: Columbia University Press, 1958.

Knight, Richard Payne. *An Analytical Inquiry into the Principles of Taste.* 1808. 4th ed. Westmead: Gregg International, 1972.

Lewis, Matthew G. *The Monk.* 1795. Ed. Howard Anderson. London: Oxford University Press, 1981.

Otto, Rudolph. *The Idea of the Holy: An Inquiry into the Non-Rational Factor in the Idea of the Divine and Its Relation to the Rational.* 1917. Trans. John W. Harvey, 2nd ed. London: Oxford University Press, 1957.

Todorov, Tzvetan. *The Fantastic: A Structural Approach to a Literary Genre.* Trans. Richard Howard. Cleveland: Case Western Reserve University Press, 1973.

David M. Miller

Mommy Fortuna's Ontological Plenum: The Fantasy of Plenitude

Peter Beagle's *The Last Unicorn* conspires in mankind's ancient hope that the universe contains creatures better and wiser than ourselves, and in the human dread of a dark, nether symmetry in the chain of being: bright Ariel above, rude Caliban below, mankind at the balance point, darkly wise and rudely great. Like most fantasy, *Unicorn* assumes an ontological plenitude with man in the middle: morally, physically, intellectually, spiritually. The interdependence of links in the chain of being projects man's potential for good and evil far beyond anything he has yet achieved. Thus no situation can ever be purely personal, no ethical decision purely situational. The universe is on its way from *gonos* to *telos*. Everything is hooked into everything else, everything changes, no change is without consequence.

In short, *The Last Unicorn* is a high fantasy, and such fantasies, whether of joy or terror, insist that mankind is not alone. Perhaps in past times fantasy was the play of a firm belief system. Perhaps for the last hundred years that has not been the case. But the lure of ontological plenitude has never really faded, and we have never ceased to respond to great authors who people their universes with beings both more and less than human: Homer, Dante, Shakespeare, and Milton are cases in point. Witness Tolkien's continuing audience. There seems reason to hope that similar fantasies will continue to be written—to challenge, to reassure, and to delight generations yet unborn. Even when literary fashion pushes fantasy from center stage, it never really goes away. Its most recent oppressor, realism, is now itself devalued, and the hundred-year-old axiom— serious fiction equals realism—grows quaint.

The emergence of various post-modern theories and fictions, though they scorn high fantasy, has had the effect of allowing fantasy out of the ghetto. At least two sorts of fantasies have already emerged: "metafiction" and the "fantastic" (Waugh; Todorov).

The "fantastic" has always been an important, if minor, aspect of both fantasy and realism. A "fantastic" character's perceptions are, by definition, indeterminate, and realism frequently gains for a moment the power of fantasy without losing its own soul by tracing supranatural trailings through imperfect (diseased) perception—Uncle Charlie's pink elephants, Little Sue's imaginary friend. Conversely, fantasy has often coddled its more literal-minded readers by employing the fantastic as a relief valve for overtaxed credulity: "and lo, it was but a dream."

"Metafiction" finesses both problems by turning ontology and epistemology back upon language and referentiality back upon fiction. In one sense, metafiction makes indeterminacy the norm as it shifts referentiality to textuality.

My premise—a major distinction between fantasy and realism is that fantasy posits a "vertical" ontological plenitude that realism either denies or flattens into a "horizontal" multiplicity—places both "fantastic" and "meta" fiction as phenomena of the margin. They are aligned with realism in their skepticism concerning being, and with fantasy in their admission of worlds beyond the psychologically and materialistically real.

The carnival episode in Peter Beagle's *The Last Unicorn*—set between an intertextual Butterfly and a metafictional Captain Cully—is a convenient miniature in which to investigate the interaction between fantasy and the fantastic (Beagle 49–57). "Creatures of night," the carnival sign says, "brought to Light." But it is not initially clear whether the "night" referred to is the habitat of beings from other ontological niches or merely the opaque screen upon which psychological bogies are projected.

Mommy's carnival has nine exhibits divided into three sets. Each exhibit has a real and a fantasy dimension. The outer ring has five real creatures: a run-of-the-mill dog and four mildly exotic tropical animals: ape, lion, boa constrictor, and crocodile. The second set, a triad within the outer ring, presents a physically unexceptional spider, an undisguisable real harpy, and a unicorn who must be disguised as a unicorn if she is not to be seen as a white mare. At the center sits Mommy—an obsessive antiquarian amid her curiosities. Mommy herself is perhaps the most intriguing exhibit of all.

Before examining the 5–3–1 mandala of the carnival in such fashion as to suggest the role fantasy seems to be playing in various sorts of postmodern literature, I wish to establish a distinction between fantasy and the fantastic that is not prejudicial to ontological fantasy. Such a distinction is perhaps the major point of this essay.[1]

In distinguishing between fantasy and the fantastic, I find myself unable to avoid two clumsy and overtechnical terms: ontology and epistemology. To say "being" and "knowing" implies both too much and too little. To speak of "stimulus" and "response" is equally misleading. I shall be grateful when proper terms are suggested. In the meantime, the very ugliness of the terms may prove an advantage.

In an "ontological fantasy," characters from "our" niche interact with sentient beings from other niches, as in Shakespeare's *The Tempest* and Tolkien's *The*

Lord of the Rings. The reader is not at liberty to doubt the existence of trolls, orcs, and elves, even if a character within the fiction does. Often the interaction borders on the sacred, as in Hamlet's encounter with his father's ghost. Walter M. Miller, Jr., in a passage from *A Canticle for Leibowitz*, makes a clear distinction between ontological and epistemological fantasy. Dr. Cors and Abbot Zerchi are debating the merits of euthanasia. The skeptical doctor speaks,

> "If I thought I had such a thing as a soul, and that there was an angry God in Heaven, I might agree with you."
> Abbot Zerchi smiled thinly. "You don't *have* a soul, Doctor. You *are* a soul. You *have* a body temporarily." (W. M. Miller 242)

Given leisure from hagiography, the abbot might enjoy an ontological fantasy. Dr. Cors might read an epistemological fantasy, though he would likely prefer psychological realism.

The issue need not be so overtly religious, but because ontological fiction is concerned with the proper unfolding of being, those who utterly deny archetypes and essences, providence and fate, gods and souls, may, I suspect, have little sympathy for ontologically based fantasy. At least some of the misunderstandings may be ideologically rooted (Zipes; Kolbenschlag; Brooke-Rose).

An ontological fantasy set in a world bursting with multiform creatures, for example, Spenser's *Faery Queene*, contrasts sharply with an epistemological fantasy, marked by a solitary consciousness solipsising the illusory world on/in which it broods, such as Poe's "Bernice."

Epistemological fantasy foregrounds problems in knowing, and at its extreme asserts that epistemology *is* ontology, or what would be ontology if there were such a thing as ontology, which there isn't, for instance, Barth's *Lost in the Funhouse*. Fantastic narrative is one long moment of doubt in which an insufficiently gifted, underinformed, overstressed "hero" attempts, unsuccessfully, to solve questions that are forever beyond his competence, as in Golding's *Pincher Martin*. Complex dramatic and romantic ironies are everywhere, and the reader is implicated in the generative dance of doubting. Each step consists of and evolves from a transitory epistemological moment that dissolves as the next crystallizes: the old *mise en abyme* (J. H. Miller). The likely upshot is yet another confrontation with a painfully ubiquitous paradox: a speaker who can't communicate and won't shut up. In such fantasies, essence is a wish, being an accident, and valid reference an *impossibility*, for example, Pynchon's *V*.

So? *Cogito ergo sum*. The mind is its own place, right? Nothing but well and fair. Except that somehow the character-reader-critic is never able to quite do away with those damn ontological longings—precisely because epistemology, like dwarf fire-magic, has got to have some *thing* to work on. And if the reader could give up ontology, there would then be nothing for epistemology to process: the game won is done. If everything is projection, then nothing is projection.

We should not forget the most stunning instance of this conundrum: how painfully and with what consequence Milton's Satan fails to learn that lesson.

The "acts" of Mommy Fortuna's Midnight Carnival are mounted in such fashion as to feed the ontological appetites of the rubes, but the "narrative" shows the reader the rubes' responses to the exhibits, not the exhibits themselves. The initial "action" of the episode is a series of fumbled problems in knowing: the rubes encounter disguise, delusion, projection, illusion, reality, and epiphany. So strong is their desire for plenitude that they see a monster in every cage, *whether it's there or not.*

When the reader is allowed to look into the cages instead of at the rubes, he finds that the cages are not empty, though he is not so gullible as to see the rubes' mythological monsters. At least not at first.

But when the unicorn (who is the reader's guide to reality) sees both what is and what is not there, the reader must do likewise or quit reading (D. M. Miller). The rubes' responses, which had seemed hysterical reactions to their own projected fears, suddenly function as affective tracings of real unknowns. Like the unicorn, the reader can see both the "real" and the "illusory" simultaneously and distinguish between them without denying either (Norford). If we are unable or unwilling to do that, we will read *The Last Unicorn* as a sort of *Alice in Wonderland*—that is to say, as a fantasy of language and epistemology. I can't read it that way, but if I could, I think it would not bear comparison with the masterpieces of metafiction and the fantastic.

I wish to focus on something Beagle does very well: encourage apperceptive growth by playing, dialogically, between ontological and epistemological fantasy. If *The Last Unicorn* were not ontologically based, the unicorn would not say to the harpy, "You are like me" (Beagle 66). By which she clearly means, "You're real too." She is not only insisting that *being* exists, but that it exists on at least two qualitatively different levels. If the novel were purely ontological, it would not concern itself so often with the transient, affective moment of ambiguity that Todorov calls the Fantastic (24–40), nor with the self-constituting (epistemological) structures favored by Brooke-Rose (231–80). Because *Unicorn* is clearly a high fantasy, we might assume that any critical stance that valorizes epistemological manipulation would find Beagle's novel uninteresting.

This is not so. A critic following Eric Rabkin's lead might profitably trace the ways in which Beagle, again and again, manages to achieve an epistemological lurch (Rabkin 3–41). A minor example: the novel puts unicorns and tacos in the same world. Most readers will have accepted the unicorn-world by banishing the taco-world; hence, when the banishment has to be rescinded, the machinery must be reset. So long as the author continues to jar the reader's achieved episteme, the work will continue to be "fantastically" interesting. One may trace a significant pattern of such dislocations in *The Last Unicorn*. David Stevens read *Unicorn* in search of the fantastic, and so finds that the taco-world undercuts the unicorn-world, à la P. D. Q. and J. S. Bach. He is quite wrong in saying that Schmendrick and Molly do not "take themselves seriously." They do not take themselves solemnly—quite a different matter. In fact, both Molly and Schmendrick achieve a sort of magnanimity because they accept both the taco and the unicorn world (Stevens 230–38). R. E. Foust, in an essay that is among the best yet written on Beagle, traces epistemological dislocations (Foust 5–20).

But in the enjoyment of "fantastic" complexity, we should not forget that there's *something* in every one of those nine cages. If we are sensitive to fantasy, we are not jolted by a series of epistemological earthquakes; rather, we gradually discover a widening space in which words, beings, and worlds that we had thought quite separate are intricately related. To oversimplify: in *fantasy* the framed is foregrounded; in the *fantastic*, the framing is foregrounded. In *Unicorn*, fantasy makes use of the fantastic: the epistemological frame-shifts mark off an area of remarkably stable ontological plenitude, claimed as not less but more real than the reader's ordinary world (Swinfen 230–34).

Check this assertion against the text. The triangle containing spider, unicorn, and harpy is ontologically firm. If there is a surprise, it is that the harpy does *not* change. Although Beagle makes rich use of the fantastic, he does not produce a fantastic tale in the sense Christine Brooks-Rose uses the term for *The Turn of the Screw* (Brooke-Rose 158–88). James never clarifies the ontological status, and the effect of the tale would be very different if he had. Certainly, there are fictions in which epistemological double-clutching dominates either the tale or the critical inquiry, or both—cases in which the key to the treasure is the treasure (Barth). Many are very fine. The fantastic is a heady trip, so is meta-fiction—John Hawkes's *The Blood Oranges* is wonderful. But to make episte-mological fantasy the standard by which all fantasy is measured is silly.

The critical stakes are high, as when Christine Brooke-Rose discusses onto-logical fantasy from an unacknowledged (and hostile) epistemological bias (233–56) or when Todorov tells us what is and what is not *interesting*. Robert Philmus has a good go at Todorov in an essay called "Todorov's Theory of 'The Fantastic': The Pitfalls of Genre Criticism."

To be fair, from the "fantastic" perspective, ontologically firm creatures may seem (in contrast to the intricately autogenerative consciousness central to epistemological fantasy) dull, "of the surface," like the characters in a Jonson comedy (Eliot 112). In an ontological fantasy, one should not expect Sergeant Steadfast to run nor Lady Fickle to be waiting.

But this does not mean that fantasy is without complexity. The complexity of ontological fantasy, since it is cast neither as perceptual static nor as psy-chological storm, is hard to find if you look inside the characters. The complexity of high fantasy is in its creature plenitude, on the outside, right there in front of God and everybody, created by the play of things that within the fictive world have being and presence. As the complexity of an ontological fantasy increases, each new facet is likely to occasion another creature. But the very existence of such creatures is what the fantastic approach to fantasy explains away: the key to the treasure destroys the treasure.

Digression. Sometimes the new creature is a thing, part of what we might mistake for setting. If, for a moment, you grant the existence of ontological fantasy, you might then discover two subdivisions: creature-fantasy and place-fantasy. In creature-fantasy, characters produce the setting. In place-fantasy, setting produces the characters. Frequently, place-fantasy will serve as ground for creature-fantasy and vice versa. The reversal of that ground-figure relationship signals extremities of plot and theme. Tolkien's *The Lord of the Rings* is primarily a place-fantasy; hence, when the generative process is reversed (Galadriel preserving Lothlorien; Sauron perverting Ithilien), the effect is impressive. In contrast to *The Lord of the Rings*, *The Last Unicorn* is primarily a creature-fantasy (the unicorn makes her wood, Mommy makes her carnival). Both Tolkien and Beagle reverse the ground when they wish to get your attention. End of digression.

"Creature of the night, brought to light," the sign says, and some of them are. Others are creatures of light brought to night. Others? Some of the creatures are frauds, some victims; some are hidden by disguise, some revealed by disguise. Some are freed by the end of the carnival, some imprisoned, some quite unchanged.

In *The Last Unicorn* (as in all high fantasy) the ability to distinguish between illusion and reality matters, a lot. To mistake a dog for Cerberus is embarrassing. To mistake a harpy for a parrot is fatal. In contrast, a character in an epistemological fiction may safely blur the distinction. Neither the dog nor Cerberus has being, or presence, or essence: harpy and parrot are signs woven on the semiotic loom—warp of signifieds, woof of signifiers—sign patterns without external referent. (Is there an "A" on Dimmesdale's chest? How did it get there?)

In ontological fantasy, the single most important piece of information about a character (person, or thing, or spirit) is the category of being to which she, he, or it belongs. The wise character in (and the skillful reader of) such fantasy discerns those categories and sets his expectations and makes his evaluations accordingly.

Why should this be so? The creature categories in an ontological fantasy are permanent. They are "out there" to be discovered by the wise, not "in here" to be projected by the clever, and they constitute a bordered hierarchy, not a fluid continuum. Movement from one ontological category to another is very rare, and therefore doubly important—as when Frank Herbert allows Leto to meld with the sand trout (*Children of Dune*). Gollum does not become an orc; Frodo does not become an elf.

There is one character in *Unicorn* who crosses an ontological boundary: the unicorn herself. That the crossing is uncrossed before the tale ends is significant. There is also one "fantastic" character in *The Last Unicorn*: the Red Bull is as purely epistemological as a character can be. These two genre-breaking creatures are in one sense at the center of *Unicorn* and that suggests . . . another time.

Back to the cages: the unhappy dog signs Cerberus, a crippled ape is seen as a leering satyr, a boa sleeps beside one fold of the midgard serpent, a crocodile shares its cage with an illusory dragon, and a "perfectly good lion" forms the biological kernel around which fear and desire may coalesce the manticore-illusion.

The three cages that form a triangle within the outer pentagram hold creatures that are more "real," more "true" than the creatures in the outer cages, though the nature of their truth and reality is various. We admire the "free" Arachne, we are awed by the fragile beauty of the disguised unicorn, and we are terrified by the harpy. The taxonomy of affective responses found in G. R. Thompson's "Gothic Fiction of the Romantic Age: Context and Mode" (6–12) is useful for understanding this aspect of the carnival. Through delusion (spider), accommodation (unicorn), and presence (harpy), we have been led toward an understanding of being.

The spider is worth a closer look. Like the outer creatures, she forms the ground for an illusion, but unlike them, she herself projects (and believes in) the illusion—even more fully than do the rubes. Unlike the outer five, who are unhappy with or indifferent to or unaware of their illusioned counterparts, the spider is one with the illusion. She believes and is happy and humble and proud—and very responsible. She strains toward being by willing to be a projected illusion of herself, not as actor or victim, but as the feminine principle that sustains the universe. Mommy's pet spider has denied any distance between herself and an archetype—and that is perhaps heroic—but she has chosen the wrong archetype (Arachne was not really a spider) and then mistaken herself for it. The spider is a character freely bound by her own epistemological fantasy in a world that is ontologically firm. When her episteme collapses, we are left not with the ululation of the female principle, nor with the boasting of human Arachne, nor with the silent dissolution of Ovid's metamorphic spider, but with the sound of a real spider crying: a hortatory instantation of another archetype. The spider's cry is a tiny version of the ur-scream shared by all who damn themselves by insisting that they have created themselves.

Where did the spider go wrong? Can't language as *langue* be substituted for logos? Escher's hand can draw Escher's hand drawing Escher's hand? One can *say* language speaks man. But that is not the same as saying that man speaks himself. Fiat saying "Fiat" saying " 'Fiat.' " No escaping *gonos* and *telos*. At least not in ontological fantasy.

And what sits in the eye of the mandala? At the center of the carnival is Mommy-Elli: double star on the blue-event horizon. Which is real? Mommy or Elli? Perhaps aspect and instance have burned so long in the slow fires of avarice and desire that no distinction is necessary, or possible. If that is true, Mommy, who seems to be the only creature in the carnival who can turn her act on and off, really has no act, no pretense. She knows what is true, what illusion. And her knowing joins epistemology to ontology. Molly Grue will achieve a good (and pleasant) version of this unity. Lir becomes the hero he studied to be. Even Schmendrick gains life (and loses immortality) by finding the vectors along which he may predicate his imprisoned essence.

But none gets quite so far as Mommy Fortuna (Olsen 133–44). She is the central paradox: a being who is wholly becoming. Perhaps the visitors find her "illusion" so terrible—more terrible even than the real harpy—because she is not an illusion at all. She is true, a presence affirming that only impermanence is permanent, and that change is always and only—when all is said and done—decay.

The harpy may do it *to* you. Will do it to you if you run. Elli reminds you that in order for there to be a you, you have to consume yourself. The harpy is "pure" presence, less human than any of the other creatures, all of whom share with humanity the stretch between presence and existence. (Except, of course, for the unicorn, who experiences the human stretch only when she "becomes" Amalthea.) Perhaps Mommy Fortuna's relationship with Elli is a model. Like the spider (and unlike Haggard), Mommy has linked herself to an archetype, to the penultimate archetype of all mortals. Unlike the spider, she has chosen appropriately—she goes with the grain of mortality. Unlike the spider, she has not mistaken herself for the chosen archetype. Perhaps that is why we pity the spider and respect Mommy. Mommy embraces first Elli and then the harpy, old age and death, two monsters no mortal can evade. Knowing what Haggard knows, she does not retire. Mommy loses, of course, but her grip on the players and audiences of the Midnight Carnival is exemplary: grab the world and time as best you can. The world is always real, and the time is always now. Join in joyous servitude with the archetypes of your ontological niche. Thus you may hold the harpy caged for another day. Such is the message of all high fantasy.

If you are evil (like Mommy), you may pander to the world's desire for spectacle by transforming illusory chaos into a "fantastic" parody of order—so that true order may be concealed (Gardner 5–6). If you are ambitious, you may display that double illusion for your own glory and profit, and when the magic fails, embrace the triumph of a lost success that was at least significant enough to be marked as it crumbles. The game is worth the price, and the cost, whether you play or not, is your liver.

Mommy has as much presence and being as mortals may achieve. One could say of her, at the end, when it counts, "Now *there* was a witch!

The fantasy I know and love is not an anomalous lichen growing in the crack between natural and supernatural, nor is it graffiti scrawled by Dionysius on Aristotelian logic. It is not subliminal programming allowing the economically privileged to perpetuate themselves; not proletarian dissimulation by which "The People Speak" despite bourgeois repression. It is not a theoretical category generated by continental structuralism, nor is it twentieth-century man's surreptitious scratch of a religious itch that cannot be tended overtly in polite society.

It is not the carnivalesque belly laugh of the sleeping giant; not feminism's etching away at "phallologocentrism"; not chauvinistic rape insensitivization. Not a waking dream, nor the day's care robed in sleep.

It is one means by which I renew my failing powers and beliefs, a means of knowing that others know what it means to live in the present and to seek to fulfill one's very own being—which is, after all, only held on loan. As Tolkien points out, that is not such a bad thing.[2] For me, the renewal is necessary, because every morning somebody shows up with a dragon to be killed or a harp to be played, and I don't know how to do either.

Five cage-wagons, surrounding three cage-wagons, centered upon one cage-wagon. A pentagram for the magician, a mandala for the mystic, and—for the literary theorist—an invitation to explore degrees of being and illusion, within and among which Peter Beagle weaves the quest of *The Last Unicorn*. If I am right, high fantasy's affirmation of presence can accommodate the postmodern critical dance without much strain.[3] It remains to be seen if postmodern criticism can come to terms with high fantasy.

Notes

1. Kathryn Hume begins her great effort to distinguish between mimesis and fantasy by ignoring a problem that all reader-response criticism eventually must confront. Who gets to say what is "usually accepted as real and normal"? (*Fantasy and Mimesis*, p. xii). Whose turn will it be in 1998? Even with all the formalist paradoxes, it is better, I think, to let the book signal that decision with the reader as tacit referee. Nevertheless, her book is much needed and very welcome. I do nothing, here, with the generative end of her model, the relationship between the author, his world, and the genre. I touch lightly on the reader's world in the envoi that closes this essay.

Hume's first chapter, pp. 5–28, provides a taxonomy for definitions of fantasy. Her model is the communication triangle: author, work, reader with the addition of world.

2. J.R.R. Tolkien, "On Fairy Stories," *The Tolkien Reader* (New York: Ballantine Books, 1966) is the classic essay on the consolations of fantasy. Beagle presents the opportunity for the reader to experience a modest version of what Tolkien calls "eucatastrophe," not by presenting a *type* of Christ, but by assembling creatures who successfully seek to grow in "being." Beagle's fantasy, because of its admixtures of the fantastic and metafiction, encourages an intensity of apperception far greater than that likely to accompany a reading of Tolkien's fantasy.

3. C. N. Manlove, "Anemic Fantasy: Morris, Dunsany, Eddison, Beagle," *The Impulse of Fantasy Literature* (Kent, Ohio: Kent State University Press, 1983) 148–54, finds none of this in Beagle.

Works Cited

Barth, John. *Chimera*. New York: Random, 1972.

Beagle, Peter S. *The Last Unicorn*. New York: Viking, 1968.

Brooke-Rose, Christine. "The Unreal as Real: The Modern Marvellous." *A Rhetoric of the Unreal*. New York: Cambridge University Press, 1981. 231–80.

Eliot, T. S. "Ben Johnson." *The Sacred Wood*. London: Methuen, 1920.

Foust, R. E. "Fabulous Paradigm: Fantasy, Meta-Fantasy, and Peter S. Beagle's *The Last Unicorn*." *Extrapolation* 21, no. 1 (1979): 5–20.

Gardner, John. *On Moral Fiction*. New York: Basic, 1977.

Herbert, Frank. *Children of Dune*. New York: Putnam, 1976.

Hume, Kathryn. *Fantasy and Mimesis: Responses to Reality in Western Literature*. New York: Methuen, 1984.

Kolbenschlag, Madonna. *Kiss Sleeping Beauty Good-Bye*. New York: 1979.

Manlove, C. N. "Anemic Fantasy: Morris, Dunsany, Eddison, Beagle." *The Impulse of Fantasy Literature*. Kent, Ohio: 1983. 148–54.

Miller, David M. "Hobbits: Common Lens for Heroic Experience." *Tolkien Journal* (1969): 11–15.

Miller, J. Hillis. "Stevens' Rock and Criticism as Cure." *Georgia Review* (Spring 1976) 30:31.

Miller, Walter M., Jr. *A Canticle for Leibowitz*. Philadelphia: Lippincott, 1959.

Norford, Don Parry. "Reality and Illusion in Peter Beagle's *The Last Unicorn*." *Critique: Studies in Modern Fiction* 19, no. 2 (1977): 93–104.

Olsen, Alexandra Hennessey. "The anti-Consolatio: Boethius and *The Last Unicorn*." *Mosaic* 13, no. 3–4 (1980): 133–44.

Philmus, Robert M. "Todorov's Theory of 'The Fantastic': The Pitfalls of Genre Criticism." *Mosaic* 13, no. 3–4 (1980): 71–82.

Rabkin, Eric S. "The Fantastic and Fantasy." *The Fantastic in Literature*. Princeton: Princeton University Press, 1976. 4–41.

Stevens, David. "Incongruity in a World of Illusion: Patterns of Humor in Peter Beagle's *The Last Unicorn*." *Extrapolation* 20, no. 3 (1979): 230–38.

Swinfen, Ann. "The Perilous Realm." *In Defence of Fantasy*. London: Routledge & Kegan, 1984. 230–34.

Thompson, G. R. "Introduction: Gothic Fiction of the Romantic Age: Context and Mode." *Romantic Gothic Tales 1790–1840*. New York: Harper and Row, 1979. 6–12.

Todorov, Tzvetan. *The Fantastic: A Structural Approach to a Literary Genre*. 1970. Cleveland: Case Western Reserve University Press, 1973.

Tolkien, J.R.R. "On Fairy Stories." *The Tolkien Reader*. New York: Ballantine, 1966. 33–90.

Waugh, Patricia. *Metafiction: The Theory and Practice of Self-conscious Fiction*. New York: Methuen, 1984.

Zipes, Jack. *Breaking the Magic Spell: Radical Theories of Folk and Fairy Tales*. University of Texas Press, 1980.

Bibliography

Aaronson, Dernard S. "Hypnosis, Depth Perception, and the Psychedelic Experience." *Altered States of Consciousness: A Book of Readings*. Ed. Charles T. Tart. New York: Wiley, 1969.

Aldiss, Brian. "T." *No Time Like Tomorrow*. New York: Signet, 1959.

———. *Frankenstein Unbound*. 1st American ed. New York: Random House 1974.

———. *Helliconia Spring*. 1st ed. New York: Atheneum, 1982.

———. *Helliconia Summer*. 1st ed. New York: Atheneum, 1983.

———.*Helliconia Winter*. 1st ed. New York: Atheneum, 1985.

———. *The Malacia Tapestry*. London: Jonathan Cape, 1976.

Aldiss, Brian, and David Wingrove. *Trillion Year Spree: The History of Science fiction*. London: Gollanz Ltd., 1986.

Alkon, Paul K. *Origins of Futuristic Fiction*. Athens: University of Georgia Press, 1987.

Altered States of Consciousness: A Book of Readings, Charles T. Tart, editor. New York: Wiley, 1969.

Anderson, Poul. "The Man Who Came Early." *The Horn of Time*. Boston: Gregg Press, 1978.

———. *There Will Be Time*. New York: Signet, 1973.

Attebery, Brian. *The Fantasy Tradition in American Literature: From Irving to LeGuin*. Indiana University Press, 1980.

A Visit to William Blake's Inn.

Barth, John. "The Literature of Replenishment: Post Modernist Fiction." *Atlantic Monthly* (June 1980).

Baudrillard, Jean. *Cool Memories*. Paris: Editions Galilée, 1987.

Baum, Frank I. *To Please a Child: A Biography of L. Frank Baum*. Chicago: Reilly and Lee, 1961.

———. *American Fairy Tales*. Chicago: George M. Hill, 1901.

Baum, L. Frank. *The Wonderful Wizard of Oz*. Chicago: G. M. Hill, 1900.

Benthall, Jonathan. *The Body Electric, Patterns of Western Industrial Culture*. London: Thames and Hudson, 1976.

Beversluis, John. *C. S. Lewis and the Search for Rational Religions*. Grand Rapids, Mich.: Eerdmans, 1985.

Bluestone, George. *Novels into Film*. Berkeley: University of California Press, 1971.

Boyer, Robert, and Kenneth Zahorski. *Fantasists on Fantasy*. New York: Avon, 1986.

———. *The Fantastic Imagination*. New York: Avon, 1986.

———. *Visions of Wonder*. New York: Avon, 1986.

Bradbury, Ray. "The Dragon." *A Medicine for Melancholy*. New York: Bantam, 1959.

Burroughs, E. R. *Tarzan, Lord of the Jungle*. 1928. Reprint. New York: Ballantine, 1963.

———. *Tarzan of the Apes*. 1912. Reprint. New York: Ballantine, 1963.

Butor, Michel. *Mobile, étude pour une représentation des Etats-Unis*. Paris: Seuil, 1962.

———. "6,810,000 Liters d'eau par seconde." *Etude Stéréophonique*. Paris: Seuil, 1967.

———. *U.S.A. '76*. Illustr. de Jacques Monary. Paris: Editions Phillippe Lebaud-Le Club du Livre, 1975.

Buttigeig, Joseph A., ed. *Criticism without Boundaries. Directions and Crosscurrents in Postmodern Critical Theory*. Notre Dame University Press, 1987.

Card, Orson Scott. *Seventh*. New York: St. Martin's, 1946.

———. *Red Prophet*. New York: TOR, 1988.

Cassirer, Ernst. *Language and Myth*. New York: 1946.

Cavell, Stanley. *The World Viewed*. Cambridge, Mass.: Harvard University Press, 1979.

Champigny, Robert. *Ontology of the Narrative*. Paris: The Hague, Mouton, 1972.

Collins, Robert, and Robert Latham. *Science Fiction and Fantasy Book Review Journal 1988*. Westport, Conn.: Meckler, 1988.

Colloque de la Sorbonne et du Senat, *Metamorphose du récit* de Voyage. Actes de la Sorbonne et du Senat receuillis par François Moureau, Paris: Champion-Slatkine, 1986.

Cox, Jeffrey N. *In the Shadow of Romance: Romantic Tragic Drama in Germany, England, and France*. Athens: Ohio University Press, 1987.

Day, William Patrick. *In the Circles of Fear and Desire: A Study of Gothic Fantasy*. Chicago: University of Chicago Press, 1985.

de Man, Paul. *The Rhetoric of Romanticism*. 1968. Reprint. Chicago: University of Chicago Press, 1982.

Dennis, John. *The Grounds of Criticism in Poetry*. 1704. Reprint. Menston, England: Scolar, 1971.

Drake, Nathan. *Literary Hours, or Sketches Critical and Narrative*. 1800. 2nd ed. 2 vols. New York: Garland, 1970.

Field, Syd. *Screenplay: The Foundation of Screenwriting*. New York: Dell, 1984.

Finney, Jack. *The Third Level*. New York: Dell, 1959.

Fletcher, Marilyn P. *Reader's Guide to Twentieth-Century Science Fiction*. Chicago: American Library Association, 1989.

Forisha, D. L. "Relationship between Creativity and Mental Imagery: A Question of Cognitive Styles." *Imagery: Current Theory, Research, and Application*. Ed. A. A. Sheikh. New York: Wiley, 1983. 310–39.

Frankowski, Leo. *The Cross-Time Engineer*. New York: Ballantine Del Rey, 1986.

Friend, Beverly. "Time Travel as a Feminist Didactice in Works by Phyllis Eisenstein, Maryls Millhiser, and Octavia Butler." *Extrapolation* 23, no. 1 (Spring 1982).

Frye, Northrop. *A Study of English Romanticism.* 1968. Reprint. Chicago: University of Chicago Press, 1982.

———. *Fables of Identity: Studies in Poetic Mythology.* New York: Harcourt, Brace, Jovanovich, 1963.

Geoffrey of Monmouth. *History of the Kings of Britain.* Trans. Sebastian Evans. Rev. Charles W. Dunn. New York: Dutton, 1958.

Girouard, Mark. *The Return of Camelot: Chivalry and the English Imagination.* New Haven and London: Yale University Press, 1981.

Gordon, Andrew. "*Back to the Future*: Oedipus as Time Traveler." *Science-Fiction Studies* 14, part 3 (November 1987).

Grahame, Kenneth. *Wind in the Willows.* New York: Heritage Press, 1940.

Grant, Berry Keith, ed. *Planks of Reason: Essays on the Horror Film.* Metuchen, N.J.: Scarecrow Press, 1984.

———. *Film Genre Reader.* Austin: University of Texas Press, 1986.

Green, Martin. *Dreams of Adventure, Deeds of Empire.* New York: Basic Books, 1979.

Hale, Edward Everett. "Hands Off." *Harper's,* March 1881. Reprinted in *Alternative Histories.* Ed. Charles G. Waugh and Martin H. Greenberg. New York and London: Garland Publishing, 1986.

Harland, Richard. *Superstructuralism: The Philosophy of Structuralism and Post-Structuralism.* London: Methuen, 1987.

Heldreth, Leonard. "Clockwork Reels: Mechanized Environments in Science Fiction Films." *Clockwork Worlds: Mechanized Environments in Science Fiction.* Ed. Richard D. Erlich and Thomas P. Dunn. Westport, Conn.: Greenwood Press, 1983.

Heller, Terry. *The Delights of Terror: An Aesthetics of the Tale of Terror.* Urbana: University of Illinois Press, 1987.

Hennelly, Mark M., Jr. "*The Time Machine*: A Romance of 'The Human Heart.' " *Extrapolation* 29, no. 2 (Summer 1979).

Hertz, Neil. *The End of the Line: Essays in Psychoanalysis and the Sublime.* New York: Columbia University Press, 1985.

Hirsch, E. D., Jr. *The Aims of Interpretation.* Chicago: University of Chicago Press, 1976.

Holtsmard, E. B. *Edgar Rice Burroughs.* Boston: Twayne, 1986.

Huizinga, Johan. *Homo Ludens.* Boston: Beacon Press, 1962.

Hume, Robert D. "Exuberant Gloom, Existential Agony, and Heroic Despair: Three Varieties of Negative Romanticism." *The Gothic Imagination: Essays in Dark Romanticism.* Ed. G. R. Thompson. Pullman, Wash.: Washington State University Press, 1974. 109–127.

———. "Gothic versus Romantic: A Re-evaluation of the Gothic Novel." *PMLA* 84 (1969): 282–90.

Irwin, W. R. *The Game of the Impossible: A Rhetoric of Fantasy.* Urbana: University of Illinois Press, 1976.

Jackson, Rosemary. *Fantasy: The Literature of Subversion.* New York: Methuen, 1983.

Jameson, Fredric. "Reification and Utopia in Mass Culture." *Social Text* 1, no. 1 (Winter 1979): 130–48.

———. "Postmodernism, or the Cultural Logic of Late Capitalism." *New Left Review* 146 (July–August 1984): 53–94.

Jones, W. L. *King Arthur in History and Legend.* London: Cambridge University Press, 1933.

Kenney, Alice P. "Yankees in Camelot: The Democratization of Chivalry in James Russell

Lowell, Mark Twain, and Edward Arlington Robinson." *Studies in Medievalism* 1, no. 2 (Spring 1982).

Kerman, Judith B. "Private Eye: A Semiotic Comparison of the Film *Blade Runner* and the Book *Do Androids Dream of Electric Sheep.*" *Patterns of the Fantastic II*. Ed. Donald M. Hassler. Mercer Island, Wash.: Starmont House, 1985.

Kermode, Frank. *The Sense of an Ending: Studies in the Theory of Fiction*. New York: Oxford University Press, 1967.

Klüver, Heinrich. *Mescal and Mechanisms of Hallucinations*. Chicago: University of Chicago Press, 1966.

Laurence, David. "William Bradford's American Sublime." *PMLA* 102 (1987): 55–65.

Lewis, C. S. *The Last Battle*. London: Chatto and Windus, 1956.

Lupoff, R. A. *Edgar Rice Burroughs, Master of Adventure*. New York: Canaveral Press, 1965.

MacDonald, George. *The Princess and the Boglin*. New York: Grosset and Dunlap, 1907.

McCormack, W. J. *Sheridan Le Fanu and Victorian Ireland*. Oxford: Clarendon Press, 1980.

McGann, Jereome J. *The Romantic Ideology: A Critical Investigation*. Chicago: University of Chicago Press, 1983.

Mellor, Anne K. *English Romancing Irony*. Cambridge: Harvard University Press, 1980.

———. *Mary Shelley, Her Life, Her Fiction, Her Monsters*. New York: Methuen, 1988.

Modleski, Tania. "The Terror of Pleasure: Contemporary Horror Film and Postmodern Theory." *Studies in Entertainment: Critical Approaches to Man's Culture*. Ed. Tania Modleski. Bloomington: Indiana University Press, 1986.

Molson, Francis J. *Children's Fantasy*. Starmont Reader's Guide 33. Series Editor: Roger C. Schlobin. Mercer Island, Wash.: Starmont House, 1989.

Moore, C. L. and Lawrence O'Donnell [Henry Kuttner]. "Vintage Season." *ASF* (1946). Reprinted in *The Science Fiction Hall of Fame*. Vol. 2A. Ed. Ben Bova. New York: Avon, 1974.

Morris, Richard. *Time's Arrows: Scientific Attitudes Towards Time*. New York: Simon and Schuster, 1984.

Nancy, Jean-Luc. *Des Lieux Divins*. Paris: Mauvexin-Trans-Europ-Press, 1987.

Naranjo, Claudio, and Robert Ornsetin. *On the Psychology of Meditation*. New York: Viking, 1971.

Nelson, Lowry, Jr. "Night Thoughts on the Gothic Novel." *Yale Review* 52 (1962): 236–57.

Neumann, Bonnie Rayford. *The Lonely Muse: A Critical Biography of Mary Wollstonecraft Shelley*. Salzburg: Institut für Anglistik und Amerikanistik, 1979.

Nitchie, Elizabeth. *Mary Shelley*. New Brunswick: Rutgers University Press, 1953.

Norris, Christopher. *Deconstruction: Theory and Practice*. London: Methuen, 1982.

Paley, Morton D. *The Apocalyptic Sublime*. New Haven: Yale University Press, 1986.

Parker, Helen N. *Biological Themes in Modern Science Fiction*. Ann Arbor, Mich.: UMI Research Press, 1984.

Phy, Allene Stuart. *Mary Shelley*. Starmont Reader's Guide 36. Series Editor: Roger C. Schlobin. Mercer Island, Wash.: Starmont House, 1988.

Pinkerton, Jan. "Backward Time Travel, Alternate Universes, and Edward Everett Hale." *Extrapolation* 20, no. 2 (Summer 1979).

Piper, H. Beam. "Flight from Tomorrow." *Amazing* (1959). Reprinted in *The Worlds of H. Beam Piper*. New York: Ace, 1983.

Rawlins, Jack P. "Confronting the Alien: Fantasy and Anti-Fantasy in Science Fiction Film and Literature." *Bridges to Fantasy.* Ed. George E. Slusser, Eric S. Rabkin, and Robert Scholes. Carbondale and Edwardsville: Southern Illinois University Press, 1982.

Ricoeur, Paul. *Time and Narrative.* 3 vols. Trans. Kathleen Blarney and David Pellauer. Chicago: University of Chicago Press, 1984–88.

Robbe-Grillet, Alain. *Projet pour une révolution á New York.* Paris: Seuil, 1970.

Ronald, Ann. "Terror-Gothic: Nightmare and Dream in Ann Radcliffe and Charlotte Bronte." *The Female Gothic.* Ed. Juliann E. Fleenor. Montreal: Eden Press, 1983. 176–86.

Saporta, Marc. *Vivre aux Etats-Unis.* Photos de Gerard Seiven. Paris: Seuil, 1970.

Shelley, Mary. *Collected Tales and Stories.* Ed. Charles E. Robinson. Baltimore: Johns Hopkins University Press, 1976.

Siegel, Ronald K., and Murray E. Jarvik. "Drug-Induced Hallucinations in Animals and Men." *Hallucinations: Behavior, Experience, and Theory.* Ed. R. K. Siegel and L. J. West. New York: Wiley, 1975. 81–161.

Slusser, George, and Eric S. Rabkin. *Mindscapes.* Carbondale, Ill.: Southern Illinois University Press, 1989.

Sobchack, Vivian. *Screening Space: The American Science Fiction Film.* 2nd. enlarged ed. New York: Ungar, 1987.

———. *The Limits of Infinity and the American Science Fiction Film.* Cranbury, N.J.: A. S. Barnes, 1980.

Sontag, Susan. "The Imagination of Disaster." *Against Interpretation.* New York: Dell, 1966. 209–25.

Stableford, Brian. *Masters of Science Fiction: Edmond Hamilton, Leigh Brackett, Barry N. Malzberg, Kurt Vonnegut, Robert Silverberg, Mack Reynolds: Essays on Six Science Fiction Authors.* 1st ed. San Bernardino, Calif.: Borgo Press, 1981.

———. *Scientific Romance in Britain, 1890–1950.* New York: St. Martin's Press, 1985.

———. *Future man.* 1st ed. New York: Crown Publishers, 1984.

———. *The Sociology of Science Fiction.* San Bernardino, Calif.: Borgo Press, 1985.

Strenski, Ivan. *Four Theories of Myth in Twentieth-Century History.* Iowa City: University of Iowa Press, 1987.

Tallis, Raymond. *Not Saussure: A Critique of Post-Saussurean Literary Theory.* London: Macmillan, 1988.

Tart, Charles T. "Guide to the Literature on Psychedelic Drugs." *Altered States.* 477–83.

Thompson, G. R. "Introduction: Gothic Fiction of the Romantic Age: Context and Mode." *Romantic Gothic Tales, 1790–1840.* New York: Harper and Row, 1979. 6–12.

Thorslev, Peter L., Jr. *Romantic Contraries: Freedom versus Destiny.* New Haven: Yale University Press, 1984.

Tolkien, J.R.R. *Return of the King.* Boston: Houghton Mifflin, 1956.

"The Transcendent Adventure: Studies of Religion in Science Fiction/Fantasy." *Study of Science Fiction and Fantasy.* Ed. Robert Reilly. Westport, Conn.: Greenwood Press, 1985.

Twain, Mark. *A Connecticut Yankee in King Arthur's Court.* 1889. Reprint. New York: Harper and Row, 1974.

Twitchell, James. *Romantic Horizons: Aspects of the Sublime in English Poetry and Painting, 1770–1850.* Columbia: University of Missouri Press, 1983.

Tymn, Marshall. "The Year's Scholarship in Fantastic Literature: 1987." *Extrapolation* 29 (Fall 1988) 238–84.

Varnado, S. L. "The Idea of the Numinous in Gothic Literature." *The Gothic Imagination: Essays in Dark Romanticism.* Ed. G. R. Thompson. Pullman, Wash.: Washington State University Press, 1974. 11–21.

———. *Haunted Presence: The Numinous in Gothic Fiction.* Tuscaloosa: University of Alabama Press, 1987.

Volkoff, Vladimir. *Nouvelles Américaines.* Paris: Julliard/L'Age d'Homme, 1986.

Wachhorst, Wyn. "Time-Travel Romance on Film: Archetypes and Structures." *Extrapolation* 25, no. 4 (Winter 1984).

Waller, Gregory A., ed. *American Horrors: Essays on the Modern American Horror Film.* Urbana: University of Illinois Press, 1987.

———. *Living and Undead: From Stoker's Dracula to Romero's Dawn of the Dead.* Urbana: University of Illinois Press, 1986.

Warrick, Patricia S. *The Cybernetic Imagination in Science Fiction.* Cambridge, Mass.: MIT Press, 1980.

Waugh, Patricia. *Metafiction: The Theory and Practice of Self-Conscious Fiction.* New York: Methuen, 1984.

Wendland, Albert. *Science, Myth, and the Fictional Creation of Alien Worlds.* Ann Arbor, Mich.: UMI Research Press, 1985.

Willard, Nancy. *Angel in the Parlor: Five Stories and Eight Essays.* 1st ed. San Diego: Harcourt Brace Jovanovich, 1983.

———. *A Visit to William Blake's Inn: Poems for Innocent and Experienced Travelers.* 1st ed. New York: Harcourt Brace Jovanovitch, 1981.

———. *East of the Sun and West of the Moon.* Illus. by Barry Moser. San Diego, Cal.: Harcourt Brace Jovanovitch.

———. *Firebrat.* Illus. by David Wiesher. New York: Knopf, 1988.

———. *Household Tales of Moon and Water.* 1st ed. San Diego: Harcourt Brace Jovanovitch, 1982.

———. *Nineteen Masks for the Naked Poet.* Santa Cruz, Cal.: Kayak Books 1971.

———. *The Nightgown of the Sullen moon.* Illus. by David McPhail. 1st ed. San Diego, Cal.: Harcourt Brace Jovanovitch, 1988.

———. *Things Invisible to See.* 1st ed. New York: Knopf, Distributed by Random House, 1984.

William, Ray. *Literary Meaning: From Phenomenology to Deconstruction.* Oxford University Press, 1984.

Wittig, Monique. *L'Opoponax.* Paris: Seuil, 1964.

Wolfe, Gary K. "Instrumentalities of the Body: The Mechanization of Human Form in Science Fiction." *The Mechanical God.* Ed. Thomas P. Dunn and Richard D. Erlich. Westport, Conn.: Greenwood Press, 1982.

Wood, Robin. *Hollywood from Vietnam to Reagan.* New York: Columbia University Press, 1986.

Zahner, Pascal. *America, America.* Paris: P. M. Favre, 1987.

Index

About the Editor and Contributors

BRIAN W. ALDISS was recently called "the godfather of British science fiction." He thinks that flattery might have been intended. His novel "Frankenstein Unbound" is being filmed by Roger Croman. Aldiss is working on an anthology of the stories of Anna Kavan while writing three other books.

JOSEPH ANDRIANO is an assistant professor at the University of Southwestern Louisiana, where he also directs the Writing Center. He recently published an article on Poe's "Ligeia" in *Poe Studies*. His book manuscript, *Our Ladies of Darkness: An Archetypal Perspective on the Female Daemon in Gothic Fiction*, was a finalist in the Midwest MLA's annual book award contest. It is currently being revised for publication.

MICHAEL CLIFTON teaches at California State University, Fresno. His work on the imagery of altered states stems from his dissertation on postmodern poetry, part of which, dealing with W. S. Merwin, is forthcoming in *Chicago Review*. His interest in science fiction and fantasy, however, is a lifelong passion, beginning sometime during the third grade. He is currently at work on a full-length study of the imagery of altered states in literature.

JOEL N. FEIMER is Associate Professor at Mercy College, Dobbs Ferry, New York, where he has taught since 1967. He received his Ph.D. from City University of New York in 1983. His last publication was "The Tender Connection: Sexuality in the Novels of D. H. Lawrence," *Antioch Review*, 1979 (coauthor, Adma d'Heurle). He has participated in the annual conferences on the fantastic in the arts since 1982. He is currently serving as secretary of the IAFA.

BUD FOOTE an associate professor, has taught English at Georgia Institute of Technology since 1957, and science fiction there since 1970. During that time he has produced numerous essays, two hundred songs, many columns for *The Detroit News* and *The National Observer*, and six children. He is finishing a book on travel to the past.

LISA M. HEILBRONN received her Ph.D. in sociology from the University of California, Berkeley, in 1986. Her dissertation, "Domesticating Social Change: The Situation Comedy as Social History," examines the relationship between the popularity of types of situation comedy and underlying ideological and sociological change in American culture. Dr. Heilbronn has done research on other popular cultural subjects, including the depiction of Vietnam veterans in television and film.

LEONARD G. HELDRETH teaches composition, contemporary drama, and literature and film courses at Northern Michigan University. He has presented papers at numerous conferences, has published chapters in several books dealing with fantasy and science fiction, and is editing a book on vampires in literature. He also writes a monthly column about films on videotape, and reviews contemporary films each week on WNMU-FM.

INGEBORG M. KOHN is Associate Professor of French at the University of Arizona, where she teaches literature of the twentieth century and women's studies. Educated in Switzerland and the United States (Ph.D., 1970, University of Arizona), she has published articles on Marcel Proust and the Nouveau Roman. She is presently at work on a book on the aesthetics of decadentism/ symbolism.

MICHELE K. LANGFORD, Professor of French Literature and Cinema at Pepperdine University, has published *Les Menageries Intimes*, a study of animal imagery in French poetry, as well as articles on poetry, novels, and film criticism in American and European journals. She is currently working on a book about Jules Verne and doing research on Belgian literature.

WILLIAM LOMAX has taught English and music in the Los Angeles Unified School District for over twenty years. He has degrees in music and music education from California State University, Los Angeles, and in English from University of California, Los Angeles. He is currently completing work on his Ph.D. in English Literature at UCLA. He has published in *California English, Extrapolation*, the *DLB, Phoenix from the Ashes*, and the ninth annual Eaton Conference volume, and has lectured for the California Writing Project.

PETER MALEKIN is a senior lecturer at the University of Durham, England. He has taught in Germany, Iraq, and Sweden. His interests include philosophy, Eastern and Western arts, and the theory of consciousness. He has published works on Shakespeare, the seventeenth century, Wordsworth, the Romantics, and Eliot, and has translated works by Böhme and Strindberg.

DAVID M. MILLER is Professor of English and Director of Graduate Studies at Purdue University, where he teaches Milton, literary theory, and science fiction/fantasy. His publications include *The Net of Hephaestus* (1971), *John Milton: Poetry* (1978), and *Frank Herbert* (1981), as well as several articles on Tolkien.

MICKEY PEARLMAN received her Ph.D. from the City University of New York. She is the editor of *Women Writing Fiction in America* (1988, University Press of Kentucky), the author of *Re-inventing Reality: Patterns and Characters in the Novels of Muriel Spark* (Peter Lang Publishing), and *Tillie Olsen: United States Authors Series* (forthcoming, Twayne Publishers). She has contributed extensively to dictionaries of British, continental, and Catholic authors, and is now writing a critical analysis of Muriel Spark's short stories and a feminist reinterpretation of Albee's *The Zoo Story*.

SHARON A. RUSSELL is a professor of communication at Indiana State University. She teaches film studies and film production. Previous publications include work on various aspects of the horror and mystery genres. Her article "The Transformed Woman: Female Clothing and the Vampire Film" appears in *Spectrum of the Fantastic*.

JOE SANDERS teaches English at Lakeland Community College in Mentor, Ohio. Besides numerous reviews and essays, he has written books on Roger Zelazny and E. E. "Doc" Smith. He is currently editing a collection of essays on science fiction fandom for Greenwood Press.

VIVIAN SOBCHACK is Professor of Theater Arts/Film Studies at the University of California, Santa Cruz. Past President of the Society for Cinema Studies, her articles have appeared in *American Quarterly, Journal of Popular Film and Television, Literature/Film Quarterly, Quarterly Review of Film Studies, Film Quarterly,* and *Camera Obscura* as well as in numerous anthologies. She has also published *An Introduction to Film* and *Screening Space: The American Science Fiction Film*.

BRIAN STABLEFORD taught in the Sociology Department of the University of Reading between 1976 and 1988, but has now returned to full-time writing. He received the I.A.F.A. Distinguished Scholarship Award in 1987. His works include *Scientific Romance in Britain 1890–1950, The Third Millennium: A History of the World 2000–3000 A.D.* (in collaboration with David Langford) and *The Empire of Fear*.

JACK G. VOLLER is an assistant professor of English at Southern Illinois University at Edwardsville, where he is introducing a course in popular literature. He has written on science fiction and on Poe, and is currently working on a full-length study of the supernatural sublime in Gothic and Romantic literature.

CYNTHIA L. WALKER is an associate professor of English at the University of Alaska. She received her B.A. from Denison University in 1970, and her M.A. and Ph.D. from Purdue University in 1972 and 1974, respectively. In addition to fantasy, her areas of interest include the history of the British novel, twentieth-century fiction, and twentieth-century drama.

JOYCE WATFORD is an associate professor of English at Kentucky State University, where she is also chairperson of the Division of Literature, Languages, and Philosophy. Her growing interest in Third World and minority literature has led her to discover a rich literary heritage indigenous to Africa and other Third World countries. One of her ambitions is to call attention to indigenous Third World and minority literature and to see that literature one day placed side by side with other great literary canons of the world.

NANCY WILLARD published seven books of poetry, a play, three collections of stories, a novel, *Things Invisible to See*, and a book of critical essays on poetry. Her work has appeared in *The New Yorker, Redbook, Esquire*, and numerous quarterlies and anthologies. Her publications include *Household Tales of Moon and Water* and *Nineteen Masks for the Naked Poet* (poetry), *Angel in the Parlor* (short stories and essays on writing), and *A Visit to William Blake's Inn* (poetry), which won the Newbery Award. Most recent publications: *Water Walker* (poems), *The Ballad of Biddy Early* (poems), and *East of the Sun, West of the Moon*, (a play, illustrated by Barry Moser). She attended the University of Michigan and Stanford, and teaches at Vassar College.

JULES ZANGER is Professor of English and Director of American Studies at Southern Illinois University in Edwardsville. He was the first president of IAFA, and has published variously in the fields of fantasy and American studies. He has been a visiting professor of American literature in Brazil, France, and, most recently, Czechoslovakia.

GREGORY L. ZENTZ has a B.A. in philosophy, with some graduate work in physics. He is a technical sales representative for Fisher Scientific Company and a free-lance writer in the field of motivation and business who has traveled to several countries on assignment. Greg has written one science fiction novel which is as yet unpublished. He is director of The Astronomical Society of the Palm Beaches and of a private astronomical observatory.